Cheshire's Famous

A Comprehensive Guide to Celebrity Cestrians

Bob Burrows

Cheshire's Famous

A Comprehensive Guide to Celebrity Cestrians

breedon **books**
PUBLISHING

Acknowledgements

Arighi Bianchi, Macclesfield; Bob Greaves; Cheshire Lawn Tennis Association, John Hoffman, Mike McAfee; *Cheshire Life* magazine; Cheshire Regimental Museum, Chester; *Chester Chronicle*; Cotton Traders, Altrincham; Crewe Library and Town Hall; Diana Bishop; Glenda Jackson, MP; Irlam and Sons, Chelford; King's School, Macclesfield; *Knutsford Guardian*; Lancashire County Cricket Club, Revd Malcolm Lorimer; Lee Dixon, Arsenal FC; Leonard Cheshire Foundation; *Macclesfield Express*; Macclesfield Library, Mrs Tweddle; Mrs Yvonne Bagshawe; *Northwich Guardian*, John Buckley; Paterson Zochonis, Cussons; *Runcorn and Widnes Weekly News*, Ray Mellor, Dave Bettley; the Manor of Gawsworth, Raymond Richards; *Sale & Altrincham Messenger*; Sandbach Gymnastic Club, Peter Aldous; Shakespeare Birthplace Trust; Sir Chris Bonington Picture Library; *Stockport Express*, Liz Pearce; Stockport Grammar School, Sara Johnson; Stockport Library; Vauxhall Motors, Ellesmere; *Warrington Guardian*; Warrington Library; Wilmslow Library.

Sources:
A History of Cheshire, by Alan Crosby.
Breaking into Heaven, The Stone Roses, by Mick Middles.
The Faber Book of Exploration, by Benedict Allen.
History of Cheshire, by Dorothy Sylvester.
History of Stockport Grammar School, by Benjamin Warley.
Old Cheshire Families and Seats, by L.M. Angus-Butterworth.
Stockport Grammar School 1487–1987, by James and William Ball.
Stockport Lads Together (6th Cheshire Territorials), by David Kelsall.
Story of the Victoria Cross, by Sir John Smyth.
Victoria History of the County of Cheshire, Oxford University Press.
William Turner – Painter, by Dave Gunning.

Dedication

To my own Cheshire set: my wife
Pat, my son Nick and his wife Lisa, my
daughter Penny and her husband David Bates.

First published in Great Britain in 2004 by
The Breedon Books Publishing Company Limited
Breedon House, 3 The Parker Centre,
Derby, DE21 4SZ.

ISBN 1 85983 397 7

Printed and bound by Butler & Tanner,
Frome, Somerset, England.

JACKETprinting by Lawrence-Allen Colour Printers,
Weston-super-Mare, Somerset, England.

Contents

Introduction: Cheshire

THIS book is ostensibly all about people, Cheshire people, Cestrians. That is to say people who were born in Cheshire or whose formative or creative years were spent in the county. However, it may first be useful to offer a thumbnail sketch of the county, its features and characteristics, without attempting to write a definitive history, something which has been accomplished by a number of far more competent historians than I. If we take the present geographical and administrative boundaries of Cheshire, following the mauling which the county suffered in 1974, then with a population of approximately 1 million and an area of 900 square miles, Cheshire is ranked 17th and 27th respectively of the 44 English counties. The statistics imply that it is a county of little consequence, something that is frequently reinforced by media comments that refer to a pleasant county of black and white country houses, renowned for dairy farming, cheese and, oh yes, that infernal Cheshire Cat.

Cheshire is much more than that. Cheshire citizens, Cestrians, have not only helped write the history of Britain but have been instrumental in turning the pages. There has scarcely been a chapter in the history of these islands in which Cheshire or its citizens have not been involved.

Ancient Cheshire was subjected to incursion and invasion at various times in its history by the Welsh, the Romans, the Irish Norsemen, the Vikings, the Danes, the Normans and the Scots. However, none of these has done more daamage than the modern administrators, the bureaucrats, who with a stroke of the pen and insensitive or oblivious to identity, history or culture, have changed boundaries for political or economic reasons.

In the redrawing of boundaries in 1974 great swathes of Cheshire were given away, including virtually the whole of the Wirral peninsula apart from Ellesmere and Neston. Other parts were lost to Greater Manchester. However, the significant towns of Warrington and Widnes were transferred into Cheshire. Unsurprisingly the losses created much bitterness as the communities being moved out did not want to leave the county where they or their families had perhaps been born or lived for generations. The administrators were oblivious to the natural human desire to belong, and to the significance of heritage to the individual and to the family. A number of communities appealed and some were successful in being permitted to stay in the county, but nevertheless Cheshire was much reduced in size. The pen is indeed mightier than the sword! However, it could have been much worse, as an earlier report in 1970, the Redcliffe Maud, recommended that Cheshire be done away with altogether!

Whatever boundaries are created, history cannot be rewritten. This book concerns itself with people who were born in Cheshire and therefore includes the 'lost territories' and takes the liberty to also include the towns transferred into Cheshire after 1974, because the inhabitants are now technically Cestrians. The book also includes those people whose formative or creative years were spent in the county.

After the Ice Age slowly receded in about 10,000 BC, exposing the Cheshire plains, the region became more habitable for the early settlers who were nomadic in nature. Cheshire, with rich forest good for hunting, access to the sea and the major rivers of the Dee and the Mersey supplying an abundance of food, had all the ingredients required to sustain a structured existence. Hill forts, stone circles, artefacts and pottery trace the historic settlements throughout the county.

However, Cheshire in the first millennium was unrecognisable, geographically, as the piece of real estate that it is today. At times it is thought to have been part of Powys, the Welsh Kingdom, and it later became part of a greater Mercia. It is believed that Edward the Elder established Cheshire in today's (pre-1974) more recognisable form in the early 900s.

For many years Cheshire was vital to whoever ruled the country, as it was very much a frontier state. Bordered on the western side by Wales, on the northern boundary by the River Mersey, to the east by the Pennines and by deep forest in the south, it was ideal for repelling the Irish Norsemen and for defending or launching offensives against the Welsh. The Norman earls of Cheshire became powerful and influential, to the extent that the county became Palatine, being almost autonomous in government but charged with settling Cheshire and keeping the Welsh under control.

It was of course the Romans who had first recognised the value of Cheshire, not only for its salt, an important commodity of the Roman Empire, but also for Chester as a base for fighting the Welsh. The Normans instigated military training for the male population, but the Cheshire barons and their forces were not obligated to fight outside of the county. Many did so anyway, and fought as mercenaries, with Cheshire archers earning a reputation second to none. Over the next 900 years Cheshire soldiers would fight with great distinction in all the major conflicts involving Britain: the Crusades, the Hundred Years War, the English Civil Wars of the 1640s when Cheshire itself was split between Royalists and Parliamentarians, the Scottish Wars, the many Victorian Empire wars and of course the major conflicts which dominated the 20th century.

Cheshire was a familiar part of the country to many of the great names of British history, including **King Alfred, King Canute, William the Conqueror, The Black Prince, Elizabeth I, Charles I, Prince Rupert** and the **Duke of Buckingham**. During the 1745 rebellion **Bonnie Prince Charlie**

Bonnie Prince Charlie at Macclesfield in 1745, from an original silk print.

invaded England and stopped at Macclesfield to rest, replenish his supplies and seek recruits. The event is commemorated in a Macclesfield silk picture showing a reluctant mayor reading out a message of welcome in the market square. In April 1746 the 'butcher' **Duke of Cumberland** also stayed in Macclesfield on his way to defeat Bonnie Prince Charlie's army at Culloden.

Milton, Shakespeare, Livingstone and **Nelson** all had Cheshire connections. **Handel** also visited the county and, it is believed, completed one of his most important works during his stay. A British Prime Minister and a Deputy Prime Minister were both educated in Cheshire.

In terms of commerce and industry Cheshire has contributed in its own unique fashion. The county was not a massive beneficiary of the Industrial Revolution but with the improvements in the canal systems, the advent of the railways and improvements in roads and motor transport it was able to supply both home and foreign markets with specific local products. At various times in its history the county was a major supplier of salt, cheese, soap and silk throughout the United Kingdom, and indeed was world-renowned for its silk. There was once a time when Nantwich supplied London with leather shoes! It was, however, the creation of the Manchester Ship Canal which made an enormous difference to the county's fortunes.

Daniel Adamson, who owned a small engineering works in Manchester, was the visionary who set the wheels of construction in motion, and after he resigned as chairman of the committee of the Ship Canal project in 1887, **Lord Egerton of Tatton** ensured that sufficient funds were raised to commence the project. Work started in 1887 and the canal was opened for traffic in 1891, but it was not until 1 January 1894 that vessels could travel the full distance of 35½ miles from Eastham Locks to Manchester.

Towns along the canal, like Runcorn, Ellesmere Port and Warrington, among others, benefited enormously from increased trade now that the movement of goods was so much easier. Heavy industry was based on shipbuilding in Birkenhead, chemicals at Northwich and Runcorn, oil refining at Stanlow where the Shell refinery was (in 1980 the biggest in the UK), coal production at Poynton, car manufacturing with

The Rows, Chester, a splendid blend of old and new.

Vauxhall at Ellesmere Port, locomotive construction and a Rolls-Royce areo-engine factory at Crewe and the installation of nuclear reactors by the Atomic Energy Authority at Culceth and Risley, Warrington. It must also be noted that Cheshire contains one of the UK's major airports, Manchester Ringway, and also has one of the world's greatest astronomical radio telescope facilities at Jodrell Bank.

Situated just outside Nantwich is a massive underground complex which was commenced in the 1950s and later enhanced in the 1980s to form a vast site on two underground levels designed to withstand the impact of a nuclear bomb. It was to be the regional government headquarters in the event of a war, but has now been turned into a highly successful tourist attraction. The 'Secret Bunker City' gives an insight into life as it might have been.

Over the years some of Cheshire's industries and activities have diminished, while others have been refined. New industries and commercial activities have grown in response to modern demands, which have brought ingenuity, invention and initiative from the latest generation of Cestrians, to match those of their illustrious predecessors. For example, Cheshire has 200 miles of canal waterways, more than any other English county, and is making great strides in clearing and improving the network to encourage tourism and leisure activities and to maximise the canal legacy.

Roman Chester, with its fabulous complete circuit of ancient walls, superb Norman cathedral and very tasteful setting of modern shops in the ancient black and white unique buildings called the Rows, is a major British attraction. Just a short distance away at Ellesmere Port is a very modern but highly successful attraction, one of the best in Europe, the Blue Planet Aquarium. The building is home to more than 2,500 species of fish, including huge sharks, and affords visitors the opportunity to walk under and through a 250ft long transparent underwater tunnel while the marine life swims alongside and above the watcher.

Chester also plays host to Chester Zoo, which was awarded the title of the UK's No.1 Zoo in the *Good Britain Guide* in 2003. The zoo, with more than 6,000 animals and 500 species, is also Britain's largest, attracting more than one million visitors per year to its well-maintained, spacious, landscaped grounds. Stapeley Water Garden near Nantwich is reputed to be the largest of its kind in the world. It not only holds the national collection of water lilies but features a Tropical House and Oasis, reptiles, a stingray pool, piranhas and virtually everything and anything to do with aquatic and angling supplies. At Ellesmere Port there is a Boat Museum which houses the largest collection of floating canal boats in the world, and at Tatton, Knutsford, the Royal Horticultural

An exhibit at the Royal Horticultural Show at Tatton Park, Knutsford.

Britain's first hat museum, in Stockport.

Stockport, uniquely displays more than 500 hats of historical and contemporary interest and conducts educational tours through the workshops with demonstrations of working machinery.

The county has made good use of its rich heritage with very skillful management of its magnificent country houses and castles. Many of these are open to the paying public to enjoy, while the revenue helps pay for the upkeep of these superb historic monuments. Bramhall Hall, Lyme Park, Arley Hall, Capesthorne and Gawsworth Hall are just a few of many which enhance the countryside.

Society annually hosts one of the largest flower shows in Britain.

A more recent innovation for the county was the establishment of the first British hat museum in the British Isles. The Museum of Hatters, at

Cheshire is picturesque, with its castles, ancient manor houses, green pastures, leafy lanes and rich farmland, and yes, it is affluent and an excellent place to reside. But soft underbelly, a small county of little consequence, a smudge on the historic

The ancient Manor House of Gawsworth Hall, home of many Fittons.

mirror of Britain, its citizens content to chew grass, munch cheese, not get involved and smile back at the Cheshire Cat? Nothing could be further from the truth. Warriors, soldiers, pioneers, adventurers, explorers, mountaineers, sports people, entertainers in cinema, television, radio, music, pop, opera, scientists, writers, artists, politicians, clergy, industrialists, entrepreneurs and academics from Cheshire have made an impact nationally on the fabric of Britain and in many cases have had international influence. The county is blessed with high-quality schools, two of which, Stockport Grammar School founded in 1487 and King's School, Macclesfield, visited by the Queen in 2002 to celebrate its 500th anniversary, have unsurprisingly produced a large number of Cheshire's famous people.

Cestrians have left Cheshire placenames all over the world. They have explored the Arctic, China, Tibet, Australia and the Amazon and have conquered and died on Mount Everest. Cheshire knights fought in the Crusades and Cheshire archers excelled at Crécy and Agincourt and were so respected that they formed the personal bodyguard of the Black Prince and later Richard II. Cestrians were Royal Standard Bearers to Richard The Lionheart and Henry VIII, and Head

The coat of arms of Edmund Shaa, placed in the wall of the house traditionally occupied by the headmaster of Stockport Grammar School, founded by Shaa in 1487.

of The King's Life Guard of Charles II. A Cestrian was beheaded by Henry VIII for having an affair with Anne Boleyn. A Cheshire girl was Maid of Honour to Elizabeth I and a Cestrian was knighted for helping to fight off the Spanish Armada. Kings were crowned and one, Charles I, was sentenced to death by Cheshire power brokers. Cheshire soldiers fought in all the great campaigns of the 19th and 20th century and won an astonishing 16 Victoria Crosses.

Cestrians have won BAFTA awards and Hollywood Oscars, brought *A Man For All*

King's Grammar School, Macclesfield, founded in 1502.

Seasons, *Lawrence of Arabia* and *Dr Zhivago* to the cinema screen and gave the theatre world *The Boyfriend* and *Love on The Dole*.

Pop stars have had No.1 bestsellers in Britain and the US and the greatest boy and girl bands of the 1990s contained Cestrians. Opera singers have appeared at La Scala, Glyndebourne and Covent Garden and composers have produced a legacy of music which has endured. Cheshire-born entertainers and presenters have been very prominent on our national TV screens and on the radio, many of them becoming household names. Cheshire's sporting record is amazing, producing Britain's greatest cricketer, golfer, cyclist and female athlete and England's greatest-ever soccer goalscorer, as well as the greatest British male and female tennis players. Cestrians have captained England at cricket, soccer, rugby union, athletics and hockey and have captained Great Britain in golf's Ryder Cup and tennis's Davis Cup, and Rugby League's World Cup. Olympic gold medals have been won and world records held and broken. A Cheshire boxer features in the New Jersey Boxing Hall of Fame in America!

Cheshire writers have given the literary world *Alice In Wonderland*, *Master of The House*, *The Owl Service* and *Hindle Wakes* to name but a few. In addition it was a Macclesfield writer who gave Shakespeare his inspiration and direction. Cheshire scientists have been prominent in the fields of computers, aeronautics, radioactivity, radar, neutrons, gene therapy and stem-cell research. One scientist received the Nobel Prize for Physics, the highest honour in science. The county has played a

Jodrell Bank, the World's third largest radio telescope.

part in three of the most momentous events of the 20th century. A Cheshire scientist worked in America on the invention of the atom bomb and a Cheshire hero was nominated as the official British observer as the bomb was dropped on Nagasaki in 1945. Jodrell Bank was used to track the successful journey of Apollo 11, which on 20 July 1969, for the first time in the history of mankind, placed a human being on the moon.

Cheshire was also involved in arguably the two greatest archaeological discoveries in the history of the British Isles. At an ancient marshy, boggy stretch of land between Mobberley and Wilmslow, Lindow Moss, now much reduced in size from that of centuries ago, men digging peat unearthed a body which was to arouse worldwide interest. Experts were called in and on 6 August 1984 the body was removed from the peat bog and housed at Macclesfield District General Hospital. During weeks of examination and study it was discovered that the body had suffered what appeared to have been a ritual killing, a sacrifice. It transpired that 'Lindow Man' or Pete Marsh, as the media nicknamed him, had been struck twice on the head, probably rendering him unconscious, before he was garroted, after which his throat was cut and his lifeless body thrown into the peat bog, which at the time was probably a small lake. When the corpse was found, half of it was missing, believed to have been cut away by previous peat cutters. What remained was in a marvellous leathery state of preservation. A neat beard, tidy finger nails and healthy teeth showed that the 25-year-old male had been well nourished and had probably been the willing victim of a Celtic custom. The body was estimated to have been thrown into the bog perhaps sometime in the first century, which made it the only surviving bog burial in England. Massive interest was created and a television programme of the find, by QED

for the BBC, attracted a viewing audience of over 10 million. But interesting as the discovery of Lindow Man undoubtedly was, a later find in 1939 made it slip down into second place in terms of British discoveries.

Raised in Cheshire, Mrs Edith May Pretty married and moved to Suffolk. In the grounds of her private estate, she was intrigued by a number of mounds. Excavations later unearthed the outline of a massive burial ship which yielded what is universally accepted as the greatest treasure hoard ever found in the British Isles. The treasure found at Sutton Hoo was virtually beyond valuation. Mrs Pretty astonishingly gave the entire collection to the British Museum for the benefit of the nation. The Sutton Hoo site now has its own visitor centre, but the main collection is still in the British Museum. The country owes a great debt to Mrs Edith Pretty, a girl from Cheshire who has left us with a priceless legacy.

In terms of conservation and environmental issues, Cheshire gave two very large tracts of land to create Britain's first national park. The Peak District National Park was established in 1950 and has been the successful forerunner of several other schemes.

Several Cheshire politicians have held national office and one Prime Minister was educated in the county. Commerce and industry have nationally benefited from Cheshire ingenuity and it is surprising how many items that are used in our daily routines are linked to Cheshire.

Sculptors, artists, inventors and poets have all contributed to the nation's cultural archives to leave Cheshire with an amazing legacy to Britain's political, social and sporting history. It is mystifying how such a small county can leave such giant footprints in the sands of time of these islands. A small, sleepy, insignificant county with a soft underbelly? I don't think so.

CHAPTER 1

Warriors and Soldiers

FOR almost 2,000 years Cheshire, because of its geographic importance, has featured prominently in the many domestic and international wars which have shaped the history of the British Isles.

The Romans regarded Chester as an important base for military operations and over the succeeding centuries, Cheshire became strategically important in the wars against the Welsh, the Irish, the Norsemen and the Scots. When Mercia enveloped Cheshire it entered into a treaty with Edward the Elder and agreed to strengthen Cheshire against the Vikings by building castles or fortifications. At Chester this meant enhancing the Roman ruins, while castles were built at Eddisbury in 913, at Runcorn in 915 and at Thelwall in 919. Offa's Dyke, which extended along the entire Welsh border, offered some protection against the Welsh raiders. Cheshire was of vital importance to succeeding rulers and many of the Cheshire earls enjoyed power and privilege.

When the Norman conquest of 1066 spread further north, the earls were replaced by Norman earls who were quick to realise Cheshire's importance. The seven earls of Chester played a prominent part in the development of this early period. Indeed **Randle the Good**, the 6th Earl of Chester, held his position for more than 50 years and was present at the signing of Magna Carta in 1215. Such was his influence that after the death of King John, he, together with two other respected men, was left to run the country and to provide a

measure of stability. It was during this time, in 1220, that Randle gave his trusted friend, **Baron Robert de Stokeport** (Stockport) the Charter of Freedom for the people.

The Norman earls started to formalise military training. All free men under the age of 60 were given instruction by Norman knights and were expected to fight as required. The Crown could insist on conscription and as the Welsh Wars lasted until 1284, and while rebellions against the Normans had to be put down, there was always a requirement for manpower, particularly when the Scottish campaigns started. At one stage Cheshire sent a contingent of 1,000 spearmen and archers to fight in a Welsh campaign and then had to supplement that with a further 620 men plus 100 archers from Macclesfield. In the fighting in Scotland in the late 13th century Cheshire supplied 2,000 men and when the Hundred Years War against France commenced in 1337, a great many Cheshire knights and men were drafted into the army.

During this tumultuous time there was also the little matter of the Crusades. From the First Crusade in 1096, to the Eighth Crusade which finished in about 1274, Cheshire's fighting men were well to the fore. A wonderful piece of history involves the Carrington family of Bowdon. **Adam de Carrington** fought in the Crusades in 1187 and later his son **Mychael** joined him, becoming, in around 1189, Royal Standard Bearer to Richard the Lionheart. Mychael must

In St Wilfred's church, Grappenhall, is this effigy of Sir William Fitzwilliam Boydel, a crusader and 13th-century knight.

have been a warrior of some distinction to have been given such an honour and he was later knighted and received the Order of the Garter. Tragically he died in the Holy Land in 1192.

John Fitz Richard, the 6th Baron of Halton, credited with being the instigator of the first ferry across the Mersey, served as a governor in Ireland and went to fight in the Crusades. He also died in the Holy Land in 1190 fighting at the siege of Tyre.

Another Crusader was Grappenhall's **Sir William Fitzwilliam Boydell,** who died in about 1275 and is commemorated in the superb St Wilfrid's Church, Grappenhall, which dates back to 1120. Lying resplendent in stone the effigy clearly shows the chain armour and breastplate of the time, decorated with three stars, with Sir

William's hand firmly clutching his sword. The figure has its legs crossed, which was an indication that the knight had fought in the Crusades.

When Edward I finally conquered the Welsh in 1284 he was much taken with their expertise with the longbow and decided to adopt the weapon, which he used to beat the Scots at Falkirk in 1298. However, it is Cheshire that is most renowned for its archers, who played a significant part in many English victories, taking centre stage in the 13th century and well into the 14th. It may well be that having a mutual border and having fought each other for years and, at one point, having been allies, that the Welsh and the Cestrians would both be familiar with the longbow, particularly as the vast forests, plentiful with game, would be hunted with the bow. When the Hundred Years War with the French commenced in 1337, Edward III, the Black Prince, chose Cheshire knights and 100 Cheshire archers to be in the vanguard of his campaigns at Caen, Crécy and at the siege of Calais. When his son Richard II succeeded him he also made Cheshire archers the core of his personal bodyguard.

The longbow was a fearsome weapon in the hands of a skilled marksman. A typical bow, made of yew, was between 5 and 6ft in length,

An English longbow.

with a draw weight of about 65 pounds depending on the individual. It had a range of more than 200 yards, even further if elevated. Arrows with broad heads were about 3ft long with goose, peacock or swan feathers and could penetrate armour at short distances. A skilled archer could fire 12 arrows a minute and a company could discharge a hail of arrows in a very short space of time. The archers became an elite body with all the arrogance prestige can bring and although they were not exactly popular, their skill was much appreciated.

Robert del Shagh of Cheshire was one such archer. Fighting with the Black Prince in the conquest of Aquitaine, he acquitted himself so well that when he returned from France to find that his house had virtually fallen down, he was granted four oak trees from Macclesfield Forest to rebuild his property.

As the war progressed many of the Cheshire knights excelled themselves with acts of daring and it was another Carrington from Bowdon, **Sir William Carrington,** who was knighted by the Black Prince for defeating the French Fleet at Sluys, off Flanders, in 1340, the first great victory of the war. Sir William was wounded and indeed lost an eye, but was not prevented from continuing to fight in the campaign.

The major victory at Crécy in 1346 was attributed to the English archers. Although the French force outnumbered the English three to one, they were slaughtered by the deadly accuracy of the longbow, and lost more than 12,000 men. However, an extremely significant moment occurred during the battle when **Sir Thomas Danyers** from Bradley-with-Appleton near Grappenhall managed to recapture the Black Prince's

Brass plaque at St Wilfred's church, Grappenhall, dedicated to the memory of Sir Thomas Danyers, hero of the Battle of Crécy in 1346.

royal standard, which had been lost in the early ferocious fighting.

The Danyers family, which ironically originated in France, lived at Bradley Hall for more than 200 years. In addition to saving the Prince's royal standard, Danyers was credited with the capture of the Chamberlain to the King of France. After the war Thomas returned home and eventually became a Justice of Chester and later Sheriff of the County of Cheshire. It is believed that he worshipped at St Wilfrid's Church in Grappenhall until his death in 1354. There is a brass plaque to his memory on a wall inside the church.

The Battle of Poitiers in 1356 was a similar story, with the English archers, many from Cheshire, killing more than 2,500 of the French cavalry. Four Cheshire squires were mentioned for their bravery during this action: **Delves, Hawkstone, Foulshurst** and **Dutton** all served under Lord Audley, and on their return to England, two of the archers were given land near Goostrey as a reward for their fighting skills. **Robert de Legh** from Adlington commanded a company of 80 Cheshire archers who fought in Gascony in 1358. He survived the war, dying in 1382.

Yet another much-honoured Cestrian was **Sir Hugh Calveley**, born in Calveley in about 1315. He owned the estate at Lea. He too served under the Black Prince in France and fought at the Battle of Navarette (Najera) in 1367, where the French and Spanish suffered heavy losses. He was made an admiral in 1378, appointed Governor of Calais and Brest, and later became Governor of the Channel Islands. He was a giant of a man, reputedly 7ft tall, a real warrior and adventurer who survived a shipwreck off the coast of Brittany with six others, while more than 1,000 perished. After many years of fighting abroad he returned home to Bunbury where he founded a college in 1386. After his death in 1394 he was entombed at Bunbury church. His effigy in the form of a prone carved statue gives an idea of his size and is magnificent in light armour.

Another effigy, this time in Bunbury church and of Sir Hugh Calveley, the warrior admiral who founded Bunbury College in 1386.

Someone else who fought at the Battle of Navarette was **Sir Thomas Carrington** of Bowdon, one of Sir William Carrington's sons. Sir Thomas was knighted by the Black Prince for his bravery at Navarette during the Gascony campaign.

Sir William Brereton of Brereton routed a much larger French force near Mont St Michel and was knighted for his bravery and leadership. He was appointed Bailiffe of Caen, later became Governor of Caen, and returned home rich from his campaigning. However, he was a fighting man and returned once again to the fray and was eventually killed in France.

Typical of the time were personal agreements or contracts. In 1379 **Sir Ralp de Davenport** was indentured to serve King Richard II with three well-mounted, well-armed archers who would serve him in warfare for one year. Needless to say they served in France and Ralp received his knighthood in 1380 and died in 1383.

The Hundred Years War raged on, and yet another massive English victory at Agincourt in 1415 was credited directly to the archers. A much superior French force with much heavier armour got completely bogged down and were massacred in great numbers by the deadly fire from the long-bowmen. It is estimated that more than 5,000 French knights died that day.

Two Cestrians who were there that day, were archer **Robertus Shawe** who fought with Henry V's forces and who carried the distinctive shield bearing the coat of arms of the family Shaa, and **Sir Peter Legh** of Lyme who was knighted banneret for his valour on the field at Agincourt. Sadly, later in the campaign in 1422, Sir Peter died of wounds and his body was brought back to Macclesfield for burial.

A few weeks before Agincourt, Henry V had besieged and then taken Harfleur and **Robert de Legh**, the grandson of Robert de Legh of Adlington, fought with great distinction during this action.

Throughout the fighting in France there had been growing unrest at home which manifested itself in 1403 in a battle near Shrewsbury, when Harry 'Hotspur' led the rebels against Henry IV. Hotspur was killed while leading a company of Cheshire archers. The dispute had split the influential Cheshire families and **Sir John de Massey** of Tatton was killed fighting for the rebels while **Sir John de Massey** of Puddlington and **Sir John Calveley** died fighting for the victorious King. During the battle Cheshire archers must have been pitched against each other. Unrest simmered, with uprisings in Wales, trouble in Ireland and expeditions into Scotland. The discontent erupted with the Wars of the Roses, which pitted Englishmen against Englishmen, family against family and relative against relative.

At the Battle of Blore Heath in 1459 Yorkists under the command of Earl Salisbury crushed the Lancastrians under Lord Audley. In a brutal battle, despite being out-numbered two to one, the Yorkists suffered minimal casualties while the Lancastrians lost over 2,000 dead including Lord Audley. Fighting for the Yorkists that day was **Thomas Fitton** of Gawsworth. Fitton, aged 27, rounded up 66 local men to join him in the struggle. Although he acquitted himself very well, and was knighted on the battlefield, he lost 31 of his men in the fighting.

The Battle of Wakefield in 1460 resulted in **Sir Peter Legh** of Lyme, whose father had been knighted at Agincourt, being knighted on the field of battle. He was later made Keeper of Rhudlan Castle for life in 1461 and held office with interests in the forest and in the manor at Macclesfield. Another relative, **Sir Piers Legh**, was knighted in 1482 while serving with the Earl of Derby in Scotland, and a descendant, **Sir Piers Legh**, was knighted at Leith, Edinburgh, in 1544.

Humphrey Stafford, Duke of Buckingham, had a large house in Macclesfield situated in a part of the town, Backwallgate, which still survives. Buckingham fought with the King and the Lancastrians at the First Battle of St Albans and was wounded by an arrow in the face. It was a bitter defeat and his son died during the fighting. At the Battle of Northampton in 1460, Buckingham led the Lancastrian army to a crushing defeat in which he lost his life and the King was captured and sent to the Tower.

The Wars of the Roses continued until Henry

triumphed at Stoke Field in 1487, but unrest continued for some time. In the Battle of Blackheath, Henry VII knighted **Sir John Shaa** of the Stockport dynasty.

Sir Ralph Egerton of Bunbury was appointed Royal Standard Bearer to Henry VIII in around 1512. Sir Ralph built the chapel at Bunbury in 1527 where there is a brass plaque to his memory.

The Breretons continued to contribute richly to British history, but tragically the last male heir to the Handforth family estate was killed fighting the Scots in the terrible carnage at the Battle of Flodden Field in September 1513. One Cheshire man who fell out of favour with Henry VIII was **Sir William Brereton** of Malpas Hall and Shocklach. Henry accused him of having an affair with his wife, Anne Boleyn, and despite his denials, he suffered the same fate as Anne Boleyn and was beheaded.

However, **Sir William Brereton** of the Breretons of Brereton line distinguished himself fighting in Ireland suppressing the rebellion led by Fitzgerald. In 1534 he stormed the heavily forti-fied castle at Maynouth, scaling the walls with his troops and leading a bloody encounter that crushed the rebellion with heavy losses on both sides. In 1541 he was made Lord Justice and Henry VIII made him Lord High Marshall of Ireland. He died in 1559.

A most unlikely Cheshire hero was **Sir George Beeston** from Bunbury, who was knighted by Queen Elizabeth I. He was knighted at the age of 89 for his bravery and skill in helping to defeat the Spanish Armada in 1588. Beeston com-manded the ship *Dreadnought*, which was one of the four ships to break the Spanish fleet's battle line, and contributed greatly to breaking their formation and making them vulnerable to attack. An experienced old warrior, he had fought with Edward VI against the Scots at Musselborrow

In Bunbury church Sir George Beeston, heroic admiral from the battle with the Spanish Armada in 1588, is commemorated.

and had been at the siege of Boulogne. During his long life he served under four monarchs and was Admiral of the Fleet. Sir George Beeston, born in 1499 died in 1601 at the age of 102. There is an excellent colourful effigy of him in the magnifi-cent church at Bunbury.

In 1596 there was an action in France which has been described by that great historian Macaulay as one of the most brilliant tactical victories in British history. Central to the action was **Sir Urian Legh** of Adlington. Philip II of Spain was ready to invade England by sea and it was decided to launch a pre-emptive strike. The British fleet arrived off Cadiz on 12 June 1596 and, in a brilliant attack, destroyed the Spanish fleet and then laid siege to Cadiz, which was deemed to be impregnable. It fell after two weeks. It was Oxford educated 30-year-old Urian Legh who led the attack and he was knighted on the field for his valour.

A romantic side story emerged when one of the Spanish ladies fell in love with Legh. By all accounts he was charming and gentlemanly but spurned her advances despite the fact that she wrote a ballad to him, called *The Spanish Lady*. When he explained to her that he was married, she forgave him and gave him a gold necklace as a gift for his wife. It is believed to be still among the Legh family heirlooms.

However, in a period of seemingly never-ending warfare the First English Civil War erupted on 23 October 1642 with the first major battle at Edgehill where the Royalists (Cavaliers), defeated the Parliamentarians (Roundheads). One of the fighting Fittons of Gawsworth, **Sir Edward Fitton**, fought on the Royalist side at Edgehill and later raised a force of 500 men to fight for King Charles. Sir Edward was killed at the siege of Bristol in 1645. However, the war once again split families and divided the county, which was largely sympathetic to the Royalist cause.

An example of the anguish and uncertainty of the time is graphically illustrated by an incident at Macclesfield. An old boy of Macclesfield's King's School, **Sir Thomas Aston**, captured the town for the Royalists only to be defeated later by the Parliamentarian **Colonel Mainwaring**, whose children attended King's School. He in turn was then attacked, unsuccessfully, by **Colonel Legh** for the Royalists, who was a governor at the school. The struggle involved an old boy, a parent and a governor. Sadly Sir Thomas Aston died of wounds in 1645.

An interesting story from the war involves **Sir Geoffrey Shakerley** of Hulme Hall, Lower Peover, who it was said crossed the River Dee in a small wooden tub to deliver a message to King Charles at the Battle of Rowton Heath. There is a memorial to Sir Geoffrey at the church in Lower Peover. Another great Royalist figure of the time was **Charles Gerard**, the 1st Earl of Macclesfield. Gerard commanded a cavalry brigade at the Battle of Newbury, where at the end of a struggle involving 30,000 men the Royalists were defeated. He spent some time in France and when King Charles II was restored to the throne in

1660, Gerard returned and was appointed Head of The King's Life Guard, a great honour. He retired in 1688, returning to Gawsworth to live out his life in splendid circumstances.

However, the commanding figure in the North, and certainly Cheshire, was not a Royalist but very much a Parliamentarian, yet another Brereton, another **Sir William Brereton** of Handforth. As the county MP, he was a strong leader who triumphed despite being in a minority. For a while he held most of the market towns, before being besieged in his stronghold at Nantwich by strong Royalist forces until rescued by Fairfax. It was Brereton who effectively ended the Royalist struggle by capturing their stronghold at Chester, which ended the Royalist resistance in the First Civil War.

The death of one of England's great heroes of the 18th century placed another Cestrian in the history books. The 22nd (Cheshire) Regiment, formed in 1689, was part of the daring British assault that scaled the cliffs below Quebec in 1759 and defeated the surprised French on the Plains of Abraham above. Tragically James Wolfe, the British general, was mortally wounded, and died in the arms of Ensign **Henry Browne** of the Cheshire Regiment. Browne was only a few feet from Wolfe when he fell and he wrapped him in the regiment's flag. For many years part of the blood-stained flag was housed in

Ensign Henry Browne attending the dying General James Wolfe in the Fall of Quebec in 1759. Cheshire Regimental Museum

Chester Cathedral. Browne confirmed in a letter home that he was indeed the man who held Wolfe as he died.

Fifty years later another Cheshire soldier achieved national recognition through a brilliant military career. **General Sir Stapleton Cotton**, 1st

Viscount of Combermere, born in Wrenbury in 1773, went to school in Audlem, became an MP, and went with Wellington to fight in the Peninsula War. He played a major role in the Battle of Talavera in 1809, where vicious fighting ended virtually in a draw, with casualties for both sides amounting to 13,000. He also fought at Salamanca in 1813, when Wellington's retreating forces suddenly turned and defeated the pursuing French, with great loss of life. Cotton later spent five years as Commander-in-Chief of the British forces in India. When he died in 1865 he was buried in Wrenbury close to his home at Combermere Abbey. There are memorials to him in the church at Wrenbury and in Chester.

Two of the major conflicts of the Victorian era, the Crimean War and the savage Indian Mutiny, provoked inspiring individual feats of heroism which will be detailed later in the section on the Victoria Cross. However, two men who did not receive awards are also worthy of mention.

Roger Barnston from Holt had the distinction of fighting in both campaigns. He survived the brutal, harsh conditions of the fighting in the Crimea, only to die at the age of 31 leading a British assault on an enemy position in the Indian Mutiny. There is a fitting memorial to his deeds and his sacrifice in his home town of Holt. Although Holt has long been recognised as being part of Denbigh, North Wales, it was regarded in ancient times as being part of Farndon, Cheshire. In 1066 for example Farndon and Holt were assessed as a '15 Hide Unit' and in the early part of the 14th century Farndon, as the mother church, absorbed Holt. When eventually, towards the end of the 14th century, Holt chapelry was returned to Denbigh, the parties nevertheless agreed that Holt was regarded as a parcel of the Farndon estates in Cheshire.

Trumpet Major **William Smith** of the 11th

Major Smith is buried in the church at Knutsford and his headstone states that he was born in 1822 and died on 16 November 1879. It carries the legend 'Honour the Light Brigade, One of the Noble 600'.

After Napoleon's defeat by Wellington at Waterloo he was exiled for the second time, this time to St Helena. One of the British officers charged with supervising him was **Sir Thomas Reade** from Congleton. Sir Thomas spent a considerable time with this leading figure of the 19th century, a man who had threatened to conquer all of Europe, and it is said that he had little respect for Napoleon and did not like him.

Two Runcorn men featured in one of history's greatest feats of arms: the defence of Rorke's Drift on 22/23 January 1879 during the Zulu Wars. On 22 January a huge Zulu force of 20,000 men had wiped out more than 1,500 British and native troops in a bloody massacre at Isandhlwana, and some 4,000 Zulus then moved on to attack the small mission station at Rorke's Drift on the Buffalo River. The garrison, led by Lieutenant John Chard, numbered 139, including B company 2nd/24th Regiment South Wales Borderers and about 35 sick and wounded. The Zulus attacked incessantly, suffering enormous casualties as they began to overrun defended positions. The battle continued overnight with desperate hand-to-hand fighting, but incredibly, as dawn broke, the Zulus, who had suffered more than 500 killed and many more severely wounded, gave up the struggle. The garrison suffered 15 killed and 12 or more seriously wounded. The battle was an epic in British military history and 11 Victoria Crosses were awarded, the highest number ever to be awarded in a single action. Private **Thomas Moffat** and Private **Thomas Taylor** from Runcorn both fought in that historic action and survived.

Moffat joined the 2nd Battalion of the 24th

The headstone of Knutsford Trumpet Major William Smith, a trumpeter at the Charge of the Light Brigade. He met a sad end and took his own life in 1879. This headstone at St John the Baptist's Church, Knutsford, was only erected in 1991.

Hussars, born in Knutsford, had the dubious distinction of entering the history books as the man who sounded the call on 25 October 1854 to commence the charge of the Light Brigade into the 'valley of death' at Balaklava in the Crimean War. The gloriously infamous charge into the valley, covered on three sides by Russian artillery, destroyed the Light Brigade but preserved it forever in legend. It was a miracle that more than 400 men survived the charge: 247 were not so lucky. It was not Smith's decision to charge, he merely gave the signal for the dash that was inscribed in the pages of history.

The headstone of Thomas J. Moffatt, Rorke's Drift veteran, in Runcorn Cemetery. *Photograph courtesy Runcorn Cemetery.*

Regiment South Wales Borderers in 1877 and, having survived Rorke's Drift, went on to serve in Gibraltar and India. He returned to South Africa some years later with other survivors to receive a framed certificate as a testimonial to their historic defence. He was also awarded the South African War Medal, with clasp, in 1879. Moffat died aged 80 in 1936 and is buried in Runcorn Cemetery.

Private **Thomas Taylor** was born in 1861 and lived at St John's Cottages, Weston. He joined the army at the age of 16 in Dover before going to South Africa and the Zulu Wars. Incredibly he was only 18 when he took part in the defence of Rorke's Drift and later served in India, Burma and Gibraltar. He too was awarded the South African War Medal with clasp and after his death in 1926 was also buried in Runcorn Cemetery. Moffatt and Taylor were both presented to King George V when he visited Runcorn in 1925.

Sergeant **P. Tanner** of the Cheshire Regiment received an honourable mention for his part in the march of General Roberts's forces from Kabul to defeat the Afghan army, led by Abyub Khan, at Kandahar in 1880. The Cheshires took part in many of the campaigns fought throughout the British Empire at this time.

John Fielden Brocklehurst, later Lord Lieutenant of Rutland, educated at King's School, Macclesfield, had the distinction of participating in two of British history's historic military actions. In 1885 he was part of the British relief force which was tragically too late to save General Gordon at Khartoum, but he did take part in the successful defence of Ladysmith during the Boer War, 1899–1900.

However the fighting which had taken place over the past 800 years almost paled into insignificance at what was to come. In 1914 World War One broke out with carnage unprecedented in the history of mankind. At its end in 1918 it was estimated to have resulted in over 20 million casualties. Many Cheshire soldiers, indeed too many to mention, were recognised for their bravery during this savage conflict.

Lieutenent-Colonel **Frank Naden**, commander of the 6th Cheshires, became one of the war's most decorated men. Stockport man Naden joined the Royal Marines as a drummer boy and went to the North West Frontier and to the Ashanti campaign in Africa. He later left the army and set up as a greengrocer in Wellington Road South, Stockport, but at the outbreak of war in 1914 he joined up. He quickly became colour sergeant and then sergeant-major, while earning the Distinguished Service Order (DSO), the Military Medal and the second most-valued medal, the Military Cross (MC). A fearless soldier, he was later crippled for life in a car crash.

2nd Lieutenant **Tom Casson**, from Turncroft Lane, Stockport, educated at Banks Lane and Stockport Grammar, earned the Military Cross at the age of 20 on 19/20 July at Givenchy. He led an attack on a German position, killed five of the enemy, captured two and destroyed their bunkers. Casson had previously served in Gallipoli, but after being seriously wounded had been sent home and, after recovering, returned to the fray, joining the 6th Cheshires in May 1916. In May 1917 he was awarded his MC at Buckingham Palace but was killed later that month in France by a faulty hand grenade.

Another MC winner was Captain **Richard Kirk** who commanded B company of the Cheshires at Hamel near the Somme. Kirk, aged 31, was a single man from Stalybridge, educated at public school. He was a bank official at the Manchester & County Bank. He joined the VBCR in 1907. On 1 September 1916 he led his patrol of six men into the German trenches, entering their dugouts. He personally killed three with his revolver and then got all his patrol safely back to English lines. His success was short lived, as he was killed by a sniper in November 1916.

Company Sergeant-Major **Arthur Bonsall**, from Back Lane, Woodley, was also an MC winner. When his company was decimated he assumed command and, leading by example, turned the situation round and captured many of the enemy. On his return home in 1917 he was given a silver watch in appreciation from the Bredbury and Romiley Soldiers and Sailors Recognition Committee.

Other MC winners with the Cheshires were **J. Hobson**, Captain **Sid Yorston** and Lieutenant-Colonel **Sydney Astle**, an old boy of Stockport Grammar School.

Lieutenant **Wilfred Owen**, among the greatest World War One poets, qualifies as part Cestrian. Despite his anti-war poetry Owen was a brave man, who while fighting with the Manchester Regiment suffered severe shell shock and was sent home to recover. Soon he was back fighting on

Lieutenant Wilfred Owen MC, soldier and World War One poet. Photograph courtesy Imperial War Museum.

the Western Front and was awarded the Military Cross for his bravery in an action in October 1918. Just a few weeks later, one week before the war ended, he was killed on 3 November 1918 at Sambre Canal. Ironically, his parents were notified of his death on Armistice Day, 11 November 1918. Although he was born in Shrewsbury in 1893, the family moved to Birkenhead in 1897. There Owen went to school and spent his formative years. The family returned to Shrewsbury 10 years later.

A Military Medal (MM) winner was Lance-Corporal **Fred Utley** from Stockport. He lived in

York Street and went to St Matthew's School at Edgeley. He won his medal at Givenchy and was brought home badly wounded. He died, aged 22, in 1917 at the Royal Victoria Hospital and is buried in Stockport cemetery.

There were other medals and honours won by Cestrians including an MM with bar for Sergeant **W. Seaton** of the Cheshires and a DCM for **H. Butterworth**.

However, one of the great heroes of World War One was **David Beatty**, born at Howbreck Lodge at Stapeley, Nantwich, in 1871. A great naval man, Beatty was the hero of the sea battles of Dogger Bank and Jutland. He was much decorated: Admiral of the Fleet, knight of the realm and Freeman of the City of Chester, and he was also given an earldom for his services to the Navy. His eventual title was 'Admiral Sir David Beatty, Viscount Borodale of Wexford and Baron Beatty of the North Sea': quite an epitaph.

One of the great characters of World War One was undoubtedly the **2nd Duke of Westminster**, or **Bendor** as he was known. His nickname was attributed to his father's favourite Derby-winning horse and a heraldic design on the coat of arms. Bendor was one of the wealthiest men in the country and with a base in London and at Eaton Hall, Chester, he lived life to the full. A long-standing love affair with the legendary French fashion designer Coco Chanel was a source of fascination in society circles. He was, however, no dandy, and when the Boer War broke out he volunteered for service in South Africa and later volunteered to serve in World War One. Winston Churchill actually gave him some credit for inspiring the invention of the tank. Bendor, it is said, remembered from his Boer War experience how some of the trains had been 'armoured' to protect against enemy fire, and experimented by reinforcing one of his Rolls-Royces with thick steel plate and fitting a machine gun into the boot space, thus creating a prototype of an armoured car. Satisfied with the first conversion he transformed several other Rolls-Royces and created his own squadron of armoured cars. On one occasion he led his squadron in a 100-mile dash across the desert to rescue 90 British prisoners of war. He was awarded the DSO for his courage and ingenuity in the fighting in the Western Desert.

Another great character was Lieutenant-Colonel **Sir Philip Lee Brocklehurst** of the Macclesfield silk dynasty. Explorer, adventurer and soldier, Brocklehurst joined Shackleton's 1907 expedition to the South Pole as a 20-year-old. He volunteered for World War One and was wounded fighting with the Life Guards in 1914–17. He later served with the Egyptian Army in 1918–20. During World War Two he commanded the 2nd Regiment of the Arab Army and was later appointed to the British Council for Palestine.

The horrors of World War One were barely dry on the pages of history when the world, disregarding the lessons learnt from that first disaster, embarked on World War Two in 1939.

Among the honours awarded to Cheshire men was an MM given to **Douglas Wright** from Poynton. Wright served with the Special Boat Squadron, operating behind enemy lines in the Greek Islands and Yugoslavia. He was part of the team that laid explosives that destroyed the German garrison at Amorgos. After the war he remained in the army, serving all over the world before returning to Poynton in 1970. His later years were spent living at the Royal Hospital, Chelsea, and becoming a Chelsea Pensioner, wearing the distinctive red tunic on special occasions.

Les Graham, born in Wallasey on 14 September 1911, was the winner of a Distinguished Flying Cross (DFC). Graham was the pilot of a

Lancaster Bomber and earned his award in action on 8 December 1944. After the war he became Britain's first 500c motorbike World Champion.

Wallasey is the birthplace of another great flyer, **Peter Parry**, a fighter reconnaissance pilot who flew Hurricanes and Spitfires and was a flight commander with 208 Squadron. At the outbreak of World War Two Peter was studying veterinary science at Liverpool University. After joining up he found himself, in 1942, flying Hurricanes over the battlefield at El Alamein. His job was to spot enemy movements of men and armour and to direct the fire of the Allied guns. It was dangerous work and several of his close friends were killed.

Later in the war he flew Spitfires over northern Italy and in July 1944 he was awarded the Distinguished Flying Cross after completing more than 100 missions. After completing 150 sorties he returned to Britain to train new pilots at the RAF college at Cranwell. At the end of the war he returned to Liverpool University to complete his studies and eventually moved to the West Country, where he had a large and highly successful veterinary practice. During his war service he was awarded the Africa Star for North Africa, the Italy Star, the Defence Medal and the War Medal with a mention in despatches, as well as the DFC.

Another flying hero, one of 'the Few', that distinguished band of pilots who, despite overwhelming odds, won the Battle of Britain during the dark days of the summer of 1940, was Sergeant **Ronnie Hamlyn**. Piloting a Spitfire, Ronnie, based at Biggin Hill with the 610 (County of Chester) Squadron Auxiliary Air Force, shot down five enemy aircraft in one day, 24 August 1940. That same day 10 other men from the squadron were killed.

One Cheshire man who did not get an award but surely deserved one, was Captain **William Higgin**. Higgin, born in 1922, was acknowledged as one of the greatest game marksmen of his time. He entered the Hall of Fame when, while home on leave in 1940, he saw a Dornier German bomber flying low over his estate at Puddington, Cheshire, about to attack a local factory. Without a moment's hesitation he took aim with his 303 and fired into the plane's engines, bringing it crashing to the ground. 'It was quite an easy shot', he said later.

Courage of a different kind in circumstances even more frightening earned **Jim Bradley** an MBE in 1949. James Bradley was born on 17 June 1911 in Stalybridge, but in childhood moved with the family to North Wales, where he was educated. He completed his education at Cambridge, where he studied engineering, and at the outbreak of World War Two he enlisted and was commissioned as lieutenant in the Royal Engineers. He sailed for the Far East in 1941. He was captured by the Japanese at the fall of Singapore in 1942 and spent more than a year in Changi jail, before being sent to work on the notorious Burma–Thailand railway. As the world knows, forced death marches, monsoons, malaria, poisonous snakes, torture and savagery from their captors led to the deaths of thousands of prisoners. Bradley arrived in camp in May 1943 with 1,600 men. Within two months 1,200 were dead and more than 200 were in hospital.

After suffering unbearable brutality, 10 men decided to risk all and escaped into the jungle. The Japanese had not fenced off the camp because they realised that anyone attempting to escape would be subjected to disease, snakes, tigers and lethal insects. Five of his companions died, but Bradley and the rest reached what they thought was the safety of a Burmese village. Sadly they were betrayed and the Japanese recaptured them. Amazingly the Japanese, perhaps astounded at their bravery at surviving for more than eight weeks in the jungle, did not execute them, but jailed them for a number of years. Bradley and his colleagues were eventually rescued by the British in 1945 and Jim was awarded the MBE for his courage. Although poor health, as a result of his wartime privation, plagued him for much of his life, he did not bear any malice towards the Japanese. Indeed for the 50th anniversary of VJ Day Bradley went to Japan to meet with the man who had controlled the camp working parties that Bradley had worked in. The man was a convicted war criminal, but Bradley forgave him. It was an emotional and trying meeting for both men and was filmed for television and released as the *Big Story*. Amazingly, despite his suffering, Bradley had a long life. He was married twice, both marriages lasting 33 years, and he died aged 91 on 19 May 2003.

Major **Harry 'Bomber' Harrison**, who was born in Chester on 1 July 1911, gave up his career as an optician and went to the Military College of Science at Woolwich Arsenal to specialise in guns and explosives. During World War Two he was mentioned in despatches but excelled himself when he was posted to Cyprus in 1955 during the Eoka campaign as the government explosives expert. The campaign was very much concerned with assassination, sabotage and booby traps. Often Harrison worked around the clock, being on call to defuse all manner of explosive devices. So effective were Harrison and his small team that it is believed that they defused more than 10,000 devices and Harrison himself was high on the terrorists' hit list.

At the end of his tour of duty he was awarded the MBE (military) and the George Medal for his bravery. He died in April 2003.

The Victoria Cross: the Cheshire Set

Over centuries of battle and struggle, bravery and loyalty has been recognised and appreciated in a variety of ways. In mediaeval times the king or queen would grant land, silver, gold, favours or hunting rights, and for outstanding acts of bravery or loyalty would knight the warrior or soldier.

However, there was a marked change to this tradition when, during the Crimean War, Queen Victoria became concerned for her army at a time when the campaign was not going too well. In consultation with her ministers she decided that an incentive or a gesture to recognise the importance of the campaign and the efforts of the British troops should be more manifest. She became involved in the design of a special medal and indeed reserved the right to have the final say on how it would look. The eventual design carried the legend 'For The Brave', but Queen Victoria changed it to 'For Valour', meaning more

The Victoria Cross, the ultimate award for bravery.

than brave. It was introduced on 5 February 1856 and made retrospective to the start of the Crimean Campaign. The first ever awards were three VC's awarded to the Navy in the Baltic. It has since become and remained Britain's highest and most coveted award for gallantry above and beyond the call of duty.

Since its inception Cheshire soldiers have won the Victoria Cross in the Indian Mutiny, the Crimean War, World War One, World War Two and the Korean War, a record of which any county can be proud.

Cheshire's first ever VC was won by Private **Anthony Palmer** of the 3rd Battalion Grenadier Guards on 5 November 1854 at Inkerman, during the Crimean War. Born in Brereton Green on 10 March 1819, Palmer performed with great courage in desperate and savage hand-to-hand fighting. The British, led by Sir Charles Russell, who was also awarded the Victoria Cross, attacked a fortified sand-bag battery held by the Russians. Palmer saved Russell's life by killing a Russian who was about to bayonet him and eventually, through their superior skill with the bayonet, the Grenadiers routed the Russians. Palmer survived the war and died in Manchester on 12 December 1892.

The Crimea yielded two more Victoria Crosses for Cestrians. Corporal **William Norman** of the 7th Regiment (the Royal Fusiliers) was awarded his for an action on 19 December 1854. Born in Warrington in 1832, Norman survived the war and died in Salford in March 1896. The last VC of the Crimean War was won by Lieutenant-Colonel **Thomas Egerton Hale**, who was born in Nantwich on 24 September 1832. Hale won his medal fighting with the 7th Regiment (the Royal Fusiliers) on 8 September 1855 at Sebastopol. At the time he was an assistant surgeon, but he took part in the assault on a day in which 10 VC's were awarded to British troops. The assault was initially successful, but then the Russians counter-attacked and when they finally withdrew the British had suffered 2,000 dead. When the great

siege of Sebastopol finally ended, it had cost the lives of 2,600 British, 7,500 French and 11,700 Russians. Thomas Hale survived the war and returned to Nantwich, where he died on Christmas Day 1909. He is buried in Acton parish churchyard.

The Indian Mutiny (1857–9) followed very quickly on the heels of the Crimean War and was the theatre of operations which resulted in the award of a VC to Stalybridge-born **John Buckley**. Buckley was assistant commissar of ordnance, working with the Commissariat Department, Bengal Establishment, in Delhi at the outbreak of the mutiny.

On 11 May 1857 the magazine in Delhi was in the charge of Lieutenant George Willoughby, with a staff of eight Englishmen, including Buckley, and a force of native Indian troops. Willoughby knew that the magazine, which contained massive stores of gunpowder, rifles, shells, guns and cartridges, would be a prime target for the rebels and he also knew that he could not rely on the loyalty of the native troops in the event of an overwhelming attack. Plans were made to blow up the magazine if it became clear that the rebels were going to overcome the garrison. Buckley was given the task, if all else failed, of igniting the gunpowder and blowing the magazine, which would result in certain death for all the defenders. Their fears were quickly realised as the fighting became fiercer and the rebels swarmed over the walls. The native troops deserted, and with Buckley and several others wounded, Willoughby himself gave the signal to destroy the magazine, which went up with a massive roar. The whole town shook with the explosion as debris and smoke spread far and wide. Incredibly four of the Englishmen, including Willoughby and Buckley, survived the carnage and, covered in dust and smoke, were able to escape in the confusion.

Buckley was badly wounded, but managed with two of his companions to reach the safety of the British garrison at Meerut. Sadly Willoughby was killed when he became separated from the group. Blowing the magazine was a selfless, calculated act of courage, because none of them expected to survive. Buckley well deserved his honour. He recovered from his severe wounds and later died at the age of 63 in East London in 1876.

World War One was the biggest and bloodiest conflict in the history of mankind. The casualties, estimated at over 20 million, were beyond the comprehension of a supposedly civilised society. The battles were numerous, involving forces on a scale never seen before and there were many deeds of heroism. Cheshire soldiers, as they have done in every major conflict, distinguished themselves and eight VC's were won in the various theatres of the war.

The first to be awarded was to Captain **E.K. Bradbury**, who commanded 'L' Battery of the Royal Horse Artillery in an action in Nery, France, on 1 September 1914. Bradbury and his battery found themselves trapped in fog in an orchard close to the village of Nery and surrounded by a much superior enemy force. The Germans poured heavy fire onto the British position, causing severe casualties, including Captain Bradbury. Despite having a leg blown off by a shell he continued to direct return fire. British reinforcements saved the battery but were too late to save the 33-year-old captain, who died from his wound. Although it is believed that Captain Bradbury was not Cheshire-born, records describe him as being from Altrincham. His VC was awarded posthumously.

Lieutenant-Commander **Edgar Christopher Cookson** RN, who was born in Tranmere on 13 December 1883, also won a posthumous VC for his action in Mesopotamia on 28 September 1915. Cookson had previously won the DSO on 9 May 1915 for his reconnaissance work up the Euphrates River, an action in which he was badly wounded. After recovering he took command of the gunboat *Comet*, which was engaged in removing an obstacle that had been deliberately sunk in the middle of the river to stop British vessels. All attempts to move the obstruction, a sunken dhow, were prevented by heavy gunfire from both sides of the river. Cookson grabbed an axe and jumped onto the dhow in an attempt to cut the hawsers but was shot several times and died at the scene.

The medals of Private Thomas 'Todger' Alfred Jones of the 1st Battalion the Cheshire Regiment, including the Victoria Cross won in 1916. Cheshire Regimental Museum.

Born in Runcorn on 25 December 1880 and educated at the Runcorn National School, Private **Thomas 'Todger' Alfred Jones** of the 1st Battalion of the Cheshire Regiment won the VC on 25 September 1916 in France. Jones had earnt a reputation as a crack shot during his service with the Runcorn Volunteer battalion, which was to serve him in good stead in the conflict to follow. In an action near Morval, Jones saw his friend killed by a German sniper. Despite being shot through the helmet and through the coat, Jones avenged his friend and killed the sniper. He was particularly incensed as the enemy was firing at him while he was holding a white flag. He

their fingers in disdainful glee."
Koelnische Zeitung, September, 1914.

Pte. T. JONES. V.C. D.C.M.
22nd (CHESHIRE) REGIMENT

Private Jones's cabinet, including his photograph, statue, picture with his parents and a helmet with a bullet hole in it. Cheshire Regimental Museum.

attacked the German trenches single-handedly, killing several of the enemy and causing the rest, 102 of them, including several officers, to surrender. In a later action this fearless man earned the DCM, an award also won by six other Runcorn men. When he came home in 1916 the town gave him a tumultuous reception and he went on to receive the VC from King George V at Buckingham Palace before returning to the fighting. He survived the war and was a much admired and respected figure in his home town, where he died on 30 January 1956. He is buried in the Runcorn cemetery at Greenway Road. His Victoria Cross medal is in the Cheshire Regimental Museum in Chester, together with the

helmet dented by a bullet and his other medals, which include an Iron Cross, the German equivalent of the Victoria Cross, which he took from a German officer after a fight to the death.

The first VC of 1917 was won posthumously by Sergeant **Thomas Mottershead** on 7 January over Belgium. Mottershead, born in Widnes on 17 January 1892, worked at Cammell Laird before the war and then joined the 20th Squadron Royal Flying Corps. While flying over Belgium he was attacked by Albatross Scouts and bullets pierced his petrol tank, setting the aircraft on fire. Although enveloped in flames, Mottershead refused to bring the aircraft down over British trenches and tried desperately to protect his observer. His skill got the aircraft down safely, but he was too badly burnt and died of his wounds. The observer survived. Mottershead's widow received his VC from King George V on 2 June 1917 in London.

Another 1917 VC winner was Captain **Hugh Colvin** of the 9th Battalion Cheshires, who excelled in an action in Belgium on 20 September. Although Colvin was born in Burnley in 1887, he earned his award fighting with his regiment, the Cheshires, and his VC is held in the Cheshire Regimental Museum, Chester. Colvin commanded two companies and led them under heavy fire to assist a battalion which had been pinned down. Accompanied by only two men, he infiltrated enemy trenches and captured more than 50 Germans. He later personally wired the positions after all attempts had failed. He died in Bangor, County Down, in September 1962.

The first of three VC's to be won in 1918 went to Corporal **John Thomas Davies** of 11th (S) Battalion, South Lancs Regiment, on 24 March 1918. His gallantry occurred in the massive offensive between the rivers Oise and Arras, an action in which British and French losses amounted to 24,000. Davies was born in Birkenhead on 29 September 1896 and survived the war, dying in St Helens in October 1955.

The second was won by Private **Wilfred Wood** of the 10th Battalion Northumberland Fusiliers. Born in Stockport on 2 February 1897, Wood was awarded the VC for his gallantry in fighting at Casa Vana, Italy, on 28 October 1918. He lived to a ripe old age, dying in his 86th year in 1982 in Stockport. He is buried in Stockport cemetery.

The last VC to be won by Cestrians in World War One went to Sergeant **James Clarke** of the 15th Battalion Lancashire Fusiliers, who was born in Winsford on 6 April 1894. It was awarded following an action on 2 November 1918 in France. Clarke survived the war and died in 1947 in Rochdale.

The world had barely recovered from the slaughter of World War One when some 20 years later World War Two broke out in 1939. This second global conflict secured Britain's highest award for valour for two Cheshire men, one of whom was appropriately called Cheshire.

Chester-born Group Captain **Geoffrey Leonard Cheshire** was one of World War Two's most decorated men. Born on 7 September 1917, the son of a lawyer, Cheshire was educated at Oxford and took up flying in 1937. At the outbreak of war he joined the RAF Volunteer Reserve and from 1940–4 he flew fearlessly with great skill. At the age of 25 he was the youngest group captain in

Leonard Cheshire VC. Photograph courtesy Imperial War Museum.

The atom bomb. See Leonard Cheshire and Sir James Chadwick. Photograph courtesy Imperial War Museum.

Bomber Command and at one stage he even commanded the 'Dambusters'. There was no one particular action which earned his award; it was given for an accumulation of daring sorties over the years. In 1940 he won the DSO, in 1941 he won the DFC, in the same year he was awarded a bar to his DSO and in 1942 he received a second bar. In July 1944, flying a Lancaster bomber, Cheshire completed his 100th bombing mission. For his astonishing record, at a time when life expectancy in the air was often measured in weeks, if you were lucky, he was awarded the VC and became one of Britain's greatest ever flying heroes. However, there was one more mission that he was asked to make by Prime Minister Winston Churchill, and that was to act as the official British observer of the dropping of the atom bomb over Nagasaki on 9 August 1945.

After the war Cheshire pioneered the Cheshire Foundation Home scheme for the incurably sick which has now attained worldwide recognition. He died in 1992 in Cavendish and is buried in the local churchyard. In a poll in 2002 he was named in the list of 100 Great Britons.

Cheshire's other World War Two VC winner was Company Sergeant-Major **George Harold Eardley** of the 4th Battalion of the King's Shropshire Light Infantry. Born in Congleton on 6 May 1912, Eardley won his VC fighting in the Netherlands, on 16 October 1944. He returned to Congleton after the war, where he died on 11 September 1991. His grave is situated in Macclesfield Crematorium.

In 1950, just as the world was recovering from the devastation of World War Two, yet another major conflict erupted when North Korea invaded South Korea and Britain was once again drawn into the fight. When the war ended in 1953, the British Army had won four Victoria Crosses, two of which were awarded to Cestrians.

A posthumous VC was awarded to Major **Kenneth Muir**, who was born in Chester on 6 March 1912 and died fighting with the 1st Battalion Argyll & Sutherland Highlanders on 23

September 1950 at Songju, Korea. The Argylls had driven the Chinese and Koreans off Hill 282 and were trying to evacuate their wounded when the enemy started an offensive to recapture the hill. Muir had arrived with a stretcher party to help the wounded, but he became involved in the fighting and in the confusion took command. A firebomb devastated his forces and only 30 men were left, with little ammunition. Despite this, Muir led a counter-attack which drove the enemy from the hill and continued to inspire his men, using a 2-inch mortar himself, to ensure that the wounded escaped safely. He received a fatal wound and his last words are believed to have been 'The Gooks will never drive the Argylls off this hill'. The position was held and the wounded got away safely. Muir richly deserved his VC, but it was won at the cost of his life.

Britain's most recent VC was won by Altrincham's Private **William Speakman** on 4 November 1951 at United Hilltop, Korea, fighting with the 1st Battalion Black Watch attached to the 1st Battalion King's Own Borderers. Born in Altrincham on 21 September 1927, Speakman was educated at Oakfield Road Infants and then Wellington Road Secondary School, Altrincham. He enlisted in the Black Watch when he was only

17 and within seven years he had won the highest military honour that Britain had to offer.

The Chinese and Koreans attacked the British position on 4 November 1951 in a series of human wave assaults which resulted in desperate hand-to-hand fighting. Speakman noticed that one section of their position was about to be overrun and gathered a small group around him and, armed with grenades, led a series of counter-attacks. Shouting ferociously Speakman, 6ft 5in tall and heavily built, must have been an inspiring figure for his men and a terrifying figure for the Chinese. Attack and counter-attack, the struggle continued with Speakman's sorties continually disrupting the enemy despite his severe leg wounds. He fought on until the company managed to withdraw in good order leaving the enemy with very heavy casualties. With no regard for his own life, but with every concern for his comrades' lives, Bill Speakman's VC was in the greatest tradition and spirit of the award. He left the army as a sergeant and later went to live in South Africa, where he still resides today. However, at the age of 76 he returned to Altrincham in May 2003, to be the official guest of the town, which was naming a bridge after him.

Iraq 2003

In the most recent conflict in Iraq a young soldier of the Blues and Royals, fighting with a unit of the Household Cavalry, brilliantly upheld Cheshire's reputation for producing fighting men of the highest quality. Trooper **Chris Finney** from Marple was driving a Scimitar armoured reconnaissance vehicle north of Basra when without warning their column was subjected to a 'friendly' fire attack from US Air Force Tankbusting planes. The earth shook as 30mm depleted uranium rounds punched into the ground around them. As the flames enveloped the column, the unused ammunition

Bill Speakman VC visiting Altrincham in 2003. Photograph courtesy of Sale & Altrincham Messenger.

started to explode, but in the confusion Finney managed to escape from his vehicle. However, as the smoke and flames intensified he realised that the gunner of his Scimitar was wounded and trapped in the turret and would be burnt to death. Finney went back and got aboard the burning vehicle and managed to drag the gunner to safety. The column was badly crippled, with wounded men desperate for attention and help some 30 miles away. He realised that someone had to radio HQ and tell them what had happened and again he went back to the blazing vehicle and made the call.

Returning to help his wounded gunner, he was carrying him to safety when to his horror a roar turned his attention to the sky and he saw the aircraft coming in once again to finish the job; both men were hit by shrapnel as the shells peppered the ground. Trooper Finney said 'I saw sparks coming from the ground, then it felt like someone had kicked me in the back of my leg. I thought at first that I had hurt Andy and he was dragging me back, then when I turned round I felt warm down the back of my leg; blood was spurting everywhere. I had got shrapnel in my legs and buttocks'.

Despite his wounds Finney got Andy to safety then went to try and rescue another gunner who had been wounded in the second attack and was trapped in the turret of another Scimitar. Despite all his efforts he was beaten back by the heat and exploding ammunition and was unable to get to the man, who sadly died.

While Finney's group were being rescued they came under attack from Iraqi tanks which were eventually beaten off. Chris Finney was awarded the George Cross, regarded as equivalent to the Victoria Cross, which is awarded for valour under enemy fire. The citation said 'Trooper Finney displayed clear-headed courage and devotion to his comrades which was out of all proportion to his age and experience. Acting with complete disregard for his own safety even when wounded, his bravery was of the highest order'. Trooper Chris Finney had been in the army only a few months, and when the action took place on 28 March 2003 he was only 18 years of age! This remarkable young man, the youngest recipient of the George Cross, is a credit to his family and to Cheshire.

For more than a thousand years Cheshire's warriors and soldiers have played an important part in the shaping of the country's history and the defence of its freedom. The significant influence of Cestrians since Norman times belies the size of the county. A Cestrian was royal standard bearer to Richard the Lionheart, another became royal standard bearer to Henry VIII, and yet another was appointed Head of The King's Life Guard to Charles II and Edward III, while the Black Prince and Richard II chose Cheshire archers to be their personal bodyguards. As well as the many Victoria Crosses and other richly deserved decorations for bravery, Cheshire citizens have also attained high-ranking military positions: Admiral of the Fleet, commander, general, group captain and squadron leader, while many others have attained high political rank, a subject which will be covered in a later chapter.

Historical titbit

- One of the great figures of British history, **Robert Clive of India**, whose victory at Plassey in 1757 ensured British dominance in India, was educated at a small Cheshire school in Allostock, Knutsford.

CHAPTER 2

Pioneers, Adventurers, Explorers, Mountaineers

THROUGHOUT its history the county of Cheshire has been enriched by the adventurous spirit of its people. The warriors and soldiers of mediaeval times, and before, who embarked on fighting expeditions to the Crusades, to France, Wales, Ireland and Scotland, returned with wondrous tales of adventure, plunder and riches in return for their services, and helped to fire the ambitions of later generations.

Such a man was **Sir Robert Knolly**, born in Cheshire in 1317 but not really the ideal role model. A professional soldier by trade he fought in France in the 1340s to 1350s and, through a combination of murder, pillage, rape and extortion, he became one of the richest men in all England. At one time he controlled and ravaged a huge part of the Loire Valley in France, where there were 40 castles and several small towns. He ingratiated himself with King Edward III by placing his assets at his disposal and at one point he lent the King money secured against jewellery and silver plate. When he helped put down Wat Tyler's revolt at Smithfield in 1381 he was given the Freedom of London and further campaigning resulted in huge estates being given to him in Norfolk, Kent and London. When he died at his Sculthorpe home in Norfolk in 1407 he left more than £60,000, a huge sum for those days, but no heir to enjoy his ill-gotten gains. Sir Robert qual-ified in several categories: soldier, villain, politician and businessman, but he was certainly a consummate adventurer.

The Civil Wars of 1642–6 and 1650–1 did grievous harm to Cheshire, with rival factions not only splitting towns and communities but also dividing families, as loyalties turned to mistrust and duplicity, never to be reconciled. This very difficult period triggered the desire of a whole generation of pioneers to get away and start a new life in some of the new colonies, particularly America, which was offering attractive incentives to those willing to take the risk. Many of those setting out on their grand adventure never made it. Sea journeys were perilous, local Native Americans sometimes fought the intruders, starvation and disease were ever-present and many early settlers died in attempting to start a new life. Yet many succeeded, and they left an indelible mark on the world. Cheshire place-names proliferate today in British Columbia, Arctic Canada, Nova Scotia, America, Australia, South Africa and New Zealand, a testimony to the determination of those hardy, brave Cestrian pioneers who while establishing new beginnings paid tribute to their past by naming their new townships or settlements after their British birthplaces.

New England in America was a magnet for the early settlers as manpower was urgently needed to build towns and farm the land. Incentives such as the indentured service scheme gave free passage to New England in exchange for five years of work, and if the contract was honoured then the worker was rewarded with 50 acres of land, a suit, shoes, a hoe, an axe and several barrels of corn. Those willing to work took advantage of the scheme and soon townships started to spring up throughout New England, reflecting the Cheshire influx.

The name of Chester occurs frequently in New England and indeed **Chester, Pennsylvania**, became, with its founding in 1642, the oldest city in the state. However, it was only given its name in 1682 when William Penn, having been given land in settlement of a debt by Charles II, arrived there and promptly renamed it Chester. The town enjoyed great prosperity in textiles, oil, machinery and metals, particularly after both World Wars. Today, with a population of about 75,000, it is an affluent town with excellent access by road that enjoys all the benefits of being sited on the Delaware River. Pennsylvania also has a town called **Warrington**, again established under the influence of William Penn in 1682. The town, with a population of about 15,000, has fruit farms, wineries and a rich history of Indian Wars and the War of Independence.

There is another **Chester** in **Connecticut**, a small town of 4,000 people founded in 1692 in a particularly beautiful area of forests and lakes offering camping, boating, sailing and fishing. This very affluent town boasts a yacht club, a private aeroplane club and a main street lined with antique lampposts, restaurants and boutiques. Community spirit is vibrant with a seasonal programme of events throughout the year with a particularly magical time at Christmas.

Chester, Vermont, **New Hampshire** is another elegant charming small town with a Victorian district of historic houses. The town was char-

tered in 1761 as New Flamstead but as more settlers arrived the influence changed, and so in 1766 it was renamed Chester. Historically interesting, the town in 1774 became the first in the county to adopt the Declaration of Independence – something to do with those stroppy Cestrians? Geographically the town is situated at the confluence of three rivers and thrives on farming, shipping and the railroad.

Chester, in Western Morris County, **New Jersey**, is another small town of about 5,000 people with a rich, colonial past. The settlement was once called Black River and originated at the junction of two major Indian trails used by the Lenni Lenapes tribe. It became a thriving transport route for goods being sent to New York, as well as a natural centre for trade. Soon taverns and dwellings were established for the early travellers, which also attracted permanent settlers, and Quaker Baptists changed the name to Chester. The area is regarded as a Garden of Eden as it farms and produces grain, apples and peaches.

A very different but nevertheless interesting **Chester** is situated in Plumas County, north **California**, on the shores of Lake Almanor near Mount Lassen, a 10,448ft volcano which last erupted in 1917. This small community is in a National Park area with sulphur hot springs, and Lake Almanor's crystal-clear blue water is renowned for its fishing, while hunting, skiing and golf are also available in the area. The land was formerly home to the Maidu Indians and then the trappers and mountain men arrived together with settlers. The community of Chester, at an elevation of 4,500ft, was formalised in around 1848, but nothing is known about who actually named it. The area is rich in wildlife with mules, deer, blacktail deer, raccoons, chipmunks, southern bald eagles, osprey and squirrels to be found.

Another superbly sited **Chester** is located in **Nova Scotia** and was founded in 1759 by New England planters. The town is protected from Atlantic swells and storms by a group of islands and a peninsula. Geographically it has everything: rugged coast, woodlands, lakes, islands and of course sailing, fishing, boating and horse carriage rides around the town and the coast, providing an enviable lifestyle. They even have an annual **Chester Race Week** to rival our own. However this particular race week involves yachts, not horses. Again, similar to Cheshire's Chester, it has fine restaurants, boutiques, art galleries, craft shops and a live theatre. There must have been a number of Chester pioneers in these various townships as, apart from William Penn, no particular person has been credited with the naming of these communities. Indeed there may well be other small places called Chester, as the name is linked with Illinois and South Carolina.

Chester pioneers clearly left their mark on America, but so to did pioneers from Stockport. **Stockport** features four times in the United States, in **Ohio, Iowa, New York State** and an area off the **Hudson River**. Stockport in Ohio, a small town of 500 people, was founded by the brothers **Samuel** and **George Beswick**, who left Stockport in Britain and eventually settled in the Ohio area in about 1833. Initially the settlement was called Windsor, but as the influence of the Beswick brothers started to grow it was changed to Stockport. The brothers built a flour mill on the Muskingham River in 1842 as the township started to grow through farming and coal mining. Sadly the coal started to run out and with it went prosperity. The small community then dwindled to its present level. Nevertheless it is still vibrant with churches, schools and the Stockport Mill Country Inn, which is the focal point of the community. The owners have restored the orig-inal turbines of the first mill to working order and they are a major tourist attraction, a living testimony to the Beswicks. The Country Inn offers boating, canoeing, sailing and a full annual social programme for the community. The Beswicks are fondly remembered – certainly more fondly than another local, an Indian called Silverheels, who was renowned for taking the scalps of white men!

Another Beswick, **James Beswick**, left Ohio in 1850 with his family and settled in Iowa. He enjoyed a prosperous time as a farmer, accumulating some wealth, so much so, that when it was proposed to bring the railroad to the area in 1882, he offered to pay for it, providing that they called the township Stockport. Even now the community is only small, with a population of around 300, and descendants of the Beswicks still live in this fertile, farming area.

Another **Stockport**, located on the banks of the Hudson River, **New York State**, a small town of 4,500 people involved in farming and small businesses, is a thriving testimony to another Stopfordian. **James Wild** left England to pursue his own American dream and he settled down in the Hudson River area buying land which had once belonged to the local Indians. In 1807 he established a textile mill on a creek just off the Hudson and the community grew rapidly and still thrives to this day. The Native Americans had occupied the land for more than 5,000 years and there are excellent archaeological sites in the area. The whole of the surrounding district, a vast reserve of five miles of coastline, marshes, a peninsula and freshwater wetland just off the Hudson River, drains a watershed of almost 500 square miles. The reserve is called Stockport Flats and is abundant with flora and fauna, freshwater fish, kingfishers, bald eagles and osprey. It certainly conjures up a different mental picture than the British Stockport flats!

One Stockport family settled very successfully in America but did not leave a calling card by naming their settlement after their home town. Nevertheless their family name has become a legacy to two legendary American institutions. The Dodge family has been established in Stockport since 1433 and historically featured prominently in the running of the town. In 1629 **William Dodge** set out for America to start a new life and was joined eight years later by brother **Richard**. They settled well and soon established a strong and numerous family base, several of whom feature in the history of America. One of their descendants, a Civil War General, **Grenville Mellon Dodge**, established a military base in 1864 in Kansas and called it Fort Dodge. In just a few short years, with the coming of the railroad and the cattle industry, it became a boom town. Infamously renowned to all Western movie lovers, Dodge City was associated with Bat Masterson, Indian fighters, buffalo hunters, ranchers, gamblers and outlaws, several of whom stayed in Dodge City for ever, in a place called Boot Hill! Later descendants established a car building business in Detroit in 1901, the **Dodge Motor Co.**, which they sold in 1917 to the Ford Motor Co. Even today the name Dodge still features on a number of models.

The Macclesfield area also has its share of pioneers spreading their local place names around the world. Orillia, 70 miles from Ontario, Canada, has its own **Gawsworth Hall**, a magnificent Victorian edifice built by **Henry Wollaston Fitton** in 1863 following his emigration from London. It was built as a reminder of, and named after, the Fitton family seat at Gawsworth, near Macclesfield. It is a superb country house hotel set in four acres of grounds on the shore of Lake Couchiching.

Other Maxonians travelled further afield and left their imprint on Australia. Melbourne, Victoria, has a small town called **Macclesfield** set in a farming community. The population of 600 lives in an area of horse breeding, rainbow trout farms and gum leaf harvesting, from which eucalyptus oil is distilled, in an area of lush rich green farmland about an hour from Melbourne. There is even an alpaca stud farm. However, when a man called **Stringer** first arrived in about 1840, it was gold he was looking for. Clearly, whether he made his fortune or not, he liked the place and named it after his British birthplace.

Another **Macclesfield**, set in the Adelaide Hills of South Australia, is again in a beautiful fertile area near the River Angus, with forest, rolling hills and a golf course. It is a wine-producing area renowned for McClaren Vale, which is exported across the world and particularly to Britain. The community was founded by the three Davenport brothers who settled there following the discovery of gold in the Angus river in 1840. The area still has an old English-style pub called the Three Brothers. The Davenports named the community after their benefactor, the Earl of Macclesfield.

Brisbane, in Queensland, Australia, has a small town called **Alderley** with a population of about 5,000, which is believed to have been founded in around 1865 by an English settler because it reminded him of home. Certainly it is a beautiful place with parks, woods of bamboo, bunyan and fig trees, and a reserve for flora and fauna set by a creek. The Brisbane area also contains a town with a population of 34,000 called **Runcorn**, named in 1887 by **Revd McLaren** after his UK birthplace.

Further south in New South Wales is an area called **Alderley Edge**, near Bowral, the home of the late great Sir Don Bradman. It comprises an area of about 2,500 acres and there is a restored historic house, the Yellow House. The area is believed to have been named by **Alexander Champion**, who settled there in about 1938 and named it as a reminder of home.

Macclesfield also has a foothold in America but not through pioneering initiatives. North Carolina was visited in 2001 by the British Mayor of Macclesfield to help celebrate the centenary of the founding of their small town, which today numbers about 500 people. The town, of some 200 families, was named **Macclesfield** on the suggestion of a niece of the railway engineer who had visited Macclesfield in England and had been very impressed by what she saw. As part of the centenary celebrations the town passed a law ordering all males to grow beards or pay a fine, which they claimed was an old English custom to help celebrate special occasions. Like its English counterpart, Macclesfield is very much a farming area, but unlike the English town it grows tobacco and beans and presumably beards!

Birkenhead has an affinity with New York but not through pioneering. **Joseph Paxton** created the first municipal park in Great Britain, starting in 1843 landscaping lakes and gardens in Birkenhead. An American, Frederick Law, was so impressed that he replicated the scheme, creating Central Park in New York. I suppose in his way Joseph Paxton could claim to be a pioneer: he was certainly the first and the best in his field.

Birkenhead Provincial Park in Whistler, British Columbia, Canada, is a magnificent natural reserve with bear and moose and wild forest. It was named by the explorer A.C. Anderson, who named it after a relative, Lieutenant Colonel A. Seton, who commanded the ill-fated HMS *Birkenhead*, a troopship which sank off the coast of South Africa in 1852 with the loss of 454 lives. The ship hit a rock and as it started to sink Seton gave the order to abandon ship: 'Every man for himself', but the troops, in an act which has

entered the history books, stayed in their ranks and decreed 'Women and children first'. There were insufficient lifeboats and the waters were alive with sharks and to enter the water was certain death. Despite that, barely a man moved and most of them died as the ship went down. The tragedy is commemorated by the Birkenhead Memorial Stone, located in the Simonstown naval cemetery in South Africa, and the rock which sank the ship is the subject of tourist boat trips to Birkenhead Rock, located just off the Cape of Good Hope.

Auckland, New Zealand, is the location of another **Birkenhead**, set into a magnificent landscape between two volcanic cones with spectacular views across the bay. The town of 42,000 is linked to Auckland by ferry and clearly reminded early settlers of the geographical similarities between their British birthplace and New Zealand. **Charles Heaphy**, a Brit and a government surveyor, is credited with the naming of Birkenhead in around 1860.

Birkenhead in Adelaide, South Australia, is a small town linked by ferry to Port Adelaide, again with geographic and historic similarities to Britain. The town was known as Birkenhead in 1862, and the ferry, the Birkenhead Ferry, was advertised in 1880 as the first one-penny fare ferry in South Australia.

Clearly Cheshire pioneers blazed a trail across the world and left a marker for all to see. Many chose to take the perilous journey to a new life and many succeeded. However, one man, typical of a number at the time, set out for Australia – not as a pioneer, but as a prisoner heading for a penal colony in Australia. His story turned out to be unique and has survived the years as a marvellous tale of adventure.

William Buckley, born in Marton near Macclesfield in 1780, came from a poor background and struggled to make a living as a brick-layer and odd-job man. In around 1800 he got into trouble with the law and found himself before the Knutsford Sessions. His crime would today be regarded as petty, but for criminally receiving stolen goods he was sentenced to be deported to a penal colony in Australia and found himself leaving Liverpool by ship bound for Port Philip Bay, Victoria. The tough regime in the convict settlement eventually caused him, along with several others, to make a break for freedom. A search party soon tracked them down and one by one they were caught. Several of his fellow convicts were killed. Buckley, however, managed to escape into the bush, which was something of a pyrrhic victory. He quickly realised that in temperatures of over 40 degrees centigrade, with little food and water, no sense of direction and a totally hostile environment, with poisonous snakes and insects at every turn, his chances of survival were slim. The police pursuing him were of the same opinion and called off the search, certain that he would perish. Buckley, astonishingly, survived for more than 32 years in that most hostile of terrains. Local Aborigines found him and, fascinated, sheltered him and taught him to hunt and survive on edible plants and shrubs. They called him the 'Wild White Man'. As time passed explorers ventured further and further into the bush and the Aborigines became more aware of them. One day Buckley chanced upon a group of white men and plucked up the courage to talk to them. They were astonished to find that this wild unkempt man who could speak Aborigine could also speak English. In July 1885 Buckley went back with them to Melbourne where he was pardoned, and he stayed to work with his countrymen as a guide and interpreter. He became a legend in Australia and tourist trails were established to enable people to trace his footsteps in the outback. This remarkable man, the Wild White Man, died in Tasmania at the age of 76 and passed into Australian folklore.

A pioneer of a different kind was **John Alcock**, who along with Arthur Whitten Brown entered the world's history books as the first men ever to fly non-stop across the Atlantic. Although Alcock was actually born in Manchester in 1892, he grew up acting as a delivery lad for his aunt, who owned a butchers shop in Heaton Moor, Stockport. It is said that Alcock day-dreamed of greater things as he worked to deliver orders around the streets of Heaton Moor. Those dreams turned into reality in 1919, when he and Brown set off from Newfoundland in a Vickers-Vimy aircraft and completed their historic flight by landing in Ireland. Memorials commemorating this stupendous feat were erected on both sides of the Atlantic and Alcock was knighted before dying from injuries received in a later plane accident.

An explorer who crossed the Australian Central Desert was **Peter Warburton**, born in Arley Hall, Northwich, in 1813. Warburton, blessed with an adventurous spirit, served with the East India Company for more than 20 years before taking up official posts in Australia. He organised and led an expedition into the great Central Desert, of which little was known. Attempting to cross from Adelaide to Perth over the Nullarbor Plain in an effort to establish an overland route, the lack of water almost proved disastrous for the expedition and led to the conclusion that an overland route was just not feasible. His book about the expedition, called *Journey Across The Western Interior Of Australia*, illustrated what an amazing feat he managed to achieve, but sadly he died in Adelaide in 1875 shortly after it was published.

In 1852, Sir Edward Inglefield, sponsored by

Lord Francis Egerton, Earl of Ellesmere, who was the President of the Lancashire and Cheshire Historical Society, led an expedition into Arctic Canada and in gratitude to his benefactor named a huge island which he discovered **Ellesmere Island.**

Perhaps the greatest of Cheshire's adventurers and explorers was **George Back,** who was born at Holly Vale House, Stockport, on 6 November 1796 and educated at Stockport Grammar School. He joined the Royal Navy as a midshipman and in 1809 was captured by the French and spent the next five years as a prisoner of war. After the war he joined Sir John Franklin's 1817 expedition in search of the North West Passage and in 1819–23 embarked on two further explorations in North America. Promotions to lieutenant in 1823 and commander in 1827 demonstrated the recognition of his abilities and in 1832 he offered to mount a search for Sir John Ross, who had disappeared while searching for the North West Passage. The expedition set out in February 1833 and spent two years travelling almost 7,500 miles in the polar region. They found a great river, 400 miles long, which they named Great Fish River. It has since been renamed, unsurprisingly, **Back River.** While Back was searching for him, Ross actually returned safe and sound and when Back returned King William IV made him post-captain. This was a great honour, because the only previous holder of the title had been the King himself.

Back's last great expedition turned out to be the most dangerous. He set out in 1836 aboard HMS *Terror* to survey the polar coast from

Admiral Sir George Back, the Arctic explorer. Stockport Grammar School.

Regent's Inlet to Cape Turnagain. The voyage was hazardous and the party endured great hardships. Temperatures reached minus 50, and they were near starvation at one point and were reduced to chewing leather shoes. They were also attacked by Eskimos and the ship suffered damage. When the expedition finally returned home in 1837, HMS *Terror* virtually limped into harbour bound together with cables, old ropes and chains. But the crew had survived and more honours were bestowed on George Back. In 1875 he was invited to unveil a memorial to his old leader, Sir John Franklin, founder of the North West Passage, at Westminster Abbey. When he died on 23 June 1878, he had attained virtually all the honours that could have been bestowed on him. His sextant can be seen in Woodbank Park, Stockport, and in Stockport Town Hall there is a stained-glass window commemorating the exploits of local hero Admiral Sir George Back, FRS, DCL. He was buried in Kensal Green cemetery.

Sir Wilfred Grenfell, born in 1865 at Mostyn House, Parkgate, was an explorer and medical missionary who did great work in Labrador. He devoted his life to improving the lives of the Eskimos and helped establish schools and hospitals. Knighted for his work, he became known as Grenfell of Labrador and died in 1940.

Cheshire can claim to have an interest in Britain's, and arguably the world's, greatest explorer **David Livingstone** of Africa. Robert Moffat, a Scottish missionary who did great work in Africa, lived and worked for a time in Cheshire. As a boy he tended the gardens in High

Legh Hall Park and it was during his time there that he claimed that he had a vision to go to Africa and devote his life to alleviating suffering. So successful was he that a copper beech tree was planted as a tribute to him near the private chapel at High Legh. In his final years Moffat returned to High Legh and it was said that on seeing the beech tree, dedicated to his vision as a young boy, he burst into tears. In 1840 Moffat met Livingstone, who had fallen in love with Moffat's daughter Mary, and, as the courtship progressed, Livingstone told Moffat that he was intent on working in China. It was Moffat who persuaded Livingstone that Africa was in great need and inspired his wonderful work on that great continent. Moffat's Cheshire vision set the country's greatest explorer on the road to his destiny. Sadly it also fell to Moffat to receive his son-in-law's body on its return from Africa in 1873.

The Moffat family was also instrumental in inspiring another unique explorer/missionary. **Annie Taylor**, born in Egremont, Cheshire in 1855, attended a talk given by Moffat's son on his father's work in Africa and was so moved by it that despite her family's protests she vowed to become a missionary. By the time of her first venture to China in 1884 the family had become reconciled and her three years in China left her with the taste for further experiences, particularly in Tibet. In 1887 she went to live on the Tibetan border doing medical work and helping educate and spread the work of God in the surrounding villages. It was in 1892 that she undertook a perilous journey through Tibet, hoping to reach the capital, Lhasa. She travelled dressed as a Tibetan woman with her head shaved, and was accompanied by a faithful Tibetan, four other people and 10 pack horses. The seven-month journey, covering more than 1,000 miles, was the first time a Western woman had ventured so far into this unknown land. Attacks by bandits, starvation, extreme cold and betrayal leading to a trial by Chinese leaders, sitting cross-legged in a huge tent, failed to quench her spirit. The Chinese did not punish her but forbade her to continue to Lhasa. They provided her with horses, tents and provisions and made her return the way she had come through northern China. When she reappeared safely in 1893 the news quickly spread to England and her adventures provoked the sending of further missionaries to assist her in her work. Annie Taylor continued her work in China and Tibet for another 20 years, assisted loyally to the end by the Tibetan Pashto, who had been by her side throughout the Tibetan expedition. Annie Taylor, missionary and explorer, died in 1920 at the age of 65.

Another intrepid, fearless Cheshire woman was Miss **Marianne Brocklehurst** of the wealthy Macclesfield silk dynasty. Born in 1832, she lived for most of her life on her brother's Swythamley estate in a house called the Bagstones at Wincle. Blessed with the family's wealth she was able to indulge her passion for travel and adventure and between 1860 and 1891 she travelled the world when it was a dangerous and unstable place, particularly for a woman. She travelled Europe and the Middle East, recording her experiences in a diary illustrated with watercolours and sketches, which is now in the Macclesfield West Park Museum. Accompanied by her friend Miss Booth and sometimes her footman, resplendent in his livery, her trips embraced Syria, Jordan, Saudi Arabia, Israel and Egypt on several occasions. Her diary of the 1873–4 trip to Egypt and the journey by boat up the Nile and return to Cairo, which took four months, gives an account of her search for antiquities. Her nephew **Alfred Brocklehurst**, who was also on this trip, spent his spare time hunting crocodile. The expedition was a success and Miss Brocklehurst brought back several artefacts, including a mummy case, which were smuggled out of Egypt and are all now housed in Macclesfield's West Park Museum, which was built with finance from Miss Brocklehurst. The family, who were mostly MPs and bankers, certainly indulged their taste for travel and adventure. **Thomas Unett Brocklehurst**, who lived at Henbury Hall, visited America, Japan and Mexico in 1879–82, while **Francis Dicken Brocklehurst** of Fence House spent the period from 1858–61 travelling in the Far East and Tibet.

However, the family member who perhaps made the greatest contribution to the family history was Lieutenent Colonel **Sir Philip Lee Brocklehurst** of Swythamley Hall, near Macclesfield, who was born on 7 March 1887. As a 20-year-old he joined Sir Ernest Shackleton's perilous expedition to the Antarctic and the South Pole. They were just 97 miles short of being the first to the Pole when they lost their last pony and, with little food left and frostbite taking its toll, they aborted the mission. Just 30 miles from safety they ran out of food, but they just about survived. The expedition, although it failed to achieve its main goal, had several major successes: the discovery of the magnetic South Pole, the first ascent of the volcano Mount Erebus, and the finding of a route to the South Pole over the Beardmore Glacier. Shackleton returned a hero and was knighted. For the young Philip Brocklehurst the expedition was a fantastic opportunity for adventure and exploration. He was one of the party that climbed Mount Erebus, and he lost two toes to frostbite as a permanent souvenir of that 1907–9 epic expedition. He went on to enjoy a very distinguished military and political career before his death in 1975. His brother, Colonel **Courtney Brocklehurst**, was an

explorer and big-game hunter who at one point in his life was game warden of the Sudan. He did, however, achieve a degree of notoriety when hunting in Szechuan province, China, in 1935. He shot a giant panda, reputed to be one of the largest ever seen. As it was even then an endangered species his foolishness was frowned upon in the best circles. An interesting incident occurred when the stuffed panda was to be shown at a Berlin exhibition just before World War Two. Hermann Goering took a liking to it and tried to buy it. His offer was rejected and the panda was returned to Macclesfield, where it still resides in the West Park Museum. Both of the brothers were keen hunters and brought home heads and specimens from their travels around the world. On the death of Sir Philip in 1975 the family decided to sell the many big-game trophies, together with rugs, carpets, furniture and artefacts collected over the years from around the world. The sale, held at Swythamley Hall by Christie's in May 1976, attracted buyers from all over the world. The big-game trophies were the special attraction: seal shot in the Antarctic, walrus shot in the Arctic, heads of wild boar from India, caribou from Newfoundland, rhino, buffalo, zebra, elephant, giraffe, crocodile, warthog and many other specimens from Africa including snakes and birds, showed a proclivity and disregard for wildlife that would not be permitted today. It was, however, a different world then, and explorers and adventurers were often hunters in order to survive. But organised big-game hunting was also accepted as a way of life and a hobby.

Wallasey-born **Harold William Tilman** was the complete all-rounder: soldier in World War One, coffee planter in Kenya, mountaineer, explorer, mariner and prolific writer. He started mountaineering in Kenya in 1930, moved on to the Himalayas and actually led the unsuccessful expedition to climb Everest in 1938. During World War Two he fought in the desert, and in France, and towards the end helped the resistance in Italy and Albania. At the war's end, unable to adapt to a normal life, his sense of adventure took him, along with his great friend Eric Shipton, to Kashmir, Nepal, through China and along the edges of the Gobi desert. In 1952 his efforts were rewarded with the presentation by the Royal Geographical Society of the Founder's Medal. For some time he preferred to explore the mountains of the Himalayas, until 1953 when perhaps his age caught up with him and he totally changed direction. At the age of 55 he took to the sea, embracing a different way of life. But leisure sailing, fishing and cruising were not for him. For the next 20 years or so, Tilman sailed the seas of the world. He sailed to the Arctic, to the Antarctic, and all round South America. At one point he left his boat to walk across the ice-pack at Patagonia. At the age of 60 he sailed round Africa, but tragically, on 1 November 1977, he left Rio heading for the Falklands and disappeared off the face of the earth. One can't help but believe that it was the perfect end for such an adventurer. He did leave behind a legacy of 15 books extolling his love of the great outdoors, sea and sailing, mountains and hills as treasures to be enjoyed.

A Modern-Day Explorer

Although these wonderful characters are from the past, Cheshire is fortunate to have a modern-day equivalent of those past masters. At a time when the world appears to have been miniaturised by computers, satellite probes and GPS to the point where there cannot be anything left to discover, Prestbury-born **Benedict Allen** continues the life of an explorer. Since he set off for the Amazon as

Benedict Allen in the Amazon. Catherine Marsh.

a 22-year-old in 1983, he has been travelling the world, returning to the Amazon basin twice more, and visiting New Guinea rainforests, Australian deserts and Siberia, in an astonishing demonstration of versatility and determination.

Brought up in a comfortable, stable, Prestbury environment, why on earth would someone suffer privation and terror on a voluntary basis? A fascination for the old stories, the magic of discovery and the joy of travel and experience, are perhaps the answers. Allen has certainly experienced privation and terror. At one time in the Amazon basin he was paddling his canoe along the Orinoco when he was attacked by gold miners who tried to kill him. In his efforts to escape the canoe capsized and he found himself alone and exposed. He contracted malaria and dysentery and almost starved to death, being forced to kill and eat a dog which had befriended him before finally getting out.

The local Indians called him 'Mad White Giant', and at 6ft 4in tall and travelling alone, filming himself, it is understandable. Allen's style is to get close to the people and wherever possible to live with them, gain their trust and try to understand their ways. He has spent weeks and months with indigenous tribes and actually made contact with two previously 'uncontacted' tribes – answering the question of whether there is anything new to be discovered. On a visit to Papua New Guinea he spent six weeks with the Niowra tribe, experiencing first-hand the male initiation ceremony, which involved the ritual of a daily beating. He has searched Sumatra in an attempt to solve the mystery of the ape man that legends say is human; he has crossed the Gibson Desert in Australia and spent almost four months crossing the Namib Desert by camel. He topped that with a five-month expedition through Mongolia, venturing into parts of Siberia, down through the steppes and finishing with a 100-mile walk with camels through the Gobi Desert.

His expeditions are all covered in a series of highly entertaining books and several of his journeys have been shown by BBC television. His trip to trace the steps and to solve the mystery of the disappearance of the explorer Colonel Percy Fawcett, who disappeared with his expedition to Brazil in 1925, was filmed by the BBC in 1999 and his programme featuring medicine men and shamen was shown in 2000. His expedition to Siberia to cross the frozen sea of the Bering Strait had viewers on the edge of their seats. There was a moment when he left his sledge and the dogs to scout ahead and when he returned they had gone.

In that vast empty freezing waste in temperatures of -40°C he was suddenly all alone. His stove wouldn't work and he curled up for warmth to try and survive the night in the hope of finding the dogs in the morning. He was lucky he did. Many had died in similar situations.

Benedict Allen's adventures bring pleasure, knowledge and entertainment to those of us who like the idea of dangerous exploits, but prefer to watch from the safety of an armchair, with drink in hand. Allen's home town, Prestbury, has a fine hotel called the Bridge, which named its restaurant Benedicts as a tribute to the local man's exploits.

Cestrians in this section of pioneers, adventurers, explorers and mountaineers have on occasions had an element of all four disciplines about them, particularly Wallasey's **Harold William Tilman**. However, the last discipline, mountaineering, really calls for specialist skills. Enthusiasm, determination, hard work and wealth are not enough. Death is a constant threat and a lack of expertise, a slip, a fall or a little carelessness can mean the end for a climber and perhaps his colleagues.

Harold Tilman was a mountaineer, and in 1936 he climbed Nanda Devi in the Himalayas, which was then the highest summit achieved by man. He also led the unsuccessful 1938 attempt on Everest. A Cestrian had first attempted the conquest of Everest in 1921 and the quest continued until eventually the dream was realised.

Everest: the Cheshire Connection

Straddling the border between China and Nepal stands Mount Everest, the giant in the impressive mountain range of the Himalayas. Identified in 1856 as the highest point on earth at 29,030ft, and named after Sir George Everest as a tribute to his work in establishing the Great Arc of the

Meridian, the mountain has posed a challenge for generations of mountaineers. It was not until 29 May 1953 that man first stepped onto its summit when Edmund Hillary and Sherpa Tensing entered the history books as the first conquerors of the highest mountain in the world. Or were they? Their magnificent achievement has always been qualified by the enduring legend of George Mallory and Andrew Irvine, who in 1924 were last seen at about 27,000ft moving steadily towards the summit, before being enveloped in mist and cloud and disappearing into immortality. Many believed, and wanted to believe, that they made it to the top and perhaps perished on the descent in a gale or in temperatures of minus 23°C, or in a fall. For over 75 years the legend endured, with no evidence, and no bodies discovered, until 1999.

George Leigh Mallory was born in Mobberley in 1886, the son of the local vicar, who had succeeded his father to become the vicar at the 13th-century St Wilfrid's parish church, Mobberley. He was a bright, adventurous, inquisitive lad with an early sense of adventure. Academically bright, he was educated at Winchester College, where in 1904 he acquired his first taste for the mountains on a school trip to the Alps, before eventually moving on to Cambridge, where he made the acquaintance of the soon-to-be-renowned poet, Rupert Brooke. When the family moved to Birkenhead in 1908, Mallory, encouraged by the climber Geoffrey Winthrop Young, began to climb in Wales, the Lake District and the Alps. It was clear from the start that he had a natural ability, combining strength with agility. After leaving Cambridge, Mallory took up the post of schoolmaster at Charterhouse, joined the Alpine Club and in 1911 climbed Mont Blanc. However, his serious mountaineering aspirations were interrupted when he

met Ruth Turner and married her in 1914, just as World War One was about to erupt. As a schoolmaster he had a reserved occupation and would not be called to the fight. However, he was conscious that many of his friends had entered the fray and some had died and he felt it his duty to enlist, so he joined up in 1915.

After the war, the Royal Geographical Society vowed to attempt the climbing of Everest and the Alpine Club offered its full support, recommending two climbers, one of whom was

The ill-fated 1924 Irvine/Mallory Everest expedition. Irvine is back left and Mallory back right.

Mobberley church. The stained glass window tribute to Everest explorer George Mallory – 'Sir Galahad'.

Speculation and conjecture have been rife for decades, due in part to the lack of any real evidence until 1999. There were tantalising clues: an ice-axe found at 27,400ft in 1933 was positively identified as belonging to Irvine, and a Chinese expedition reported in 1975 that they had seen a body and described it as 'old English'. It is now believed to have been that of Irvine. However, on 1 May 1999 a real breakthrough occurred when an American expedition found the body of George Mallory after almost 75 years.

There was no doubt that it was Mallory. His shirt bore his name tag, there were personal family letters wrapped in a silk scarf, a knife, a watch, snow goggles and an altimeter with the hands frustratingly missing. Broken bones and a severed rope fastened round his waist indicated that he had fallen from a great height. Of Irvine there was no sign and therefore no verification of the Chinese sighting. Experts deduced from the evidence that Mallory and Irvine were unlikely to have reached the summit. Is the legend of Mallory and Irvine therefore over? Does the stained-glass window in Mobberley Church dedicated to his memory, showing St George slaying the dragon and a panel depicting Sir Galahad (Mallory's nickname) merely commemorate a good try and not an historic first? Let us say that the romantics among us have not given up hope. There is still one piece of vital evidence missing. It was known that Mallory had with him a Kodak vest-pocket camera, no trace of which has yet been found. It was not on his body. Where is it? If it had not been used, surely it would have been in his pocket. Was it used to capture the triumphant ascent? Does Irvine have it because he photographed Mallory, the senior climber, at his moment of glory? The search for the missing camera, the missing link which may one day complete this fabulous but tragic story, goes on.

Mallory, who would be up to the task. The British Expedition of 1921, the first fully organised attempt, sadly failed. George Mallory, as acting climbing leader, was forced to call off the attempt when the group was driven from the mountain by vicious, freezing gale-force winds. Nevertheless, 1922 brought a further attempt. Mallory reached 27,000ft, a world altitude record, before the expedition was abandoned following the deaths of nine of the party.

A further expedition, which would enter the history books for all time, set out on 29 February 1924 and culminated in the disappearance of the 38-year-old Mallory and the 22-year-old **Andrew Irvine** as they neared the summit on 8 June.

When Mallory died he left a widow and three children and it was his son John, who together with his own son, George Mallory II, visited Everest in 1995 to replace the memorial erected by the survivors of the 1924 expedition. It was a proud moment for John but even better was to come. John left the group after replacing the memorial and returned to his home in South Africa. A few days later he received the call that told him that his son George, Mallory's grandson, had reached the summit of Everest and had left a photograph of his grandparents there as a tribute.

Mallory of Cheshire will be forever linked with Everest, whether he reached the summit or not. However, one Cheshire man who definitely reached that peak was Bramhall's **Peter Boardman**, one of Britain's greatest mountaineers. Educated at Stockport Grammar School from 1956–69, he acquired his taste for climbing on a school trip to Corsica in 1964. His love for the sport and his expertise were recognised when he was appointed national officer of the British Mountaineering Council based in Manchester, and he spent his later years as the director of the International School of Mountaineering in Switzerland, based in Leysin – recognition indeed. Although he was a modest, unassuming man it

Peter Boardman on Everest in 1975. Chris Bonington Picture Library

gave him enormous pleasure to return to Stockport Grammar School and give talks on his incredible experiences. He was the youngest member of Chris Bonington's successful expedition and stood on the summit of Everest in 1975. Later, with his great friend Joe Tasker, he climbed Changabang and wrote his first book *The Shining Mountain*. When Chris Bonington started to select a team for another attempt on Everest he had no hesitation in asking Boardman and Tasker.

Peter Boardman was excited by yet another challenge and actually wrote to the Stockport Grammar School Parents Association Newsletter, reminiscing about early map-reading lessons. In January 1982 so many people wanted to attend his talk at the school that it had to be switched to the Town Hall. Tragically, later that year history repeated itself, when Boardman and Tasker, attempting the same route as Mallory and Irvine, suffered the same fate, disappearing without trace on 18 May. The expedition was abandoned and Bonington was devastated by the loss of his friends. Peter Boardman's body was found in 1992 and a Japanese team discovered Joe Tasker in 1995. Such was the respect felt for these two great mountaineers that an award founded as a tribute to their memory, the Boardman Tasker Memorial Award For Mountain Literature, with a prize of £2,000, is awarded annually and has since 1984 become international.

Everest has many tales of tragedy attached to it and another much-respected Cheshire climber, **Nick Estcourt** from Bowdon, experienced despair and triumph. Nick was part of the successful attempt in 1975 but did not actually reach the summit, it being his role to prepare the route for Boardman's assault on the last leg. They were good friends and together with Bonington they used to meet at Estcourt's house in Bowdon to plan expeditions. Tragedy decimated the friend-

Nick Estcourt, who died in an avalanche on K2 in 1978. Chris Bonington Picture Library

Wallasey that he saw a book of photographs of the Cairngorms, the Cuilins of Skye and Glencoe, which fired and inspired the 16-year-old to plan his first trip to Snowdonia. Although he was born in London he moved with his wife Wendy to the Lake District in 1963. However, Manchester was where most of the mountaineering business was taking place and in 1968 they moved to Bowdon, Cheshire, where they stayed until 1974 before returning to the Lakes. When Bonington was organising his earlier expeditions it was good to be close to Estcourt and Boardman and it fostered great understanding. This elite group of mountaineers were renowned as the **'Altrincham All Stars'**.

Sir Christian Bonington. Chris Bonington Picture Library

ship when Bonington, Estcourt and Boardman were climbing the world's second highest mountain, K2, in 1978. Bonington had paused at one stage to rest and suddenly noticed a huge avalanche sweeping down the opposite slope. He reached for his camera to get a picture. Horror-stricken, he suddenly realised that some of his team were on that slope. Nick Estcourt died in the avalanche.

Sir Christian Bonington, knighted in 1996, is probably Britain's greatest-ever mountaineer and Cheshire has a claim on him. In his autobiography he states that it was while visiting an aunt in

Despite his earlier success it was not until 1985 that Bonington, after several expeditions, finally stood on the summit of Everest. At the age of 50 he became, briefly, the oldest man ever to have climbed Everest. His record lasted nine days! He recalls movingly the moment of triumph and then the heartache, as the memory of the loss of so many close friends and colleagues hit home. Today Chris Bonnington, who during his career climbed Annapurna, Mount Vinson in the Antarctic, Everest and K2 to name just a few, is a much-respected writer with several books to his

Chris Bonington at the summit of Everest with Sherpa Anglhakpa in 1985. Chris Bonington Picture Library

credit, including a superb autobiography. As a photographer he has a comprehensive library.

Since Mallory's attempt and the successful expedition of 1953, Everest has been climbed by more than 1,000 different climbers. The first British woman, Rebecca Stephens, reached the top in 1993. However, few will match the feat of Mallory and Irvine. If they did not reach the summit they must nevertheless have been very close, with none of the sophisticated climbing aids of today: the all-weather suits, lightweight equipment, specialised oxygen, scientifically advised foods and high-tech communications. What, I wonder would Mallory have achieved with that sort of support? Biscuits, tweeds and a vest-pocket Kodak camera and he almost made it, or did he?

Cheshire has certainly contributed commendably to the conquest of the greatest obstacle on earth and its mountaineers are known and respected throughout the world.

CHAPTER 3

Entertainers

CHESHIRE has a particularly good record in the performing arts of theatre, cinema, radio and television. Its good fortune is to have on its doorstep the cities of Manchester and Liverpool, where television and radio stations, together with excellent theatres, provide a superb spawning ground for aspiring thespians and entertainers.

Northern soaps like *Emmerdale, Brookside, Hollyoaks* and the ever popular *Coronation Street* have been the springboard for many talented local actors to move on to greater things. However, with one or two notable exceptions, I have concentrated on those entertainers who were actually born in Cheshire, because the excellent theatres, studios and soaps have attracted a transient thespian population, similar to that of the soccer players, who move into the county on short-term contracts before eventually moving on.

Entertainers have come from all over the county with a particularly rich seam coming from Birkenhead, and many have established themselves as household names and faces. Indeed Cestrians have given the country and the world *The Big Breakfast, Lawrence of Arabia, A Man For All Seasons, The Boyfriend, 'Allo 'Allo, Are You Being Served?* and *Love on the Dole*, to name but a few.

However, if we step back in time, Cheshire has the distinction of having had the last professional jester. **Samuel 'Maggoty' Johnson**, from Macclesfield, or rather Gawsworth, was born in 1691, and appears to have been a bit of an all-rounder. He could play the fiddle and he taught dance, wrote an opera, and wrote a play called *Lord Flame*. Records show that he, like so many after him, set off to find fortune and fame as an actor in London. Samuel eventually returned home, and died in Gawsworth in 1773 and is buried in Gawsworth Wood.

Moving on a few generations, a most popular Victorian and Edwardian pastime grew up on the back of seaside holidays. At that time trips to the seaside were always highlighted by the shows on the piers, which were attended by huge crowds. Open-air family entertainment with slapstick, knock-about comedy routines and audience participation was massively popular for many years. One of the greatest of these entertainers, at one time called the 'King of the Pierrots', was **Fred Walmsley**, who was born in Cranage in 1879. After his father died Fred sold the family grocery business and went to New Brighton to perform on the pier. He later moved to Blackpool to form the pier comedy group the Tonics. After working on the South Pier and enjoying huge popularity he joined the North Pier Pavilion show, *On With The Show*, which ran from 1924–34. Fred died in 1943.

Sadly that way of life never again enjoyed such mass popularity, as other forms of entertainment started to take over. It was said that cinema would put paid to the theatre and that television would put paid to the cinema. Fortunately those prophets of doom have been proven wrong, as each form of media has survived, by getting better at what it does. Indeed it can be argued that cinema is now proving to be more popular than ever before, producing massive blockbuster epics, with superb graphics, large screens and surround sound to engender a feeling of realism and involvement for the viewer. Huge Hollywood productions like *Titanic*, *The Lion King*, *Harry Potter* and *The Lord Of The Rings* trilogy have set new box-office records, as well as raising standards.

Cinema: Stars of the Silver Screen

The film industry salutes itself with its annual awards ceremony for all the cinematic and acting categories and is currently in its 76th year of awards. Certainly, as a measure of standard and achievement the 'Oscar', a gold-plated statue about 13in tall weighing 8lb, of a man holding a sword and a reel of film, is the ultimate award in this most competitive of all media. The Academy Awards night, held in Los Angeles, brings the stars out in a frenzy of self-congratulation. Outrageous dresses, elaborate hairstyles, borrowed jewellery, dazzling white teeth (probably borrowed) bronzed skin, fixed smiles and gushing air kisses catch the flash lights of the myriad of media photographers from around the world. Those fortunate to have been nominated for an award pretend not to care and then feign surprise and shock if they win, while pulling out a 100-page document in the form of a carefully prepared acceptance speech.

In recent years some of the acceptance speeches have been worthy of an award. Who can forget the excruciatingly embarrassing speech given by Gwyneth Paltrow, whose flowing tears were matched, if not beaten, a year later by Halle Berry. The front row audience thought that they were extras in *Titanic* and, as the tears continued to flow, they were issued with lifejackets! American winners usually thank their schoolteachers, parents, driving instructors, psychologist, personal trainers, sex therapist and dog walker and then go on to plead for world peace, an end to poverty and close with a prayer for thanksgiving. Not so the Brits, who continue to gatecrash this American event with regular successes. Jim Broadbent memorably accepted his award as Best Supporting Actor for *Iris* recently by saying 'stone the crows', and when Judi Dench won she simply said 'thank you very much, it's very nice, thank you'. Astonishingly, five times Cestrians have mounted the stage in Los Angeles and have held aloft the ultimate symbol of acceptance and achievement in their art.

The best known of all Cheshire's actors, to use the politically correct expression, is undoubtedly **Glenda Jackson**. Born in Birkenhead on 9 May 1936, Glenda is considered by many to have been Britain's finest-ever actor. Certainly her credentials: four Oscar nominations for Best Actress and two Oscar wins, place her at the very top of the list of Hollywood greats.

Raised in Hoylake in a modest house, she enjoyed the comfort and support of a large close-knit family, both in Hoylake and her home town of Birkenhead. During her teens she worked in Boots at West Kirby, and had a spell as a waitress, shop assistant and receptionist while working with amateur theatre groups. Eventually she enrolled at RADA, the Royal Academy of Dramatic Art, and spent more than 10 years working in repertory theatre. She made her theatre debut in *Separate Tables* in 1957 at Worthing and her London debut followed with *All Kinds Of Men*. By the time of her film debut in 1963 in *This Sporting Life* she was regarded as a versatile, highly accomplished stage actress with appearances in *Alfie* and *Hamlet* underlining her talent. However, she was on the verge of an astonishing film career and in 1970 she won the Oscar for Best Actress in the film *Women In Love*, which featured Oliver Reed and Alan Bates. 1971 saw her nominated as Best Actress, this time unsuccessfully, for *Sunday, Bloody Sunday* but a further nomination for the 1973 light comedy film, *A Touch Of Class*, with George Segal, brought her second Best Actress Oscar. For Cheshire film buffs it is interesting to note that the apartment in the film, in which the lovers secretly met, was located in Macclesfield Road! Another nomination for *Hedda* in 1975 was unsuccessful, but Glenda Jackson had already established that whatever the role, comedy, serious, light or dramatic, she had the talent to meet the challenge. She was awarded the CBE for her services to the British film industry.

Totally unmoved and unswayed by her film career she retired from acting and turned her attention to politics, entering Parliament in 1992 as the elected Labour MP for Hampstead and Highgate. She has remained an active MP and has proven to be an honest and uncompromising politician adapting to a life away from the footlights. Nevertheless, the sneaking suspicion remains that it was she who was responsible for coaching Cherie Blair for her tearful Oscar performance in front of the cameras following the Peter Foster affair! Only kidding.

Another Cheshire Oscar winner was **Wendy Hiller**, born in Bramhall on 15 August 1912. She attended drama school as a child and went to the Manchester Repertory Theatre in the 1930s before making her London stage debut in *Love On the Dole* in 1935. She married in 1937, the dramatist **Ronald Gow**, from Altrincham, the man who adapted and converted *Love On The*

Bramhall-born Oscar-winner Dame Wendy Hiller.

Dole for the stage. They stayed married until his death in 1993. Her first film appearance came in 1937 in *Lancashire Luck* but it was the invitation from George Bernard Shaw to play Eliza Doolittle in *Pygmalion* which pushed her into the spotlight in 1938. She became the first British actress to be nominated for an Oscar in a British film, but came second to a Hollywood legend, Bette Davis, who won the Oscar for *Jezebel*. Further film roles came her way: *Major Barbara* in 1940, *I Know Where I'm Going* in 1945 and then her Oscar-winning performance in the 1958 film *Separate Tables*. She received the award of Best Supporting

Actress for playing Miss Pat Cooper, the lonely owner of an English seaside hotel, in a film whose cast reads like a Hollywood roll of honour: Burt Lancaster, Rita Hayworth, David Niven, Deborah Kerr, Gladys Cooper and Rod Taylor. Wendy Hiller must have been an actress of considerable talent to shine in that company.

She was nominated yet again in 1966 as Best Supporting Actress when she played the wife of Sir Thomas Moore in the magnificent film, *A Man For All Seasons*. The film won many awards, including Best Film, which may have influenced the judges to redirect the best supporting actress award elsewhere. Once again she was in the very best of company in a film which featured Paul Scofield, Orson Welles, Robert Shaw, John Hurt, Leo McKern and Susannah York. In 1971 Wendy was awarded an OBE for her services to British acting and the demand for her as a stage actress continued unabated: *Crown Matrimonial* in 1972, *Ghosts,* also in 1972, *John Gabriel Borkman* in 1975, and others well into the 1980s. In the meantime she was of course still sought after for movie roles: *Murder On The Orient Express* in 1974, *The Elephant Man* in 1980 and *The Lonely Passion of Judith Hearne* in 1987, while in 1988 she embarked on a long-running stage version of *Driving Miss Daisy*. She continued working into the 1990s in television and radio and died in May 2003 at the age of 90. Dame Wendy Hiller (she was honoured in 1975) was one of the great ladies of British and world cinema. Renowned for her clear diction and feisty personality, she stood out in an era frequently described as the 'golden era' of Hollywood.

Robert Donat is believed to have been born in Withington on 18 March 1905, although two other sources claim that he was born in Sale. Nevertheless Withington, old Withington, is right on the Cheshire border, and Withington Golf

Club is in Cheshire, although the town is now regarded as part of Greater Manchester. The lines are so blurred that I will claim him for Cheshire. The son of a Polish immigrant, Donat wrote a page into cinematic history with his 1939 Oscar-winning performance as the shy, bumbling schoolmaster Mr Chips in *Goodbye Mr Chips*. It was his performance in this film which prevented *Gone With The Wind* from winning every category that year, thwarting even the great Clark Gable. However, Hollywood was well aware of Donat's talent as he had also been nominated in 1938 as Best Actor for his role in *The Citadel*, a film which also included Rex Harrison, Ralph Richardson and Emlyn Williams. Recognition indeed. Donat was tragically beset by ill health for most of his life, suffering greatly from asthma, which restricted his appearances on stage and film. He died in 1958 just one week after completing the film *Inn Of The Sixth Happiness* with Ingrid Bergman.

Sale-born **Robert Bolt** is among the very best of the cinema industry's screenplay writers and was responsible in the 1960s for several of the greatest epics ever to have graced cinema screens. His birthplace, at Northenden Road, Sale, and a later

The birthplace of screenwriter and playwright Robert Bolt. A blue plaque is situated on the wall of the house in Northenden Road, Sale.

residence at 68, School Road in Sale, were adorned with blue plaques in 2000, certifying that this highly-talented man had once used the buildings. Born in 1924, Bolt did not go into the family furniture business but followed his own love of writing and drama.

He wrote a play and called it *A Man For All Seasons,* and later adapted it for the cinema screen. This historical drama concerned the struggle between Henry VIII and Sir Thomas More and won a stack of Oscars, including Best Film. Bolt received the Oscar for Best Writer/Screenplay. As mentioned it had a most impressive cast and another Cestrian, Wendy Hiller, was nominated as Best Supporting Actress. It is unique to find two Cheshire artists involved in the universally accepted best film of the decade. The 1960s were a particularly prolific time for Bolt. He wrote the screenplays for two more blockbusting epics: the swashbuckling adventure, *Lawrence of Arabia,* and the lilting, romantic *Dr Zhivago* both won Academy Awards. Another popular film was *Ryan's Daughter* and later in 1972, Bolt wrote and directed *Lady Caroline Lamb,* which starred his wife Sarah Miles. Bolt continued to write, turning out film scripts for Mel Gibson and Robert de Niro, among others, while writing plays for television and children's stories. He died in 1995 but has left a legacy which many have strived to emulate.

An easily recognisable, craggy, lived-in face has become familiar to many of us through our television screens over the years, but has now started to appear on the big screen. **Pete Postlethwaite,** born in Warrington, has appeared in many TV dramas over the years, too numerous to mention, but perhaps his most popular was the late 1990s series *The Sins.* However, his reputation as an international actor soared when, playing alongside Daniel Day Lewis, in the film *In The Name*

Actor Pete Postlethwaite.

Of The Father, he was nominated in 1992 for Best Supporting Actor. Although on this occasion he was unsuccessful, he found himself in great demand and appeared in several box-office smash hits: *Jurassic Park: The Lost World* and *Amistad.* His star is in the ascendancy and one of these days he may well add to the Cestrian roll of honour by collecting that much-coveted Oscar. In 1996 he appeared with another highly popular and much-respected Cestrian actor, **Sue Johnston,** in the film *Brassed Off.* Sue, also from Warrington, is very much a permanent fixture on our television screens but has several films to her credit, including *Brassed Off* in 1996, *Face, Preaching* moving on to the London stage and thence to Broadway, New York.

Her striking dark looks and her acting ability led her to Hollywood to pursue her film career. Very early in her career she met and married Hollywood actor Val Kilmer, already well known and accepted as the star of *Batman Forever*, *Tombstone*, *Topgun* and *Willow*, in which he appeared alongside Joanne. Joanne has made several films, with perhaps her best role being Christine Keeler in *Scandal*. She also played Scarlett O'Hara in the television production of *Gone With The Wind*. However many men will always remember her for her extremely sensuous role in Dennis Potter's television play, *The Singing*

Sue Johnston. Ken McReddie Agency

To The Perverted and a number of cameo roles. Sue's career is covered in more detail in the section on television.

Another fine actress, never mind the political correctness, who has felt the slings and arrows of Hollywood fortune but has yet to savour the joy of an academy award, is Bredbury girl **Joanne Whalley**, born in August 1964. Joanne went to Strines Drama School, Marple and Harrytown Sixth Form School, Romiley, and actually appeared in *Coronation Street* at the age of nine and in *Emmerdale* as a 13-year-old, before having an unsuccessful go at *Opportunity Knocks*. She appeared in several television dramas before

Joanna Whalley. Stockport Express

Detective. Yet despite the fame, the glamour of Hollywood and a £2 million house in New Mexico (a far cry from those early modest days in Bredbury), her marriage to Val Kilmer sadly broke up in 1996. She has two children, and still has the ambition to succeed in Los Angeles, where she continues to reside. Her latest work is a television series called *40* which features Kerry Fox and Eddie Izzard and was premiered on Channel 4 in April 2003.

Another great favourite of the British public is Bramhall-born **Peter Barkworth**. Peter, born in 1929, endeared himself to British audiences with such popular television dramas as *The Power Game* and then played the wronged bank manager in *Telford's Change* opposite Hannah Gordon. Both series became compulsive viewing, attracting massive audiences. Peter attended Stockport School and played several dramatic roles as a teenager in the Mile End, Stockport Dramatic Society and at the local Hippodrome before he joined the Royal Academy of Dramatic Art, where he eventually attracted the attention of theatre and television producers and embarked on a hugely successful career. His popularity led to a

Actor Peter Barkworth. JAA

spate of film offers and he moved into that genre most comfortably. *Two a Penny* in 1968, *Where Eagles Dare* in 1969, *Patton* in 1970, *International Velvet* in 1978 and *Winston Churchill – The Wilderness Years* in 1981 are just a few of his film credits. His talents earned him BAFTA awards as Best Actor in 1974 and again in 1977. While his parents were alive Peter made many return visits to Bramhall and his old haunts in the Stockport area. He has been an actor since 1948 but since 1980 he has concentrated mainly on directing and has been responsible for many West End stage successes.

Bramhall is also the birthplace of another fixture on the British film scene. What is it about the rarefied air in Bramhall that promotes the development of thespians? **Peter Butterworth**, the chubby, smiling, genial children's television host spent some time as a prisoner of war but during this time learnt the basics which were to stand him in good stead as a show business career started to unfold after the war. He learnt his trade working with Ted Ray and Frankie Howerd and eventually found himself working in television. Among his very many TV credits were *Hugh and I*, *Emergency Ward 10* and *Doctor Who*. However, although his film career had started in 1948 with bit parts, it was only when he was invited to appear in *Carry On Cowboy* that he became an instant hit and permanently recognisable to the film public. The films were basically comedy nonsense, but became compulsive viewing for many and Peter appeared in 16 of them, including the very last of the originals, *Carry On Emmannuelle*. He was married to the comedienne Janet Brown for many years but Peter sadly died in 1979 at the age of 60 from a heart attack.

Another instantly recognisable face and instantly recognisable deep, throaty voice was that of Wallasey-born comedy and character actor **Deryck Guyler**, who was born in 1914. Deryck too was an almost permanent fixture on our television screens, but did make a number of film appearances. He cut his teeth in the World War Two radio hit series *ITMA* with Tommy Handley and featured in the 1947 Royal Command Performance for King George VI and Queen Elizabeth. However, for 20 years he featured in the popular TV series *Sykes*, appearing as the gormless, friendly neighbourhood policeman who was the bane of Eric Sykes. In 1970 he took on the role of the put upon ex-desert rat caretaker in Fern Street Secondary School, in the popular sitcom *Please Sir*. He made many other appearances on stage, radio and TV, with the occasional foray into films in cameo roles. He too joined the cast of the *Carry On* company and was particularly good in *Carry On Doctor*. Deryck enjoyed many years of retirement in London with his wife and family but passed away in 1999 at the grand old age of 85.

The 1960s were a prolifically successful era in terms of film appearances for an adopted Cestrian, even if the quality of the films left much to be desired. Nevertheless, that fun era of permissiveness, outrageous clothes and joyous living spawned a whole series of light, cheap, easy-to-make comedy films. **Jeremy Lloyd** was a fixture in many of these productions. Born in London in 1930, he went to live with his grandparents in Didsbury when only a few months old. He lived at No.1, Winster Avenue, off Barlow Moor Road, and attended the South Manchester Junior Grammar School in Didsbury village. Later he was sent to boarding school at Harden House, Alderley Edge, Cheshire, where his sense of fun and mischievousness, which characterised the rest of his life, came to the fore. Following the death of his grandfather Jeremy moved back to

London in 1945 to be reunited with his father. He embarked on a whole series of jobs before getting a break, via script writing, to appear on television with Billy Cotton. He quickly became a regular on the *Billy Cotton Show* as a well-dressed, bowler-hatted, umbrella-carrying well-spoken toff who was a bit of a twit. His punchline became 'I say Mr Cotton, I've got a splendid wheeze'. A whole series of films followed, with the tall, blonde-haired Jeremy enjoying small cameo roles. *School For Scoundrels*, *Man In The Moon*, *We Joined The Navy*, *A Very Important Person*, *Those Magnificent Men In their Flying Machines*, *The Wrong Box*, *Just For Fun*, *Smashing Time* and *Doctor in Clover* had him appearing alongside Kenneth Moore, Leslie Philips, Rita Tushingham, Shirley Ann Field, Alastair Sim, Peter Sellers, Terry Thomas and James Robertson Justice. The 1960s were a great time for Jeremy even if he was stuck in a one-dimensional type-cast role. However, his scriptwriting was proving very successful, with several TV credits, but Hollywood was beckoning and the 1970s would prove to be even more successful. His contribution to television will probably be best remembered and that will be dealt with in that section.

Another character of that era cannot really be classed as a film star, nor would her greatest fans regard her as an actress – yet for several years she graced our television screens and made several film appearances in small cameo roles. Stockport girl **Norma Sykes**, born in 1937, was appropriately enough once a Stockport breaststroke swimming champion. She later made her name as Britain's answer to the busty Hollywood dominance of Marilyn Monroe and Jayne Mansfield, as **Sabrina**. She made her first television appearance on Arthur Askey's *Before Your Very Eyes*, and very quickly became a permanent pin-up

Sabrina. Stockport's answer to Monroe and Mansfield. *Stockport Express*

Sabrina will stir fond memories in many a not-so-young man of today.

Many other Cheshire television and stage actors have made short appearances in films but one young man who certainly picked out a plum is Stockport's **Dominic Monaghan**.

Although he wasn't born in Cheshire, Dominic grew up in Stockport, spending his childhood in Heaton Moor. He attended St Anne's RC School in Heaton Chapel, where he got his first taste of the acting bug by appearing in school plays. He later moved on to Aquinas College and thence to the Manchester Youth Theatre and work in repertory theatre in Greater Manchester. His talent was quickly recognised and he won the part of the

Dominic Monaghan, star of Lord of the Rings. *Stockport Express*

feature. Tagged with the busty, dumb blonde stereotype it was hard for her to be taken seriously and although her acting career never really took off, she was, nevertheless, a household name for several years. She left Britain in 1967 to marry a Hollywood surgeon, but retained contact with Stockport over the ensuing years. The name juvenile lead opposite Patricia Routledge in the BBC TV series *Hetty Wainthropp Investigates*. This national exposure stood him in good stead and led to a part in the film *Boomber* with Martin Sheen and Rutger Hauer. He was later asked to audition for a part in *Lord Of The Rings*, a story which he already knew having been encouraged to read Tolkien's work by his father, who was a school teacher. While waiting for the result of the audition he was offered a lead role opposite John Thaw in *Monsignor Renard*, which was to be filmed in France. It was six months before he learnt that he had won the part of Merry (Meriadoc Brandybuck) in *Lord of the Rings*, second cousin to the main character Frodo Baggins and one of the hobbits to accompany him on his dangerous quest. Merry is feisty and cheeky, a characterisation which suits Dominic perfectly. *Lord Of The Rings* was filmed as a trilogy and the first part, *The Fellowship Of The Ring*, was released to incredible acclaim in 2001. The second part, *The Two Towers*, came out in 2002, breaking all box-office records. The finale, *The Return of the King*, followed in 2003, and the trilogy has set new standards in graphics and cinematography. Although he now lives for much of the time in Los Angeles, Dominic has returned to his old school, St Anne's, to visit the drama department and talk to the young pupils. He was full of praise for the coaching and encouragement he received from the school, which inspired him to embark on a career in which, at the age of 25, he is an internationally recognised face. Dominic appears to be a young man with a highly promising cinema career.

The recognition of cinematography as an art form by the Hollywood Film Academy underlines the enjoyment that superb photography can bring to any film production, particularly with today's wide screens and surround sound. Birkenhead-born **Tony Pierce-Roberts** is one of the film world's leading cinematographers. Although he was brought up mainly in central Africa and began his career there, he started working for the BBC on a number of TV series, including *Tinker, Tailor, Soldier, Spy*. His first film production was *Caught On A Train* in 1980, but his first real popular appreciation came from his work on *Moonlighting* in 1982, which established London in a drab, grey, atmospheric setting. Since then his work has been prolific as his reputation has grown and his film credits are most impressive: *Underworld* in 2003, *The Importance of Being Ernest* in 2002, with a film every year including *Disclosure*, *Surviving Picasso*, *The Client*, and *The Remains Of The Day*, right down to *A Room With A View* in 1986.

Finally, there is another fascinating link between Cheshire and Hollywood films. One of the most amazing blockbusters of the 1990s, *Titanic*, starring Kate Winslet and Leonardo di Caprio, has two connections with Cheshire. Captain **Edward Smith** came to live in Warrington in around 1901, married a girl from Winwick and settled down in a cottage in the village. It was Captain Smith who was blamed for allowing the *Titanic* to sail full speed into the iceberg which resulted in the deaths of more than 1,500 people in the freezing waters of the North Atlantic ocean, on that fateful night in 1912. Smith himself drowned in the disaster. The *Titanic* also features in Cheshire history because it was one of the ships of the White Star Shipping Line, which was owned by **Thomas Ismay**, who lived at Thurstaston Manor, in Thurstaston village, Cheshire.

Television and Theatre

Television really started to take off as the major means of entertainment in the 1960s. The economy had fully recovered from the effects of World War Two, and the new prosperity meant that many households were able to afford a television, which brought drama, comedy and adventure into the living room. The faces of many entertainers became well known through soaps, plays, serials, comedy and talent shows and advertisements. Their exposure and popularity also resulted in a revival for theatre, as many of the new stars capitalised on their celebrity by touring the country in shows and revues. During this time several Cheshire entertainers became almost permanent fixtures on the nation's TV screens and enjoyed high-profile careers. For example, although I have placed **Deryck Guyler** in the cinema section, he featured on our television screens in two series for more than 20 years.

Russ Abbot, born in Chester on 18 September 1948, was educated at Queens Park school, Handbridge, before leaving and setting out for a career in show business. He enjoyed early success with a comedy/singing group, the Black Abbots, in the 1960s, before embarking on what was to prove to be a hugely successful solo career. His mischievous grin, easy charm and an ability to impersonate, sing and act gave him a longevity beyond the norm. The public did not grow tired of him. Indeed he won the much respected *TV Times* Funniest Man on TV award five times, and was a frequent guest on chat shows. His many TV shows included: *London Night Out*, *Who Do You Do*, *The Comedians*, *Bruce Forsyth's Big Night Out*, *The Russ Abbot Show*, *The Russ Abbot Christmas Show*, *Wogan*, *Tarby And Friends*, *Bob Monkhouse Show*, *Live From The Palladium*, and six series of *Russ Abbot's Mad House*. Not as prolific as he once was, in recent years Russ has attempted straight acting with a degree of success.

One of Russ's early madcap contemporaries was **Freddie Starr**. Born Freddie Fowell in Liverpool, in 1943, Freddie burst onto the entertainment scene following a short spell as a lead singer with a pop group. He spent the creative and formative part of his career in Birkenhead, where he married in the 1960s and moved into a flat. His days were spent working at Cammell Laird and his nights performing in the Birkenhead and Liverpool clubs and pubs. His talent for mimicry, ability to sing and his pure zany feel for comedy was like a breath of fresh air to television audiences. His first television appearance was on the talent show *Opportunity Knocks*, which was followed by an invitation to appear on *Who Do You Do*, a programme specifically for impersonators. The public took to his cheeky, irreverent style and very soon he became a fixture on television and in theatres across the country. *The Freddie Starr Show* and *The Freddie Starr Showcase* were followed in 1980 by *Freddie Starr's Variety Madhouse*, in which he shared the spotlight with Russ Abbot. Eventually, Freddie left the show, which was then renamed *Russ Abbot's Madhouse*.

Starr appeared on many chat shows and panel games and always tried to do the unexpected. However, some of his stunts got out of hand and producers became wary of trusting him on live shows. It was Des O'Connor who kept the faith and enjoyed a particularly rewarding camaraderie with Starr, who was a frequent guest on his chat show. Marital problems, adverse publicity with the alleged hamster-eating episode and health problems dogged Freddie for a while, but he bounced back with a straight acting part in *Supply and Demand* and became the host of Sky TV's game show, *Beat The Crusher*. At his peak Freddie Starr was a comic genius, a modern clown. His superb impersonations of Mick Jagger and the many cameo roles he played as a ludicrous Hitler figure will stay in the annals of television entertainment history.

However, the supreme impersonator of the era was undoubtedly **Mike Yarwood**. Born in Stockport in 1941, Mike lived in Prestbury, near Macclesfield, at the height of his career. His early skills were practised and honed working in the local pubs and clubs in the Stockport and Manchester area in the 1960s before an appearance on *Sunday Night At The London Palladium* in 1964, which was televised, exposed him to a nationwide audience who showed their approval. For almost 20 years he ruled the roost. *Will The Real Mike Yarwood Stand Up*, *Look Mike Yarwood*, and *Mike Yarwood In Persons* were his main television series, and he appeared on chat shows, in showcases and at Royal Command Performances. He was the Rory Bremner of the time. His impressions of the era's notables: Brian Clough, Eddie Waring, Robin Day and the Prime Minister Harold Wilson became almost an art form. It is said that his decline in popularity stemmed from the election success of Margaret Thatcher in 1979 and his inability to impersonate her. Whatever the reason, Mike, never the most confident of people, suffered health problems and his marriage broke down. His later attempts to make a comeback were only moderately successful. Nevertheless, for a time Cheshire could claim to have the country's greatest impersonator.

Sue Johnston, from Warrington, already mentioned briefly in the cinema section, is better known to British audiences for her versatile television acting ability, which has covered the entire range from drama and soap to comedy. Sue was born on 7 December 1943 and actually worked for a time as a tax inspector, before moving over to acting. As well as her cinema appearances Sue has made stage and TV appearances, far too many to be listed. She has featured in the major soaps *Coronation Street* and *Brookside*, and was nominated for a BAFTA award in the 1992 drama mini-

series, *Goodbye Cruel World*. Her latest major TV series has been the very popular *The Royle Family*, which started in 1998 and has enjoyed a long run. Sue plays chain-smoking Barbara (she hates smoking) in the biting comedy and plays the part so well that she won the Best British Comedy Actress Award. No doubt she will continue to grace our screens for many years to come.

The other actress whose face is instantly recognisable is that of **Patricia Routledge**, born in Birkenhead on 17 February 1929. Patricia gained an Honours Degree in English Literature and Language at Liverpool University following her basic education at Birkenhead High School. She decided that the theatre was the direction she wished to take and enrolled at the Bristol Old Vic Theatre School, making her first appearance with the company at the Liverpool Playhouse in Shakespeare in 1952. After leaving the company she gained experience with other repertory groups and made her London debut in a musical adaptation of the operetta *The Duenna* in 1954. For many years Patricia was a much-respected actress in the world of stage and theatre, having both an excellent singing voice and the light touch of a gifted comedy actress, for which she would earn everlasting fame in her later years. She appeared in many musicals on Broadway, where she was very much in demand in the 1960s. Although the show in which she starred, *Darling Of The Day*, closed after a short run, Patricia received the Tony award for Best Musical Actress on Broadway. Despite this personal acclaim, several of the shows with which she was associated came to premature ends and her musical career in America came to a halt in 1976. Nevertheless, during this period she appeared in a number of films and many television shows, including films such as *To Sir, With Love* in 1966, *The Bliss of Mrs Blossom* in 1968, *Lock Up Your Daughters* in 1969 and

Keeping Up Appearances
star Patricia Routledge.
John Timbers

Egghead's Robot in 1970; and television shows like *David Copperfield, Nicholas Nickleby, Beggar's Opera, Talking Heads, Missing Persons, Funny Women, Victoria Wood As Seen On TV* and many, many more. However, her early career as a talented musical stage actress is largely unknown to the public at large, in view of her two most popular TV characters.

Patricia took the title role in the television series *Hetty Wainthropp Investigates*, which first started in 1996, but it is the part of Hyacinth Bucket (which the character insisted was pronounced 'Bouquet') which she took in 1990, that has enshrined her in memory. The snobbish, precise neighbourhood bore, who was forever trying to get the vicar to attend one of her 'candle-light suppers' but was always let down by her vulgar family was a perfect vehicle for her comedic skills. Patricia Routledge will also continue to entertain us for many years to come.

The joys and the dangers of being remembered for one particular role are a two-edged sword for the jobbing or career actor. On the one hand it brings fame and sometimes financial stability, but on the other hand it can negate, or make the public forget, previous excellent work. A perfect example is **Kathy Staff**, born in Dukinfield in 1928, who has been ever-present on British television for almost 30 years, an astonishing record. Kathy's close family and her roots are firmly in the area in which she was born and she is still a choir member and attends church in Dukinfield every Sunday. Like a number of northern actors Kathy had experience at the Oldham Coliseum repertory theatre as a teenager, before joining a touring theatre company. She certainly served her time, gaining experience before breaking into films with small roles in the 1960s in *A Kind Of Loving* and *The Family Way*, with two more in the 1980s, *The Dresser* and *Little Dorrit*. It is,

however, television which has proved the main-stay of her career, with appearances in *Within These Walls, Coronation Street* and, in the 1970s and 1980s, in *Crossroads*. She was asked to return in the revamped version in the year 2000.

Nevertheless, the role with which she is most associated is that of Nora Batty in *Last Of The Summer Wine*. Kathy's character, playing opposite Compo (the late Bill Owen), who was always in trouble with her, became an easily identifiable figure that spawned many impersonations. A stern face, hair curlers, pinny usually under a cardigan and the trademark baggy, wrinkled stockings, indicated a no-nonsense temperament. Kathy Staff's career spans 50 years in acting, and the Nora Batty character has lasted more than 20 years in one of the longest-running series on British television. It will remain in the archives as a highly memorable characterisation from a first-class professional.

In the cinema section I mentioned **Jeremy Lloyd** and said that I would return to his career in the television section. In the 1960s Jeremy became a minor cult figure with small parts in a whole series of films, while he also made a name for himself writing scripts for *Six Five Special*, the *Billy Cotton Show* (in which he appeared), *The Dickie Henderson Show* and several more, before being invited by Harold Robbins to Hollywood to write scripts, an experience which he hated. He soon returned to England. However, his star was in the ascendancy and he appeared in a musical, *Robert and Elizabeth*, and on Parkinson's *Desert Island Discs*, and found time to become engaged to Charlotte Rampling. In 1969 America called again and Jeremy Lloyd found himself writing scripts for the American cult TV show *Rowan and Martin's Laugh In*. During his two years on the show, in which he sometimes appeared, he met and worked with Merle Oberon, Danny Kaye and Sammy Davis Junior, along with a host of other Beverley Hills stars. On a break from the show, back in England, he met, and, after a whirl-wind romance, married Joanna Lumley. Lloyd later resigned from the show, because Joanna didn't want to bring up children in America. Sadly the marriage didn't last long, but they have remained friends to this day.

During this down period he submitted a script for a department store comedy to David Croft, the writer of *Dad's Army*. He liked it and they formed a partnership and so commenced *Are You Being Served*, a comedy series which ran on the BBC and all over the world for 10 years. When the series started to flag, they decided that a new concept was needed and once again came up with a long-running comedy series, *'Allo 'Allo*, set in wartime France and concerning the French Resistance. 'Listen carefully, I shall say this only once' quickly became a catchphrase in the English comedy dictionary. *'Allo 'Allo* ran for more than 10 years with the last series being filmed in 1993. It is still being shown around the world. Jeremy Lloyd, an adopted Cestrian, educated at a Cheshire boarding school, has left a legacy of wonderful comic scripts to cherish.

Another Cestrian with a more acerbic take on modern comedy is **Paul O'Grady**, born in Tranmere in 1955 and brought up in Birkenhead. Paul has established a show business niche for himself with his drag queen character, **Lily Savage**. Tall, brassy, peroxide blonde and vulgar with a vicious tongue, Paul named the character using his mother's maiden name. The character quickly became popular and very soon the TV credits started to roll in: *The Big Breakfast*, *The Lily Savage Show*, *Brookside*, where he appeared in character, *Lily Live*, and then, in 1998, he hosted *Blankety Blank*, an ideal vehicle for his brand of blunt humour. He appeared on numerous chat shows, hosted *Top of the Pops*,

Lily Savage/Paul O'Grady.

guested on the Harry Enfield show and performed on a Royal Variety Show with his great friend Cilla Black. A new departure came in 2001 when he appeared as himself as host of a documentary called *Paul O'Grady's Orient*. Blunt and uncompromising, it was very different. A heart condition that surfaced in 2002 at the early age of 46 caused a great deal of anxiety, but Paul recovered very well and appeared on *Celebrity Driving School* towards the end of the year. Since his heart attack he has established a more healthy lifestyle and in July 2003 he began filming a new BBC sitcom, *Eyes Down*, which hit the television screens in August 2003. The series does not feature Lily Savage, but has Paul cast as a raucous, bullying bingo-caller, giving full vent to that unique scouse humour.

One of the most difficult of all the entertainment disciplines is that of stand-up comedy, and a Cheshire man who had a successful career in stand-up, before moving on to greater success, is Heswall-born **Jim Bowen**. Born on 20 August 1937, Jim struggled hard to make a living, holding down a variety of jobs encompassing dustbin man, labourer and driver before finally settling down to teaching and eventually attaining deputy head status in a Lancashire school. All the while his gift for telling jokes, in a relaxed, easy-going style in the local pubs, clubs and cabaret started to get him noticed. Following his first appearance on the excellent series, *The Comedians*, in 1973, he quickly became a regular. His appeal resulted in him being appointed host of the popular game show *Bullseye*, which ran for many years. Jim's sometimes inane interviewing of the contestants was an art form. He would welcome a guest and then ask 'How are you?' The contestant would reply, 'I've just been made redundant,' and Jim would respond 'Great, smashing, terrific'. He later said that it was nerves, but his self-deprecating style endeared him to the public. Jim later turned his attention to serious acting and put in appearances in *Muck and Brass*, *EL CID* (playing himself) and, more latterly, *Jonathan Creek*.

Another Cestrian who succeeded in the very difficult world of stand-up comedy is **Vince Earl**. Born in Birkenhead, he started in show business with his own singing act, *The Vince Earl Attractions*, but his ability to entertain and tell a joke earned him many appearances on the local circuit before, in the 1970s, he appeared on the talent show *New Faces* and went from there to *The Comedians* and regular television exposure. Vince also appeared on the theatre circuit as well as in more TV shows, including *The Video Entertainer*, *Starburst* and *Boys From The Blackstuff*, in addition to a film appearance in *No Surrender*. However, the role which has made him a household name came in the Liverpool soap, *Brookside*, in 1990, when he was given the character of Ron Dixon. The character had endured for almost 14 years when the soap finished in 2003. Ron still lives in the Birkenhead area with his family and performs at a whole range of func-

tions, including after-dinner speeches, as well as in his television work.

Another Birkenhead-born, easily recognisable face is that of actor **Lewis Collins**, born on 27 May 1946. It was always his intention to get into acting and he undertook formal drama training. He had valuable experience in his early days on the theatre circuit before breaking into television, where his rugged good looks and partnership with Martin Shaw in the TV series *The Professionals* soon thrust him into the spotlight. The show, which ended in 1981, was tremendously successful and earned him star status. Other television work included *Warship*, *The New Avengers*, *The Cuckoo Waltz*, *A Night On The Town* and *Jack The Ripper*, as well as a starring role in the SAS movie, *Who Dares Wins*. After a lull in demand for his services, Collins moved with his family to make a new start in America. However, he did make an appearance on our screens in 2002, in an episode of *The Bill*.

Birkenhead is also the birthplace of **Pauline Daniels**, who has managed to succeed in the diffi-

Pauline Daniels, the stand-up comedienne.

cult world of stand-up comedy, a traditional male preserve. Born on 30 June 1955, Pauline started working the clubs and pubs, doing cabaret and gaining experience and acceptance. Theatre work allowed her to develop and broaden her range, in such productions as *Aladdin*, *Chicago*, *Gypsy* and the title role in *Shirley Valentine*. She made the breakthrough into that male bastion of TV comedy *The Comedians*, and added *Bread*, *Brookside*, *Mike Reid Mates and Music*, *The Tom O'Connor Road Show* and several other shows to her CV.

There are very few excellent female impressionists at the moment in the world of show business. One thinks of Ronnie Ancona and then the list starts to dry up. However, a lady challenging Ancona's supremacy is Bebington's **Jan Ravens**. Born on 14 May 1958, Jan was raised in Hoylake and attended West Kirby Grammar School before going on to Cambridge. At university she took charge of the Footlights Revue and found herself directing such luminaries as Stephen Fry, Hugh Laurie and Emma Thompson. Her first real sortie into the business was as a radio comedy producer, a role that she found frustrating as she really wanted to perform. She also had a desire to become a serious actor and spent 1994 with the Royal Shakespeare Company. However, her gift for mimicry led to regular voice appearances on the cult show *Spitting Image*, and demand from the world of television advertising for voice-overs. Her theatre credits are numerous and varied. However, it was television that provided the vehicle for her talent. *Just Amazing*, *Getting Into Shape*, *Carrott's Lib*, the *Lenny Henry Show*, *Whose Line Is It Anyway*, *Smith and Jones*, *One Foot In The Grave* and *Just For Fun* ensured her exposure to a national audience. Her most recent work has been on *Dead Ringers*, a Radio 4 show for impressionists which due to its popularity was

quickly moved to BBC 2 television, for a repeat series where it won a comedy award and is still going strong in 2003. Jan is the only female in the cast, and does a wide range of impressions, including Anne Robinson, Kirsty Wark, Kirsty Young, Hyacinth Bucket, Kate Adie, Ann Widdecombe, Nigella Lawson and Thora Hird. Jan is married with four children from two marriages, but still manages to continue with her career and busy life. Her face is now well known, but who can tell which is the real voice?

The highly talented **Ann Bell** has a film CV that includes *Fahrenheit 451*, *To Sir With Love*, *The Reckoning Spectre* and *The Statue Champions*. Born in Wallasey on 29 April 1940, Ann trained at RADA and then served her time in local stage and theatre work before getting her first break in television. Since those early days Ann has featured in such perennial favourites as *The Saint*, *Callan*, *Inspector Morse*, *Danger Man*, *War and Peace*, *Tumbledown* and many more. However the role which perhaps she is best remembered for was as the leader of the female prisoners of war in the popular but harrowing television series *Tenko*.

Another talented actress, **Jean Boht**, born in Bebington on 6 March 1936, also enjoys a distinguished acting career but has achieved lasting popularity for one role. Jean trained at the Liverpool Playhouse Theatre and like many before her, gained her experience the hard way, through local drama and stage. Despite film credits in such productions as *Distant Voices*, and *Still Lives*, and a string of television credits for *Juliet Bravo*, *Spyship*, *Funnyman*, *Boys From The Blackstuff*, *Scully*, and *Some Mothers Do Have 'Em*, Jean is best remembered for her role as Mrs Boswell in the scouse comedy series, *Bread*.

Ronald Pickup is another actor whose face is familiar to all. He has an impressive list of film appearances, including *The Day Of The Jackal*, *Zulu Dawn*, *Never Say Never Again*, and *The Mission*, as well as an increasing list of television credits. Ronald was born in Chester on 6 June 1940 and after formal training at RADA, commenced his acting career. His television roles reflect the respect the industry has for his talent. He has graced a number of excellent television shows, and *All Good Men*, *King Lear*, *Henry VIII*, *From A Far Country*, *Einstein*, *Ivanhoe*, *Bergerac* and *Inspector Morse* all serve to underline his quality.

Another familiar face is that of **Tim McInnerny**, from Cheadle Hulme. Tim also has a film pedigree, having appeared in *Wetherby*, *Eric The Viking*, *August Saturday* and *Spaghetti Hoops*, and it is his versatility as an actor that has made him so much in demand in the television studios. *Edge of Darkness*, *Anastasia*, *Shadow of The Noose*, *The Adventures of Sherlock Holmes* and *A Very British Coup* are in complete contrast to *The Comic Strip Presents* and the cult TV series *Blackadder*, which ran from 1983–9. Tim showed his superb comedic ability playing Lord Percy in the first series of *Blackadder* and then in the 1989 series *Blackadder Goes Forth* he played the devious, scheming Captain Darling with exquisite mischievousness.

The very mention of mischievousness brings to mind the delicious comedy character played by **Emma Wray**. Emma, born Jill Wray in Birkenhead on 22 March 1965, played the part of Brenda in the popular ITV comedy *Watching*, which ran for 53 episodes from July 1987 until 1993. Her character, small, dark and pretty with a caustic wit, captivated audiences and for a time the show was high in the ratings. Emma had trained at Rose Bruford College and initially started out as a singer in a harmony group, The Blooming Tulips. Her television appearances to

date include *Minder*, *Boon*, *Stay Lucky* and *Defrosting The Fridge*.

Yet another highly versatile actress is **Helen Atkinson-Wood**. Helen was Head Girl at Macclesfield High School for Girls, where she first developed the acting bug. It was an invitation to appear in a production of *Twelfth Night* in what was usually an all-male preserve at the King's School, Macclesfield, which fired her thespian ambitions. After High School, she studied drama at London University, but quickly realised that teaching was not for her and enrolled at Oxford University, where she joined the Drama Society. Rowan Atkinson and the writer Richard Curtis formed part of her circle of friends. Her television break came in *OTT*, the wacky live show starring Chris Tarrant and Lenny Henry. She made the first of her many stage appearances in the West End in a Ben Elton play. She worked in revue with Angus Deayton, which led to the popular radio show *Radio Active*, which then led to the even more popular television series, *KYTV*. Helen has many stage appearances to her name and has travelled the country in a whole range of productions. She has played the role of Polina in *The Seagull* by Chekhov, and has featured in *The Magistrate*, *The Moonstone* and *High Places*. Television credits display her versatility and gift for light comedy. She appeared in *The Young Ones*, *Alas Smith and Jones*, *Call My Bluff* and *Have I Got News For You*, as well as starring as Mrs Miggins in *Blackadder The Third* in 1987. She is also in demand for presentations and voiceover work. Although Helen has twice been nominated for Best Female Comedy Perfomance at the British Comedy Awards, the ultimate accolade has eluded her to date. Fittingly, in May 2003, while appearing in a three-month run at the Royal Exchange in Manchester, she found time to return to where it all began, the King's School Girl's

Actress Helen Atkinson-Wood visiting her old school, King's Girls Division, Macclesfield. Simon Carter.

Division (the schools have merged since Helen's time) to give a master class and to talk of her career and to give advice to those wishing to tread a similar path.

Nicholas Frankau, born in Stockport on 16 July 1954, has appeared in a number of theatre productions and films, including *Plenty* and *Gunbus*, as well as several television productions – *Play For Today*, *The Last Term*, *I Remember Nelson*, *C.A.T.S. Eyes* and *Paradise Postponed*. However, many will remember him for his wonderful portrayal of the tall, silly French policeman who murdered the English language in the long-running comedy series, *'Allo, 'Allo*.

Meryl Hampton, born in Chester in August 1952, trained at the Guildhall School of Music and Drama and then started out on a theatrical career of music, light comedy and indeed straight roles. An all-round entertainer, her TV credits are impressive: *Softly, Softly*, *Knock For Knock*, the soaps *Crossroads* and *Brookside*, *Casualty* and the *Harry Enfield Show*.

Another actor who appeared in *Softly, Softly* was **Geoffrey Hayes**, born in Stockport on 13

March 1942. He also appeared in that other 'cops and robbers' epic series of the time *Z Cars*, which began in 1962 and ran until 1978. Geoffrey played the part of DC Scatliff. He had a variety of jobs before settling on an acting career and enrolling at the Royal Northern School of Music and Drama in Manchester. Before getting his break he worked as a backstage boy at Oldham Rep and worked in local theatres. Another police series was added to his CV when he appeared in *Dixon of Dock Green*. In 1973 he accepted the role of front man on the immensely popular children's TV show *Rainbow*, which ran for 22 years! It was his job to read the stories and to try to control George, Bungle and Zippy, who were always interrupting and arguing. Geoffrey was truly the face of children's television for many years.

Someone else well known on children's television is **Chris Sievey** from Timperley, better known as the large, gormless character with a papier mâché head, Frank Sidebottom, whose Saturday morning kid's show *Frank's Fantastic Shed Show* ran for eight years. His alter ego has had rather a bizarre career, appearing on such diverse programmes as *The James Whale Show*, *Match Of The Day* and his own radio show. He also achieved notoriety when he recorded versions of songs extolling the virtue of his beloved Timperley, a town in which he lived for more than 18 years. The songs, *Mull Of Timperley*, *Next Train To Timperley* and *Wild Thing In Timperley*, were all recorded on compact discs which are now perhaps being used as tea cup stands!

Back now to the serious world of drama and another excellent Cheshire actress, **Anna Keaveney**. Born in Runcorn on 5 October 1949, Anna trained at Studio 68 and followed that with repertory work all over the country. She appeared in the hit film *Shirley Valentine*, but has made her mark in television. *Within These Walls, Enemy At The Door, Widows, Brookside, Emmerdale, Divided We Stand* and a Channel 4 film, *Security*, give an indication of her range and appeal.

Cheshire girl **Louise Plowright**, born in 1956, appeared in *Eastenders* playing the part of hairdresser Julie Cooper. She also has *London's Burning, Palmer, Beaver Road* and *Families Do The Right Thing* among her credits as her career continues in theatre and television.

Margaret Blakemore from Warrington is another fine actress currently gracing our television screens in the popular BBC 2 series *The Cops*.

A popular Stockport actor, **Will Mellor**, has enjoyed considerable success in two television shows. Born in 1976, he appeared in a series of small roles until he got a part in the popular soap *Hollyoaks* and his face started to become known. He then got a starring role on prime-time television in the hugely popular BBC series *Casualty*. He has also featured in *Sport Relief, Is Harry On The Boat* and *Fat Friends*, and he gave an excellent performance in *Two Pints of Lager and a Packet of Crisps*. Will, it is said, always wanted to become a singer, but had little success in breaking into the pop world. However, in March 2003 he entered, for charity, the Fame Academy singing competition in support of Comic Relief. At the end of a gruelling but very popular series of shows, the public voted him the winner. Time will tell whether he gets the much-desired recording contract.

For many local thespians the proximity of Manchester and the world's longest-running soap *Coronation Street* has provided a starting point for those with acting aspirations. Actress **Jane Hutcheson**, born in Stockport, has an appearance in *Coronation Street* on her CV, and has also played in *Emmerdale* and taken the part of a lawyer in *The Bill* to add to her list of acting credits.

The soap also brought national exposure to Cheadle-born actor **Nicholas Cochrane**, who made many appearances as part of the McDonald family, playing Andy. Born on 16 December 1973, Nicholas was discovered by Granada TV while appearing in local theatre and, although currently out of the soap, his long-term career looks assured.

The latest local lady to have become a fixture in the nation's homes is Stockport-born **Sally Lindsay**. In July 2002 Sally, playing the part of barmaid Shelley Unwin, became the youngest boss of the Rovers Return in the soap's history. Since then strong story lines involving Shelley have made Sally a real favourite with the viewers.

Coronation Street was first broadcast to the nation on 9 December 1960 and in all that time only one cast member has been ever-present – **Ken Barlow**, played by that fine actor **William Roache**. William was born in Ilkeston, Derbyshire in 1932, but is without question an adopted Cestrian. His very early involvement with Cheshire came when he was a Cadet Training Officer based in Chester and he fell in love with

William Roache in 1963.

Bill Roache. The longest-serving soap actor in the world. Cheshire Life

the region. He also fell in love with a local girl, Sarah Mottram from Wilmslow, whom he married in 1972. They have lived in the area ever since. William's acting ability and popularity with the public have sustained him in the longest running part in British soap history. Along the way he has won several awards and in 1993 published his autobiography, *Ken And Me*. His part and career continue unabated and at the time of writing his character continues to grace 'The Street'.

A more recent convert to the world of television is **Christine Hamilton** from Nether Alderley, the wife of the disgraced former MP, **Neil Hamilton** of Knutsford. The crippling costs of the struggle with Mohammed Al-Fayed over the 'cash for questions' affair left the Hamiltons having to use their ingenuity to meet their commitments. Christine, in particular, has rein-

vented herself and is proving to be popular with the media and more popular with the public as her vulnerability has been exposed through personal appearances on TV and radio that have shown her 'warts and all'. In a charity version of *Who Wants To Be A Millionaire* she became very emotional when she failed to win sufficient cash for the charity. In *I'm A Celebrity Get Me Out Of Here*, she was revealed as caring and conciliatory and the public warmed to her. Christine and her husband have appeared on many chat shows, and Christine even had her own chat show on BBC Choice. In 2002 she and Neil starred in a pantomime, *Jack and the Beanstalk*, in Guildford. However, in September 2003 they said goodbye to Cheshire when their home was finally sold and they moved to London.

As television became the main source of entertainment and commercial television came into being, with its culture of advertising, a whole new genre came to our screens. Although many advertisements were irritating, others became mini-cinema productions, which caught our interest and stopped us from heading straight for the kitchen to put on the kettle. Those featured in the popular adverts became mini celebrities, able to make appearances opening supermarkets, night clubs and the like, and carved a niche for themselves.

One such advert featured Macclesfield-born **Johnny Maxfield**. Johnny, born in 1931, had worked as an actor for many years obtaining small parts in several of the soaps and walk-on parts in other productions. However, he was catapulted into the nation's living rooms with a whole series of adverts in the 1970s and 1980s, acting as the kindly, white-haired old granddad encouraging his little grandson to eat Heinz soup. Sadly Johnny died in 2002, but he has left behind his own little bit of television history.

Cheshire has provided Britain with one of the truly great musical writers of stage and theatre. **Alexander Galbraith Wilson**, or Sandy as he was known, was born in Sale on 19 May 1924. Sandy was a composer, an author and a lyricist. Educated at Harrow and Oriel College, Oxford, he graduated in English Literature. While at Oxford he wrote material for plays and revues. Several productions were featured in the West End. In 1948 he wrote the songs for *Slings and Arrows*, followed in 1949 by *Oranges and Lemons* and then he wrote, in 1950, a musical play, *Caprice*. Two more followed: *See You Later* in 1951 and *See You Again* in 1952. However, in 1953 he really hit the jackpot, writing the book, the words and the music to a musical play which has endured to this day and is continually being revived throughout the world: *The Boyfriend*. A light-hearted, comedic spoof of the 1920s in the era of flappers and extravagant clothes, it has appealed to audiences down the years and is still a wonderful way to appreciate theatre. In those early days the show ran from January 1954 for five years, which was regarded as phenomenal. It has now been running somewhere in the world for almost 50 years.

The memorable songs which have endured will be featured in a later section. Sandy Wilson wrote several more musicals – *The Buccaneer* in 1955, *Walmouth* in 1958, *Divorce Me Darling* in 1964 and *I Could Be Happy* in 1975 – but they could not recapture the magic of *The Boyfriend*. How could they?

Further mention must also be made of **Ronald Gow** – it is not sufficient to remember him as the husband of the brilliant Dame Wendy Hiller. Ronald was a very fine dramatist who was a pupil, and then a teacher, at Altrincham Boys' Grammar School. Although he had a number of works to his credit, his gift to British theatre is the adaptation for the stage of Walter Greenwood's novel, *Love On The Dole*. It was this play, in which Wendy Hiller appeared, that first attracted the attention of George Bernard Shaw and launched her highly successful career and marriage. Ronald continued to write and adapt plays for her, for example *Tess of the d'Urbervilles* by Thomas Hardy, and during World War Two he wrote propaganda scenarios to support the war effort. However it is *Love On The Dole* that has stayed the course and the play is still revived from time to time and enjoys success around the world. Ronald Gow died in 1993, 10 years before his wife, leaving behind a son and daughter.

Television Announcers and Presenters

Television brought with it the need to create different types of presenter. The diverse range of programmes, outside of film and drama, continued to grow as the public demanded a greater variety of entertainment. Documentaries, news programmes, game shows, sports programmes, quizzes and music programmes all required someone to front the show, to act as host and explain what was about to happen. Many of these presenters became household names and stars in their own right. Cheshire, with its proximity to Manchester and its BBC and ITV television stations, has had more than its share of television announcers and presenters.

For almost 30 years, two men dominated sports coverage on BBC and ITV with an easy versatility which made them instantly acceptable. The doyen of all sports announcers/commentators was **David Coleman** OBE. Born in Alderley Edge on 26 April 1926, Coleman was himself a useful athlete and became Cheshire mile champion with aspirations to represent his country at the very highest level, in the Olympics. He would go to several Olympics, but alas, not as a competitor. His early days in Cheshire were spent

Famed BBC sports commentator David Coleman, host of Match of the Day, Sportsnight, Olympic Games coverage and Grandstand during a long career in broadcasting. BBC

as a reporter and journalist with radio, commentating on soccer matches and other sports events. Eventually he became editor of the *Cheshire County Express*, before getting his big break and joining the BBC. Very soon there was not a sports event or programme which did not involve him. He was the front man for *Match of The Day*, *Grandstand* and *Sportsnight With Coleman*, and he compèred several Sportsman of the Year awards. In 1979 he chaired and presented the

hugely popular *A Question of Sport*, which he fronted for almost 20 years. The programme is still running. In his time David Coleman attended all the major sporting events, including the football World Cup and several Olympics. Although he was the consummate professional, calm, unflustered and always seemingly in control, he was, like anyone else, prone to saying things he later wished he hadn't. He added a new word to the English language 'Colemanballs', and several editions of small books were compiled of other commentators' errors or slip ups under that title. Several of those gaffes attributed to David are as follows: 'This man could be a black horse', 'Lillian's great strength is her strength', 'He just can't believe what's not happening to him', 'There is Brendan Foster, by himself, with twenty thousand people'. Now we all know what he meant, but in a lifetime of commentating on world sport, it was bound to happen.

For many years it could be said that another Cestrian, on ITV, was Coleman's greatest rival. Certainly **Dickie Davis**, born in Wallasey on 30 April 1933, was equally as dominant on the rival television channel. Richard Davis had a number of jobs in his early days, including being the entertainment purser on board the *Queen Mary* and the *Queen Elizabeth II*, before moving into television. His first front of screen role was that of announcer, where his cheerful, unhurried style caught the eye of his superiors and he soon graduated and became a fully fledged presenter. *World of Sport* and *Sportsmatters*, which he produced and presented, became fixtures on ITV and together with his appearance at all major sporting events including the FA Cup, Olympics and other world events he was a definite rival to David Coleman. In later years a 'white rabbit's tail' sort of blob in the front of his hair became a source of amusement to all. To the ever-cheerful, likeable

Dickie Davis it didn't seem to matter much. He was first-rate at his job, although he too suffered from 'Colemanballs' syndrome: 'You can imagine how they feel surrounded by their manager Ron Greenwood'.

Stuart Hall, born in Ashton, was raised in Hyde and has for many years endeared himself to radio and television audiences. Ebullient and effervescent, Hall's style revealed an enthusiasm that quickly involved the listener or viewer. He loves to play with the English language and treats his audience to

Colourful sports broadcaster and Wilmslow resident Stuart Hall. Cheshire Life

lavish adjectives which bring a sense of fun into whatever he is describing. He first came to prominence reading the BBC North news and followed that with presenting *North West Tonight*. He is particularly remembered for presenting the 1980s show *It's A Knockout*, a show that was compulsive viewing for several years. Hall would poke fun at

his fellow presenter and fall guy Eddie Waring, and, at regular intervals, would descend into a maniacal giggle, which despite his efforts to suppress would be clearly heard by all the viewers. It has to be said that it was in keeping with the general tenure of the show and was therefore accepted. Stuart is a frequent broadcaster, well known for his radio soccer commentaries and his many television appearances. In 2003 he was back on our screens, combining his great loves of sport and presenting, hosting a new sporting quiz show called *Anyone's Game*. His great hobby is collecting antique clocks, which fill his home in Wilmslow, the town in which he has lived for 40 years.

Another great, instantly recognisable broadcaster is **Bob Greaves**, born in Sale on 28

The changing face of Bob Greaves the TV presenter. Bob Greaves

November 1934. Bob, of the dark glasses, no-nonsense style, started out as a junior reporter on the *Sale/Stretford Guardian* before working in Nottinghamshire and then returning to Cheshire to work on the *Daily Mail* in Manchester at the age of 22. At 29 he became news editor at Granada TV. For a time he fronted *People and Places*, as well as being news editor, newsreader, and the presenter of *Police File*. Eventually he went into full-time presenting, working with and interviewing such luminaries as Bill Grundy, Michael Parkinson, Stuart Hall, Prime Minister Harold Wilson, Les Dawson, Matt Busby and Tommy Cooper, to name just a few. Retired now, he can reflect on a superb career during which John Birt, who eventually became the head of the BBC, worked for him as a researcher!

A contemporary of Bob Greaves was Marple's **Bill Grundy**, another no-nonsense presenter. For a time he worked locally but very soon developed a reputation and was sought after for television work across the country. A true professional, radio, news, interviews, football reporting and commentating and quiz shows came easily to him. He moved south to work for Thames Television, where his most notorious interview, which resulted in national headlines and outrage, took place. In December 1976 he interviewed the punk rock group the Sex Pistols live on the *Today* programme. It was an awkward interview, with the group being difficult, and it soon degenerated into a stream of foul-mouthed language in response to Grundy's questions. They were abusive to Grundy and the 'F-word' was used on several occasions, as well as other expletives that shocked the live audience. The following day the national newspapers were full of it. Banner headlines from one newspaper screamed out 'The Filth and the Fury'. Bill Grundy was suspended for allowing the programme to degenerate to such a

TV presenter Bill Grundy, probably most famous for goading the Sex Pistols into swearing on live TV in 1976. Stockport Express

level and the Sex Pistols were shunned by a number of promoters. It's a shame that such a polished presenter should have such an interview logged on his CV, but that's what makes experience and Bill Grundy's career was not diminished by it. He died in 1993.

Female presenters from Cheshire have also dominated the nation's screens and two in particular, with very different styles, became household names and faces. **Judith Chalmers** OBE, born in 1937, was raised in Gatley and went to Withington Girls' School. She had some experience as a child actor, appearing on BBC Radio's *Children's Hour* in Manchester before leaving school and enrolling at a Manchester secretarial college. However, she still had aspirations to get into show business and had her first big break in 1960, when she became BBC TVs *In Vision* announcer, a post which she held until 1963. Very quickly her style and polish were recognised by the BBC and further appointments came her way. She appeared in *Town And Around* in 1960 and was presenter and compère of the immensely popular *Come Dancing*, which thrust her into the national spotlight from 1961 until 1965. Judith has had a number of roles, presenting *Miss World*, *Radio Family Favourites*, *Woman's Hour* and the Radio 2 *Morning Show*, but the show with which she has become most associated is ITV's holiday programme, *Wish You Were Here*. Judith's heavily-tanned face would beam out at us from all over the world, from 1973 until 1987, when she ceased to be the main presenter, but still, poor thing, she continued as an occasional reporter for the programme. She finally announced her departure from *Wish You Were Here* in July 2003, after 30 years of what she described as 'one of the best jobs in television'. She said that she was looking forward to other challenges. Judith always seems friendly, polished and chatty and certainly these qualities have helped to fashion a career that has resulted in the award of an OBE and a permanent place in television history. Judith lives in London and continues to make radio and television appearances.

Another supremely polished, professional presenter is Stockport's **Joan Bakewell**. Joan, who was born Joan Dawson Rowlands in 1933, was raised in Cheadle and attended Stockport High School before moving on to Cambridge University, where she came into contact with Brian Redhead, the President of the University Labour Club (more of him later). When Joan eventually moved into presenting she had a reputation for intelligent, persistent questioning which was skilfully balanced with a sympathetic, warm approach, which earned her the memorable sobri-

quet of 'the thinking man's crumpet'. Dark and attractive, she did not let her obvious appeal detract from her professionalism. Her major programme, the BBC's *Heart of The Matter*, was a heavyweight documentary series in which Joan interviewed, among others, the murderers Myra Hindley and Rosemary West. She graced many other programmes on TV and radio. She is now a grandmother and lives in London, but still appears on our television screens. In October 2003 her memoirs *The Centre of The Bed* caused a great deal of interest when she revealed that she discovered that her husband was having an affair while she was conducting her own affair with the playwright Harold Pinter in the 1960s. They agreed to continue discreetly with their affairs but eventually their marriage broke up.

Steve Jones, born in Crewe on 7 June 1945, trained as a teacher, had spells as a professional musician and was an ice-cream salesman before getting a break as a radio disc jockey. It was his radio career which set him on the path to television. After starting at Radio Clyde, he won the Scottish Radio Personality Award and in 1989 won the Variety Club Independent Radio Personality Award. Television came calling and soon he was fronting *Battle of The Comics*, *It's The Jones Boy*, *Watch The Space*, *Saturday Morning Show*, *The Steve Jones Game Show*, *Search For A Star* and *The Pyramid Game*. Now seen less often on our screens, Steve lives in London with his family.

A man who was easily identifiable on our screens was the handsome, blonde haired, full-faced young presenter **Chris Kelly**. Born in Cuddington on 24 April 1940, Chris served behind the bar of the family's White Barn Hotel and went to school at Dunnside before moving on to Cambridge to study modern languages. A real local lad, he grew up in the Delamere Forest area and his granddad was a Northwich baker. Chris had early spells as a television announcer and worked on *Wish You Were Here* and the BBC's *Food And Drink*. However, since those days Chris has expanded his interests and is now a writer/producer. He has written a book based on his childhood and written dramas for television – *Zero Option* and *Saracen* – as well as producing such favourites as *Soldier, Soldier* and *Kavanagh QC*. Chris now lives in Cambridge.

Born in Poynton on 11 April 1959, **Howard Stableford** started his career as a reporter for BBC radio in Northampton before moving into television. He can list *Jigsaw, Puzzle Trail, Newsround* and *Tomorrow's World* among his presenter's roles to date.

Born in Chester in 1972, **Claire Smith**, who won the beauty title Miss UK in 1992 and went on to become runner-up in the Miss World contest in 1993, embarked on a television career, gaining experience through a number of appearances on programmes such as *Kilroy, Whickers World, This Morning* and *Time & Place*. Her striking looks and bright personality brought her a more permanent job as the presenter of the *Sky Travel Guide*.

A nationally known face is that of ITN news presenter **Katie Derham**. Katie went to Cheadle Hulme School and then on to Cambridge, before joining the BBC. One of her first jobs was as a researcher on Barry Norman's *Film Night*. However, she was hankering after a role in front of camera, and ITV spotted her and made her, at 31, its youngest news presenter. Although Katie lives in London with her husband and daughter, her parents live in Wilmslow and her brother and sisters live in Cheshire. Katie enjoys classical music and was therefore delighted to be chosen to present the 2003 British Classical Awards at the Royal Albert Hall. She undoubtedly has a great future

ahead of her and will be seen on our television screens many more times in the years to come.

Another young lady who has enjoyed success in a career change is Wilmslow's **Jeanette Lanz-Bergin**. Jeanette, who was educated at St Hilary's School, Alderley, started out as a stewardess with British Airways before having a spell as a *Cheshire Life* columnist. Since then she has presented on children's television, presented *Reds At Five* on MUTV and fronted Granada's *Men and Motors*. In addition she has appeared in a film, *The Law Boys*, and on the *Esther Rantzen Show*.

One of the most easily recognisable figures in the world of children's television in the 1980s was **Timmy Mallett**. Born in Marple in 1955, Timothy hosted the children's show *The Wide Awake Club* for TVam in 1984. He was undoubtedly popular with the youngsters and when, in 1985, *Wacaday* was first screened, it became one of the most popular of all the children's programmes. His gimmicks of very loud shirts, awful Edna Everage glasses, together with an inane giggle, made him irritating to most adults. However his show continued and featured such items as a huge sponge mallet, which was liberally used in a quiz game called 'Mallett's Mallett'. Yes, it was as annoying as that, but the kids loved it! Blessed with enormous courage, Timothy recorded a song, *Itsy Bitsy Teeny Weeny Yellow Polka Dot Bikini*, which promptly went to No.1 in the 1990 record charts. He did of course make many appearances on the media circuit and then, in 1997, he was the star of *Timmy Towers*, a programme made for CITV which was last shown in 2000. Although rarely seen today on our screens, he has a show on an Internet radio station, *Ozone*, does pantomime and occasionally revives *Wacaday* in a live show format. Timothy lives in Berkshire with his wife and family.

Cheshire has a tiny claim on television's most

Antiques Show and
Bargain Hunt presenter
David Dickinson, from
Cheadle Heath. John
Cocks

Newscaster and TV presenter Fiona Bruce.

highly paid news reader. The talented **Fiona Bruce**, who has worked for the BBC as a reporter and presenter on *Breakfast News*, the *Six O'Clock News* and the corporation's flagship *Ten O'Clock News*, and replaced Jill Dando on *Crimewatch*, accepted £400,000 a year to host *Call My Bluff* and is contracted to appear in a series of programmes yet to be finalised as part of the package. Cheshire's tenuous claim is that Fiona lived on the Wirral and attended Heswall Primary School before her father moved the family to Kingston-upon-Thames with his job.

A very definite Cheshire girl is Stockport's

Tess Daly, the popular TV presenter from Stockport.

vivacious **Tess Daly**, who brightened up our Saturday morning television screens as the host of SMTV on ITV 1 until leaving in August 2003. Tess left school with nine O-levels and shortly afterwards was spotted by Models One. She embarked on a successful modelling career, travelling the world and appearing on the front cover of many magazines. She thoroughly enjoyed the opportunity to see the world and welcomed the experience of visiting northern Thailand, Japan, Morocco, New York and much of Europe. It was while she was in New York that she got her first taste of presenting, when she made a documentary, *Brits Abroad*, in which she interviewed a number of celebrities. Her first big break came in 1999 when she worked for a time on *The Big Breakfast*'s Find Me A Model competition, and after that she featured on the BBC's *The Phone Zone*, ITV's *The Mix*, *Singled Out* for Channel 5, *Surf Out* for Channel 4 and *Smash Hits* for Sky One. Tess's bubbly personality, blonde hair and big smile have made her popular with the various television companies and to date she has presented the Dancestar Awards for MTV, *Exclusive* for Channel 5 and *LA Pool Party* for the BBC. She is also in demand on ITV, having already presented *Britain's Brainiest Kids*, *The Clothes Show*, a live presentation of the National TV Awards and *Home On Their Own* for ITV 1 in 2003. Tess clearly enjoys life and is always prepared to take part in new ventures; she writes, has featured in a number of pop videos dancing to top artistes, enjoys the company of her friends, champagne and chocolate and is due to marry another popular presenter, Vernon Kay, in 2004. I think that she will join the other Cestrians who have had an enduring appeal to the public.

David Dickinson is a man for whom the expression 'it's never too late' could not be more appropriate. Born in Cheadle Heath in 1943,

David spent more than 30 years in the antiques business before being 'spotted' by a television producer and invited to appear in a documentary. His impact was immediate and was followed by an invitation from the BBC to appear in the BBC 2 programme *The Antique Show*. More television followed, including *The Holiday Show*, and then he really became a television fixture, when at the age of 57, in 1999, he was asked to host *Bargain Hunt*. The show gives contestants a sum of money and with the advice of experts they buy antiques or collectibles, which are then sold at auction to see who makes the most profit. It is a simple concept, but with David's particular style, the show took off and was watched by several million day-time viewers. It has to be said that David is distinctive – he has a permanent deep tan, sharp pin-stripe suits, silk handkerchief, colourful ties, bright jackets – all topped off with a Frankie Vaughan hairstyle and a voice and presentation reminiscent of a cross between Danny La Rue and Betty Boothroyd! It certainly works, because the show was voted the Most Popular Daytime Show in the National Television Awards ceremony, and after its transfer to prime-time television the viewing figures leapt to almost 10 million. This was a far cry from those early Cheadle Heath days and his first job at Fairey Aviation in Heaton Chapel, which was followed by a spell in a Manchester textile warehouse. At one point David owned several antique shops, all in the Cheshire area, before getting his big break in the autumn of his life. After living in Bramhall, London and Wilmslow, David now lives in the Macclesfield area with his wife Lorne, who was a respected international cabaret singer for whom David acted as manager in the late 1960s. Lorne does the looking after now, as David is, to use the show business jargon, 'hot' and is in regular demand on the chat show interview circuit.

It is difficult to leave the world of television without mentioning a lady who, from about the mid-1960s, was seldom off our screens complaining about what was on them! **Mary Whitehouse,** who was born in Nuneaton in 1910, became the self-proclaimed champion and guardian of public morals. Her family moved to Cheshire, where she was educated at Chester Grammar School. She was a promising tennis player and at the age of 13 actually reached the final of the County Tournament, where she was narrowly beaten by the captain of the Cheshire team. An indication of what was to come was revealed when she was congratulated on such an impressive performance and replied 'I was not a push-over. Oh no.' Mary Whitehouse was never a push-over. Her grim school-teacher approach and 'Edna Everage' glasses would underline her uncompromising style in the years to come. The Cheshire selectors were impressed by her talent, but she had already committed to teacher training when they approached her about a future in tennis. She attended the Cheshire County Training College and became part of the Moral Rearmarment group, where she met her future husband for life. In the mid-1960s she became concerned about the effect of sex, violence and bad language on television on her pupils in particular and the public in general. She campaigned relentlessly to clean up the BBC, making speeches all over the country, writing in magazines and newspapers and appearing on countless television programmes, attacking all and sundry. She did gain a great deal of support, but gradually lost it, seeming at times too narrow-minded and even arrogant when it came to knowing what was best for everybody. Nevertheless, this fighter for public morals was appointed CBE in 1980 and carried on her campaigns well into old age. Her formative years were spent in Cheshire and the county can accept the blame, or the praise, for the effect she had on the nation. Her husband died in 2000, and Mary followed him in November 2001.

Radio

Many television presenters started their careers as radio presenters and then moved on. Some, however, made their names on radio and stayed there, and radio is still as popular as ever.

Brian Redhead was one of the old guard of broadcasters and perhaps more a devotee of the news magazine programme. Although Brian was born in Newcastle, he came to Manchester, following his education at Cambridge, to join the *Guardian* newspaper in 1954, and he settled down in Cheshire. Associated with Cheadle Hulme, Brian later moved to Rainow, near Macclesfield, to live in the countryside. He never lost an opportunity to praise Cheshire in his programmes and was forever extolling the virtues of Manchester and the north-west. Although well known as a broadcaster, Brian was a first-class journalist and became Northern Editor of the *Manchester Guardian* in 1965 before taking on the editorship of the *Manchester Evening News* in 1969. However, he will always be remembered for his time on the long-running BBC Radio 4 programme *Today*, which he presented from 1975 until his death in 1994.

Whereas Brian was regarded as the old guard, a serious or career broadcaster, radio did throw up an entirely different species that became known as DJ's (disc jockeys), who played music. Some played popular music all day, some played music interspersed with chat, but either way they became immensely popular. So much so that one of them, **John Peel**, was nominated as the 43rd ranked Briton in a BBC viewers' poll in 2002 to find the 100 Greatest Britons. To me it seems

extraordinary that John, born in Heswall in 1939, good as he is as a radio and television presenter, is rated higher than Drake, Bell, Elgar, Chaucer, Raleigh, Tolkien and Livingstone, among others. But many people voted for him, so he must have made an impression.

John came from a wealthy family and got his first job in the States as an office clerk, before finding his way into a DJ job on American radio. He came back to Britain and joined Radio 1 when it was launched in 1967. Thirty-six years later he is the only original DJ still working for the station. He has certainly had a colourful life, although he has been married to the same lady, Sheila, for 29 years. His decision to write his memoirs in 2003 caused a rush among publishers with the highest offer, of £1.5 million, being accepted. Peel's contribution to radio and his longevity were recognised in 1998 when he was awarded the OBE for his services to radio. In 1998 he also underwent a style makeover and launched a Saturday morning radio show called *Home Truths*, in which listeners rang in to talk about themselves, their problems, fears and frustrations. Typically, although he is now 63, the rebel instinct of the 1960s was revealed when he agreed to do *Home Truths* on condition that no celebrities were involved. The show was about ordinary people, for ordinary people, and that was the way he wanted it. No air kissing! There appears to be no sign of retirement on the horizon for John Peel.

One brash young man, who was perhaps inspired by the great DJ, is Warrington's **Chris Evans**, born in 1966. With red hair and black 'geeky' glasses, Evans certainly could not rely on a heart-throb image. However, he had undeniable talent and quickly established himself at Radio Piccadilly in Manchester before moving to London and GLR. Radio 1 saw him established with a large audience who responded to his unique approach, which included being rude to his staff on air. He became known for his laddish style, but it must be said that whatever the criticism, Evans was shrewd and inventive, with fresh ideas that appealed to many. He moved into television and created the hugely popular *The Big Breakfast* and *Don't Forget Your Toothbrush* and then the cult weekend series *TGI Friday*. He then founded the Ginger Media Group. Virgin Radio bought his breakfast show in a deal worth millions and Evans got married for the second time, to the singer Billie Piper, in 2001 in Las Vegas. He is now a multi-millionaire with homes around the world. However, in 2003 he was involved in a bitter court struggle with the Scottish Media Group, the owners of Virgin Radio, whom Evans was suing for wrongful dismissal and £8.6 million for withholding share options. Virgin had sacked Evans after what they described as unacceptable behaviour. Evans lost the case and it was estimated that the decision would cost him £15 million pounds. When the judge gave his verdict in June 2003, he scathingly described Evans as 'unprofessional, manipulative, insecure, sulking and childish'. If that was not enough, he added that he was 'lying and petulant' and was the kind of man who would resort to any means 'foul or fair' to get his way. Chris Evans continues to work in television with his production company UMTV.

A young lady DJ who looks set to make a big name for herself is Chester's **Charlotte Horne**, whose alter ego is house (music) diva **DJ Lottie**. Lottie is now one of Radio 1's rising young stars and is very much in demand as a featured DJ, appearing at gigs all over the country. Indeed her schedule has her flying to Los Angeles, New York, Miami, France and Italy, where she can earn several thousand pounds in one night. It is believed that some of the very top DJs can earn £30,000 in one night and that the top five DJs in the country are all millionaires. Although Lottie is not yet in that bracket she is glad that she swopped her first ambition to be a ballet dancer and her later ambition, to dance like Michael Jackson or Prince, for a record deck and the determination to become a DJ and radio presenter.

Music

The major link between the various entertainment media is music. Popular music really exploded in this country in the 1950s and the record industry became very big business, spawning songwriters, artists and groups, many of whom became very wealthy indeed as the public not only bought their records, but also flocked to the theatres as the artists toured the country, cashing in on their celebrity. The job of disc jockey evolved, as well as television shows devoted to pop music and a whole genre of cinema musicals. It must be said that Cheshire has not really produced many outstanding individual recording stars but has contributed richly to British music culture.

In terms of memorable songs that have survived and enjoyed success on the stage, and are still frequently heard on the radio and revived in shows, **Sandy Wilson** will be forever enshrined in show business history. Sandy, from Sale, gave the country such musical gems as *I Could Be Happy With You* and *It's Never Too Late To Fall In Love* among many others that he wrote for West End shows.

In the boom of the 1950s and 1960s, although Stockport featured as a venue for touring bands and the Strawberry Recording Studios hosted many of the top names, like 10CC, it was Birkenhead's **Lance Fortune** who made the first impact as a recording star. Born in 1940, Lance was spotted in 1959 by Larry Parnes, a top impresario of the time, and signed with Pye Reords. The following year, in March 1960, he had a hit record, *Be Mine*, which reached No.4 in the UK charts. He followed this with a tour of the UK with the legendary Gene Vincent. Sadly, although Lance made one more appearance in the charts with *This Love I Have For You*, it was to be his last.

A Cestrian who did change the face of 1960s rock and was later acknowledged as 'the father of British blues', was the very talented **John Mayall**, who was born in Macclesfield on 29 November 1933. John, a thorough professional, wrote

John Mayall, father of British rhythm and blues. *Courtesy Rod MacSween*

songs, played guitar, sang, produced and played the harmonica. From an early age he collected records and it was in 1955, while still at college, that he founded his first group. However, music took a back seat while he served his time in the army in Korea, before returning to civilian life as a commercial artist. But the pull of music was too strong and he went to London in 1962, where he formed his second and most famous group, the Bluesbreakers. Shortly after the group was formed, Eric Clapton joined from the Yardbirds, so starting a legendary partnership. A measure of their quality was evident on the album *Bluesbreakers*, which went to No.6 in the UK charts. Although Clapton is considered by many to have been the finest guitar player of the era, it was Mayall who was the innovator, the primer for much of the music of the 1960s and 1970s. Clapton left in 1966 to form the group Cream, and after several more changes, John McVie, one of Mayall's original members, and Peter Green also left, to form Fleetwood Mac along with Mick Fleetwood, who had also played with the Bluesbreakers. For quite some time the Mayall influence on British rhythm and blues was obvious and he continued to write his own albums. In 1971, joined by Eric Clapton, they reached No.1 in the charts with the album *Back To The Roots*. John was continually changing his group and spent almost 10 years touring and playing in the US. At one point, in 1991, he backed ZZ Top on their tour. Even during the mid-1990s he was playing 100 gigs a year. Some of his many other works include *Crusaders* in 1967, *A Hard Road*, also in 1967, *The Turning Point* in 1970 and *Wake Up Call* in 1993, with *Steppin' Out, An Introduction To John Mayall*, a compilation, issued in 2000. There are videos of his work and a book *John Mayall, Bluesbreaker*, by Richard Newman. Mayall played with and influenced many of the great names of the music industry of the time – a marvellous contribution to popular music.

Another major breakthrough into national prominence for Cheshire artists was by **Joy Division**. Founded by **Stephen Morris** and **Ian Curtis**, both born in Macclesfield in 1957, the group enjoyed huge success in the 1970s with *Love Will Tear Us Apart* and *Unknown Pleasures* in 1979. However, following the tragic suicide of

The headstone in Macclesfield Cemetery which has become a shrine to Joy Division lead vocalist Ian Curtis, who committed suicide at Barton Street, Macclesfield, in May 1980, the day before the band were due to fly out on an American tour. The inscription 'Love Will Tear Us Apart' is the title of Joy Division's Top 20 single.

Ian Curtis in May 1980 the group reformed in 1981 and called themselves **New Order**. In 1983 they had the distinction of having the biggest selling 12-inch single of all time with *Blue Monday*, a song which was said by many to have kick-started the British dance music scene. In fact, in a survey conducted by *Q* magazine in 2003 to discover the Top Twenty Songs That Changed The World, *Blue Monday* was ranked at No.8. The group produced several more quality albums including *Low Life* in 1985. Ian Curtis has a simple memorial stone placed in Macclesfield Cemetery with the inscription 'Ian Curtis, 18-5-

80, Love Will Tear Us Apart'. Staff at the cemetery told me that they get frequent requests from tourists, mostly Americans, asking for directions to visit his resting place and pay their respects. His memory and his talent linger on.

An artist who really made an impact on the pop scene in the late 1980s was **Rick Astley**. Although Astley's birth was registered in Newton, Lancashire, his birth certificate shows that he was born in Great Sankey, Warrington. Richard Paul Astley started out as a drummer in a local band, before becoming the lead vocalist in another band, the FBI. It was Pete Waterman, the producer and writer, who spotted his potential and in 1987 Rick had his first big hit, *Never Gonna Give You Up*, which not only went to No.1 in the UK but also won the Brit Award for the best single of the year. His first album, *Whenever You Need Somebody*, also went to No.1 in the UK album charts. In 1988, Rick was launched on the American market with immediate and spectacular results. He became the first artist to top the American charts with his first two singles over there, *Never Gonna Give You Up* and *Together Forever*, and was voted the best club act in the US for 1988. Rick was certainly different: with his shiny quiff, suits and ties he looked as if he were going for an interview. But the bouncy, disco beat to his music, allied to a strong voice, certainly appealed to the market. However, perhaps due to criticism that Stock, Aitken and Waterman, his management company, had manufactured him to a formula, he split from them and enjoyed a break from the business. Whatever the reasons, they had all been incredibly successful during their partnership, with seven UK top 10 records and four US top 10 records. In 1991 Rick produced an album called *Free*, which won some acclaim, but it was a single from the album, *Cry For Help*, which he wrote and produced, that projected him back into the top 10 both here and in the US. Again after a break from the industry he was believed to have signed a record contract with Polydor in 2001. Rick is one of this country's most successful recording artists and is young enough, at 37, to go on to even greater success.

A founder member of a very talented group of the 1980s, the Housemartins, was **Paul Heaton** who was born in Birkenhead on 9 May 1962. The group got together with no intention of staying in the business long-term, and despite a No.3 hit with *Happy Hour* and a 1986 No.1 UK hit with the a cappella version of *Caravan Of Love*, which was followed in 1987 with the award of Best Newcomer Of The Year, they disbanded in 1988. One member of the group, who joined them in 1985, was a man called Norman Cook who went on to make a name and several million pounds for himself as DJ Fatboy Slim. Paul Heaton went on to form a pop/rock combo, the Beautiful South, and with Paul as leader, lyricist and vocals they had their first hit with *Song For Whoever*. They made several albums and one track from *Welcome To The Beautiful South* gave them a UK No.1 with *A Little Time*. In 1991 at the British Music Awards they won Best Music Video.

Another hugely influential rock group during this period, which enjoyed world wide success and frequent chart exposure, was the Stone Roses. Founded by lead singer **Ian Brown**, born in Warrington on 20 February 1963, and **John Squire**, lead guitar, who was born in Broadheath on 24 November 1962, the group inspired others, including the Gallaghers, who would go on to form Oasis. Brown and Squire are said to have first met in a sand pit as infants, but years later at Altrincham Grammar School they got together and started their first group, Patrol, rehearsing in a scout hut in Sale and playing gigs at local spots including Hale Methodist Church! For a time

Ian Brown, former lead singer of the Stone Roses.

they also rehearsed in the cellar of band member **Andy Couzens**'s parents' home in Macclesfield. Whilst waiting for their big break Couzens and Brown both worked for Couzens's uncle in his caravan business in Poynton. Larger venues, studio sessions at Strawberry Gardens, Stockport and a record contract quickly followed. One hit single, *One Love*, made the top 10 and a couple of albums sold well. But sell-out tours of the UK, America, Japan and Australia could not prevent the group from self-destructing in 1996. Riven by discord over the rebellious, in-your-face style of Ian Brown and the quieter temperament of John Squire, the group parted company with their manager Gareth Evans and when Squire left in March 1996 the group disbanded after a final concert at Reading in Ocotber 1996. Squire started a group called the Seahorses and Brown, after moving to Lymm and a period of soul-searching, launched himself into a successful solo career, with hit singles, an album and personal appearances. However his metamorphosis was sadly interrupted when he was jailed in October 1998 following an incident with a stewardess on an aeroplane. The Stone Roses left their mark on the world rock scene but never really reached their full potential. Strangely, following the break up of the band and their subsequent solo careers the prime movers eventually finished up living very close to each other in Cheshire. John Squire moved to Morton, near Macclesfield, Ian Brown moved to Lymm and Gareth Evans, their former manager, moved to Knutsford.

Paul Young, who was born in 1947 in Wythenshawe (now part of Greater Manchester), which used to be part of Cheshire, was an original member and vocalist with Sad Café, whose first really big hit was *Run Home Girl*, which was a big hit in the US. Paul enjoyed more success with them in 1979 with *Every Day Hurts,* which went to No.3, before he left to join Mike and the Mechanics. Their first hit came with *Silent Running*, which made the top 30 in the UK but reached No.6 in the US when it was adopted as the theme music for the film *On Dangerous Ground*. However, the group's mammoth hit – No.1 in the US, No.2 in the UK – was the 1989 song *The Living Years*. Several albums sold reasonably well but their last hit of any consequence was *Word Of Mouth*, which reached No.13. However, the group was shattered by the untimely death of Paul Young, who died in Hale, near Altrincham, in July 2000.

In 1990 a Cheshire singer (hardly the word) became the first Cheshire artist to achieve a UK No.1 chart topper in his own right as an individual. **Timmy Mallett**, the children's television presenter from Marple, actually had a No.1 hit with *Itsy Bitsy Teeny Weeny Yellow Polka Dot Bikini.* Yes, some people – many people – actually bought it!

Cheshire can claim part ownership of the two biggest pop bands of the 1990s, boy band **Take That** and girl group the **Spice Girls**.

Take That were five young men fashioned into what was hoped would be a singing band that would appeal to the young end of the market.

Take That member Gary Barlow.

They were Mark Owen, Howard Donald, Jason Orange, Robbie Williams and **Gary Barlow**, the song writer, who was acknowledged to be the most talented of the boys. Gary was born in Frodsham on 20 January 1971 and from an early age had an aptitude for music. At the age of 14 it is believed that he played the backing on a Ken Dodd show and featured in local talent shows. He entered a BBC TV song-writing competition and his entry, *Let's Pray For Christmas*, was well received. During the five years that the group were together they dominated the charts. Early successes resulted in *Could It Be Magic*, a Manilow cover, receiving a British Music Award as best single before their first UK No.1, *Pray*, in 1993. Best-selling albums with *Everything Changes* at No.1 and three successive No.1 hit singles followed in 1994/5, with the best-selling song, *Back For Good,* a hit on both sides of the Atlantic. After their last No.1 UK hit, *How Deep Is Your Love*, a Bee Gees cover, the group split up. Gary Barlow continued with his song-writing and the others set out to pursue different projects. One of them, a certain Robbie Williams, appears to have done very well for himself. Gary continues to live in Cheshire, assured of his place in British pop music culture.

Unquestionably the Spice Girls were a phenomenon of their time. Five feisty girls with attitude, gathered together, perhaps in response to the glut of boy bands of the period. They had a vitality, a 'girl power', which appealed to the young girls' market, and it has to be said that their simple, uncomplicated music did have an appeal. Even if it wasn't to your taste, you would often find yourself humming or whistling their latest offering. The girls got together in 1993 after a series of auditions and started writing and practising their routines until they were taken over by Simon Fuller in May 1995. Victoria Adams – Posh Spice, Emma Bunton – Baby Spice, Geri Halliwell – Ginger Spice, Melanie Brown – Scary Spice and Melanie Chisholm – Sporty Spice, set the pop world alight with their first hit, *Wannabe,* which went to No.1 in June 1996. The criticism levelled at the girls was that despite their success, they were manufactured and not naturally talented. However, **Melanie Chisholm** is generally regarded as the most talented of the girls and is certainly a very good singer. Melanie was born in Prescot on 12 January 1974 and moved to Runcorn as an infant and then to Widnes when she was eight. During her time at Fairfield High School,

Mel C, Cheshire girl Melanie Chisholm. The former Spice Girl is now a successful solo artist. Rankin

Widnes, which she left at the age of 16, she excelled at music and dancing classes and it was obvious where her future lay as she set out for stage school. The Spice Girls were the most successful girl band in the history of pop culture and had three successive Christmas No.1 hits, as well as chart-topping albums both here and in the States. It is believed that two of their albums, *Spice* and *Spiceworld*, are the two most commercially successful albums ever made. However, just a few months after their very successful film *Spiceworld the Movie* came out, Geri Halliwell abruptly resigned from the group. The initial shock was absorbed when the four remaining girls had an immediate No.1 hit with *Viva Forever* in August 1998. Gradually the remaining girls turned to their own projects, releasing records, presenting TV shows and making chat show presentations. All the girls have had individual No.1 UK hits except Victoria, who achieved No.2 spot. Cheshire girl Mel C, Sporty Spice, has started her solo career with some excellent work and first-class results. She had a long-running hit with Bryan Adams, *When You're Gone*, which was in the charts for weeks, peaking at No.3. She had her first solo No.1 with *Never Be The Same Again*, which was followed by her second No.1, *I Turn To You*, in 2000. Her 1999 album *Northern Star* was a massive success, going multi-platinum in sales. In March 2003 her latest album, *Reason*, entered the top four in the charts. It is clear that Melanie Chisholm, who lives in North London with her boyfriend, but who is also proud to be called a Cheshire girl, has made the very best of her talent and looks set to have a long show business career.

Another designer group, five bright and bubbly attractive girls and boys, **Steps**, was formed after responses were made to an advert in *Stage* magazine in 1997. With pop impresario Pete Waterman

producing them the future looked fair. One of the young men was **Lee Latchford-Evans** from Ellesmere, who it is said turned down the chance of playing professional soccer to join the group. For Lee it was certainly the right decision. After *Last Thing On My Mind* reached No.6 in 1998, other successes included *One For Sorrow* – No.2, *Heartbeat/Tragedy* – No.1, *Better Best Forgotten* – No.2 in 1999 and another No.2, *Love's Got A Hold On My Heart*, in the same year. The album, *Spectacular*, topped the charts in 1999 and in 2000 *Stomp* reached No.1. Manufactured they might be, but they must be doing something right.

Atomic Kitten, an all-girl trio, came to the fore in 1999 and have since had a number of hit records including several No.1s. Warrington's **Kerry Katona** was a founder member of the group which signed for Innocent Records (Virgin) in July 1999. Kerry, born on 6 September 1980, attended her local school in Padgate before leaving and embarking on a successful, if short-lived, pop career. After almost two years of constant touring, in the UK, Japan and elsewhere, with the media pressure and attention constant, Kerry left the group having become engaged and pregnant to Westlife singer Bryan McFadden. During her time with Atomic Kitten, which ended in February 2001, the group had enjoyed several hits. Their first, *Right Now*, went into the top 10 in December 1999, followed by *See Ya*, which reached No.6 in April 2000, and *Whole Again*, from their highly-successful album, hit No.1 in February 2001. Since leaving the group Kerry has had two children, has presented *This Morning* with husband Bryan, written a magazine column and appeared as a television presenter. She has made several guest appearances on chat shows where her feisty, frank, bubbly personality has been a breath of fresh air. Still only 24, Kerry McFadden is now branching out into acting roles.

In February 2004, 17 million viewers watched her win *I'm A Celebrity... Get Me Out of Here!*. She received a rapturous homecoming at Warrington Town Hall. The media believe that her win will earn her around £2 million from public appearances, advertisements and so on.

The latest Cestrians to enjoy pop success are Poynton's **Sarah Harding** and Runcorn's **Nicola Roberts**. Sarah entered and won karaoke competitions at local pubs like the Flowerpot in Macclesfield and the Kingfisher in Poynton before entering a national talent competition to select five girls out of thousands of entrants to form a new all-girl pop group. The show, *Pop Stars – The Rivals*, was televised week after week with viewers voting to select the five members. The judges in the studio included Pete Waterman and Geri Halliwell

Sarah Harding from Poynton joined girl band Girls Aloud. Stockport Express

and eventually Sarah triumphed and was selected for the 'glamorous five', who were named Girls Aloud. Ginger-haired Nicola Roberts was also selected for the band although at one point it looked as if she was going to miss out. Nicola, a dance student from Runcorn, is the youngest member of the band at 17 years old and her shy manner belies a strong voice and good stage presence. It is said that as a young girl she would dance around and do Geri Halliwell impressions, but it may be that she follows other local girl Mel C, from Widnes, into pop history. Girls Aloud's very first record, *Sounds Of The Underground*, reached No.1 at Christmas 2002. Their second single, *No Good Advice*, reached No.2 in 2003 and their first album, issued in 2003, *Sounds of The Underground*, had the critics proclaiming that they could be the best girl group since the Spice Girls. The future looks promising for these two young ladies and let's hope that Sarah, a former waitress at the Legh Arms in Prestbury, never needs to return to waiting on tables.

One man who has seen it all and has now left it behind him is Bollington's **Andrew Pearson**. Andrew started as a an office boy in Strawberry Studios, Stockport, in 1981, and got the show business bug and became a roadie. During his career Andy travelled all over the world working with the giants of the business: U2, Bono, Simply Red, Pink Floyd, Spandau Ballet, Van Morrison and Lisa Stansfield. However, he gave it all up for love after meeting and marrying Helen, an Alderley Edge girl, and he eventually decided that home was where the heart should be. Andy has now established himself running his own business, Hobson and Son, making wooden toys, based in Clarence Mill, Bollington. He is a member of the British Toymakers Guild and enjoys the peace and the creativity and does not miss the travel and constant pressures of being on the road.

> ## Pop music titbits
>
> - One of the great songs of World War One, *It's A Long Way To Tipperary*, which became famous all over the world, was written in 1912 in a Stalybridge pub called the Stalybridge Grand. It was written for a bet by Jack Judge, a visiting comedian, who was challenged to write and perform a song for later that night. He is reputed to have written it in 20 minutes and did in fact sing it later that night to win his bet. If he had received a shilling every time it had been sung since he would have been a rich man.
> - Widnes railway station is the unlikeliest of all places to have inspired a wistful, romantic song. Clearly Paul Simon had the genius to translate his misery at waiting on a cold, lonely platform after performing at a local gig to write the haunting, beautiful, big-selling hit *Homeward Bound*.
> - Foden Brass Band from Sandbach were at one time acclaimed as Britain's Best Brass Band.

Classical music – opera

The rapid and huge growth in the field of popular music, did not of course detract from the more classical aspects of music which also enjoyed a massive increase in appeal as the public became more aware through the variety of modern entertainment media. Television, for example with it's advertising culture, used many classical music pieces to support a whole range of advertisements: Hamlet Cigars, Levi's Jeans, Stella Artois, British Airways, etc. Very soon beautiful pieces of music, whose names we couldn't remember became regulars in our households, prompting viewers and listeners to go out and buy the record or later, the CD, featuring a selection of favourites. Classical radio devoted programmes to 'serious music' and television screened opera to an ever widening audience. Just as it has to UK popular music culture, Cheshire, has also commendably contributed to our classical music culture with performers, administrators, teachers and composers.

One of England's finest composers was **John Nicholson Ireland**, who was born in Bowden on 13 August 1879. In his early years Ireland studied as a pianist before widening his talents to composing and for about 10 years, from 1897, he wrote lyrical pieces for the piano. From 1904–26 he was choirmaster and organist at St Luke's in Chelsea, a period during which he wrote memorable chamber music and two much-heralded violin sonatas, particularly the *Violin Sonata No.2*, which was regarded at the time as setting new standards for English classical music. He took up a teaching post at the Royal College of Music in 1923. In 1921 he wrote the excellent symphonic rhapsody *Mai-Dun*, followed in 1930 by the *Piano Concerto* and another piano piece, *Legend*, in 1933. Throughout his career he wrote many pieces of music: piano, orchestral and songs. He was commissioned by the BBC to write a choral work, *These Things Shall Be*, for the coronation of King George VI and in 1946 he wrote the splendid film score for *The Overlanders*. Ireland died on 12 June 1962 at Rock Mill, Washington, in Sussex, but his music lives on, especially the *Violin Sonata in A*, the song/poem *Sea Fever* and the superb orchestral prelude, *The Forgotten Rite*.

Basil Dean Winton, born in Birkenhead on 18

March 1916, was a much-respected writer on music, especially on Handel. During his Cambridge University days he became a great admirer of Handel through watching the 1930s university productions of his music. However, his first acclaimed book in 1948 was an analysis of Bizet as a dramatist. He wrote many articles and reviews and featured in many of the periodicals of the time. His opinion was much-respected, particularly on French and Italian opera. In 1959 he produced what was regarded as his best work, on the oratorios of Handel. In later years he co-wrote with J.M. Knapp, analysing Handel as a musical dramatist.

Peter Forbes Robinson, born in Macclesfield in May 1926, was a very fine bass singer. Educated at King's School, Macclesfield, and then Loughborough College, he won several singing competitions in the 1950s and his promise was such that he studied at La Scala in Milan. In 1954 he joined the Covent Garden Opera and embarked on a hugely successful career, in which he played more than 60 roles. He played the title role in the 1962 production *King Priam*, played Claggart in *Billy Budd* and had the major speaking part of Moses in Schoenberg's *Moses und Aron* in 1965. He memorably played Don Giovanni and Boros Godunov for the Welsh National Opera. Robinson had a voice which could be adapted to a variety of moods and was respected for his expertise as an oratorio exponent. At his peak he was one of our finest opera singers in a career which took him all over Europe and to various other parts of the world.

A soprano from Birkenhead, **Valerie Masterson**, is without question one of the finest of all the UK's classical singers. She studied at the Royal College of Music, Milan and then London, before making her first appearance in *Carmen* when she was a one-year contract soprano with the Landestheater in Salzburg in 1963. From 1966–70 she was the principal soprano at the D'Oyly Carte Opera, which gave her the opportunity to experience a wide variety of roles. As her reputation grew she was in demand not only at Sadler's Wells, Glyndebourne and at La Piccola Scala, Milan, but also across the world, visiting the US, France, Spain, Argentina and many other countries. In addition she made regular appearances in concerts, recitals and on television and radio and made many recordings. In 1972 she was appointed professor at the London Royal Schools Vocal Faculty and also became vice president of British Youth Opera, as well as finding time to look after a home and two children. In her career she won several awards including the 1983 Society Of West End Theatre Award, and she was made a CBE in 1988.

Ian Comboy, born in Northwich on 19 February 1941, started out as a research chemist before turning to music and studying at the Royal Northern College of Music in 1962. From 1966 until 1968 he studied at the Vienna State Academy. From 1968–70 he was the principal bassist at the Sadler's Wells Opera and in 1969 played Osmano in *L'Ormindo* at the Glyndebourne Festival Opera. His career has taken him to Covent Garden, Wales, Germany and Scotland in a variety of roles, and at he same time he is a devoted family man with three children.

Born in West Kirby on 18 April 1946, **Robin Leggate** was a late entrant into the world of opera. He studied engineering at Oxford, attended business school and from 1970–2 managed a cement firm. However, in 1973 he turned to his first love, music, and was coached privately by David Keren at the Royal Northern College of Music until 1975. His first part of note was in 1975 with the Kent Opera and then in 1977 at Covent Garden he played Cassio in *Otello*. A popular tenor, Robin has performed in France, Germany, Austria and Spain, as well as Covent Garden and Glyndebourne. He has been a member of the Royal Opera, Covent Garden, since 1976 and has played more than 30 roles with the company. He has also made a number of recordings and videos, and has the distinction of holding the much-coveted Richard Tauber Memorial Prize award, which he won in 1975.

Rita Cullis, soprano, born in Ellesmere Port on 25 September 1949, was trained at the Royal Manchester College of Music and had her first part in the chorus with the Welsh National Opera in 1973, before enjoying a variety of roles in her three-year stay. In 1977 she appeared as Leila in *The Pearl Fishers* and in 1979 played Titania in *A Midsummer Night's Dream*. Her career has embraced the English National Opera, the Welsh Opera, Covent Garden, the Glyndebourne Touring Opera, Holland and Canada. In addition she has appeared in concerts and recitals and has made a number of recordings.

Another Cheshire soprano who has enjoyed a highly distinguished career is **Susan Margaret Bullock**, who was born in Cheadle Hulme on 9 December 1958 and attended Cheadle Hulme School. In her formative years she studied at the Royal Holloway College, London, the Royal Academy of Music and the National Opera Studio. From 1985–9 Susan was the principal soprano for the English National Opera and as such played virtually all the major roles in a whole series of productions: *The Magic Flute*, *King Priam*, *Carmen*, *Rigoletto*, *Faust*, *The Mikado*, *Hansel and Gretel* and the title role in *Madam Butterfly* to name but a few. Glyndebourne, Covent Garden and all the other great opera venues feature in her professional career. She has sung all over the world and made many appearances on radio and television, as well as featuring in concerts with the country's leading orchestras. She had an acting role in the BBC TV production of *La Traviata* and among several

other television performances she featured in the Thames Television productions of *The Little Sweep* and *The Mikado*. Among her awards are the Royal Over-Seas League Singers Award, the Decca/Kathleen Ferrier Prize and the Worshipful Company of Musicians Silver Medal.

Kim Begley, tenor, born in Birkenhead in 1955, was an actor before he turned to opera singing. In his acting career he appeared in repertory productions in the West End and had a spell with the Royal Shakespeare Company before enrolling with the Guildhall School of Music and Drama from 1980–2 and then having a year with the National Opera Studio. He made his opera debut in *Taverner*, playing the Archangel Gabriel, and since then has made appearances with the Glyndebourne Touring Opera, performed at Covent Garden and worked abroad, particularly in the US, as well as making recordings and videos. Kim has also made many appearances on radio and television as well as featuring in concerts and recitals.

Another tenor is Crewe's **John Mark Ainsley**, who was born on 9 July 1963. John studied music at Oxford and made his debut in 1984 at the Royal Festival Hall in Stravinsky's *Mass*. But it was in Innsbrück, at the festival in 1988, that he made his opera debut with the English National Opera. In 1992 at the Glyndebourne Festival Opera he played Ferrando in *Cosi Fan Tutte*. John appears in concerts and recitals all over the UK and Europe, where his expertise in Baroque music is much in demand.

Chester's **Kenneth Woollam** is a singer-turned-teacher. Kenneth, born on 16 January 1937, trained with the Chester Cathedral School Choir and then the Royal College of Music before making his first appearance in the chorus at the Glyndebourne Festival Opera in 1962. From that modest early beginning, Kenneth spent eight years

Classical music titbits

- **Bishop Heber,** who was born in Malpas and founded the Bishop Heber High School in the village, and later became Bishop of Calcutta, gave the world the hymn *Holy, Holy, Holy, Lord God Almighty*.
- Macclesfield's **J.L. Riley Choir** won the 1951 Festival of Britain Competition to become the best choir in the UK.
- In 1996 16-year-old **Helen Massey** from Northwich won Radio Two's Choir Girl of The Year in a competition judged by Sir Harry Secombe.
- In 2003 the **King's School, Macclesfield,** with a 100-strong choir, reached the last six in a competition where the final was held at the Birmingham Symphony Hall. Hundreds of schools had entered and in the final, judged by Pete Waterman, Carrie Grant of BBC's *Fame Academy* and Malcolm Archer, the choirmaster of Wells Cathedral, the King's School was voted the Songs of Praise Senior School Choir of the Year 2003. They not only won the title but also £1,000 in prize money and were said by the judges to have had vitality and originality as well as musical excellence.
- It is known that **Handel** stayed at the magnificent 16th-century Adlington Hall just outside Macclesfield and played the superb organ in the organ gallery in the Great Hall. Furthermore, he is believed to have completed his work on *The Harmonious Blacksmith* during his stay as a guest of **Colonel Charles Legh.** It is also believed that when visiting Parkgate, he was delayed for a week waiting for a boat to take him to Ireland. During this delay he used the time to complete what some say is his finest work, *The Messiah*.

Handel stayed at Adlington Hall, Macclesfield, and composed both there and at Parkgate.

with the BBC Singers before making his debut in 1972 as Pierre in *War and Peace*. In 1984 he joined the English National Opera tour of America and performed in Copenhagen, Germany and many parts of the UK. He also made a series of appearances at concerts and recitals and on radio and television, both at home and abroad. In 1985 he was appointed Professor of Singing at the Royal College of Music and took up the position of music voice teacher at Reading University.

Steven Pimlott, born in Stockport on 18 April 1953, is not a singer but a highly acclaimed opera director. After studying English at Cambridge, he made his professional debut with a touring production of *Seraglio* with the English National Opera. From 1976–8 he was the staff director for the English National Opera before taking the decision to go freelance. As an opera and theatre director he operates both in the UK and abroad. He has directed *Carmen Jones* at the Crucible Theatre, Sheffield; *Carousel* at the Royal Exchange, Manchester; and *Julius Caesar* at the Royal Shakespeare Company. His opera credits include *La Bohème*, *The Pearl Fishers*, *Don Giovanni*, *Tosca* and *Prince Igor*. Video productions include *Carmen* and *Bizet* and Steven is very much one of the leading theatre directors in the UK.

Designer **David Fielding**, although born in Ashton on 8 September 1948, was raised in Dukenfield and attended the School of Art and Design before engaging on his first professional assignment in 1969, at the Nottingham Playhouse, with the production of Pinter's *The Homecoming*. He made his opera debut with *The Magic Flute* in 1974 after taking the decision to go freelance as a theatre and opera designer both here and abroad. Indeed David's list of clients is most impressive: the English National Opera, the Welsh Opera, the Scottish Opera, Covent Garden, the Vienna State Opera, the National Los Angeles Music Centre, and the Long Beach Opera, California, are just some of the major names who have utilised his skills.

One of the men at the forefront of British opera is Altrincham's **Nicholas Kenyon**, CBE. Nicholas, born on 23 February 1951, has for many years been an administrator, a writer with many of the leading newspapers and periodicals, and a broadcaster. After leaving Oxford, where he studied Modern History, he worked from 1973–6 with the English Bach Festival and followed that from 1976–9 as music critic for the BBC Music Division. Frequent career moves from 1979 until 1992, writing and commenting on music, embraced *The New Yorker*, *The Times*, *The Observer*, *Music Editor*, *The Listener* and a spell as editor of *Early Music* before he became a consultant to the Mozart Now Festival. From 1992–8 he was controller of BBC Radio 3, and in 2000 he headed the BBC Proms and Millennium Programme. He is now controller of BBC Proms-Live Events and Television Classical Music. Nicholas has also been the author of several books, such as *Simon Rattle – The Making of a Conductor*, and has jointly edited other books including *The Viking Opera Guide,* 1993, and *The Penguin Opera Guide,* 1995. He was awarded the CBE in 2001 for his services to the art of opera and classical music.

The year 2003 saw the culmination of a dream for a 31-year-old soprano from Audley, **Denise Leigh**. Denise won Channel 4's *Operatunity* competition and received a flood of professional engagement offers following her success. What made her win even more special was the fact that she is blind, but is still able to look after a husband and three children and develop her music. Talent will conquer all, if it is backed by determination. One of her concert appearances was scheduled to be before the Queen at St James's Palace, sharing the stage with the world-renowned blind tenor, Andrea Bocelli.

CHAPTER 4
British Sport

Cricket

For the lovers of the game, cricket has a timeless fascination: a world of quaint villages, thatched houses, village greens, emerald green manicured cricket squares, ivy-covered pubs, spreading oaks, white-clad players, leather on willow, teas on tables, salmon on sandwiches and spectators on deck chairs. A charming world of gentility and grace easily found among the leafy lanes of Cheshire.

However, in pure cricketing terms Cheshire is not in the mainstream of the National County Championship but competes in the Western Division of the Minor Counties championship along with the likes of Cornwall, Wales and Oxfordshire in a nine-team league. Nevertheless, in 2001 Cheshire figured prominently in two national competitions. In September, Bramhall defeated Bath at Lord's to become the first Cheshire County League team to win the highly-coveted National Club Championship, a superb achievement. In addition the prestigious Wisden *Cricket* magazine launched a nationwide search for the most picturesque cricket ground in the country. From hundreds of nominations the final six included **Cholmondley**, whose ground, nestling at the foot of Cholmondley Castle amid a setting of gardens, lakes and trees, I have been fortunate to have played on several times in the past. Keswick was adjudged to be the winner, although the competition must have been severe as Cheshire alone has many very attractive cricket grounds, including Toft, Over Peover, Pott Shrigley and Bramhall.

Indeed, club and village cricket throughout the county is thriving. Thirty-six teams play in the Murray Smith Cheshire County League, 31 teams

The picturesque setting of Cholmondley cricket ground, ranked one of the UK's top six most beautiful in a national competition.

in the Shammah Nicholls Cheshire Cricket Alliance and a further 35 play in the Meller Braggins Cheshire Cricket League, in addition to the very many village and community friendly matches. **Toft** became the first Cheshire village team to achieve national recognition when it won the National Village Championship at Lord's in 1989, having been losing finalists in 1978.

However, in terms of Minor Counties achievements Cheshire has, it must be said, a modest

Freddie Millett, captain of Cheshire and the Minor Counties.
Macclesfield Express

record. The county won the championship in 1967, 1985 and 1988, won the MCC trophy in 1983, 1987 and 1996 and was the losing finalist in the ECB County Cup at Lord's in August 2000. Prior to the championship in 1967, Cheshire's first success, interest had been low and results poor. It is not unrealistic to state that Cheshire's resurgence in the 1960s was due to the ability, drive and tenacity of one man, the late **Frederick W. Millett** MBE. Millett captained Macclesfield for over 14 years, captained Cheshire for 10 years (1960–70) and played for the English Minor Counties League on seven occasions. Such was his quality that leading the Minor Counties side against the touring 1969 West Indies side he scored 102 not out, at the age of 41. A hard-hitting batsman who could bowl, he was a tough skipper who did not contemplate defeat. He was a fixture in Cheshire cricket for more than 40 years and in 1979 received the MBE for his service to the game. He served on the MCC committee for 15 years, managing a touring side to America in 1982, and when he died at the age of 63 in 1991 he was chairman of the Minor Counties selection committee, still serving the game he loved.

This writer had the distinction of claiming Millett's wicket in 1958 during the annual King's School, Macclesfield, match against Macclesfield Cricket Club. The newspaper report of the day stated that 'Millett was splendidly caught by Burrows', but what it failed to say was that if I had not jack-knifed to take the catch, the ball would have drilled a hole in me on its way to the boundary! Freddie was not amused. The catch was talked about for years afterwards – I know because I was the one who talked about it!

Cheshire cricket owes a huge debt to Frederick W. Millett, a true contributor to the raising of standards. A successful businessman, Millett resisted offers from the larger counties to turn full-time professional. However, many other promising Cheshire players did join the major counties, with Lancashire in particular, due to its proximity, being the obvious beneficiary. Cheshire has enjoyed a very close relationship with Lancashire County Cricket Club over the years and several Cheshire born players graduated to the England team via Lancashire CC.

The roll call of Cestrians who went on to play for Lancashire and England is most impressive. If taken in chronological order, the **Revd Vernon Peter Fanshawe Archer**, who was born in Brooklands in 1854, is perhaps the first. He played for Lancashire and was regarded as an excellent fielder, aggressive bat and a useful slow bowler. His first-class career lasted from 1873–91 with the highlight being a cap against Australia in 1878.

Birkenhead-born **Sandford Spence Schultz** (later changed to **Storey**) also toured Australia with Lord Harris's side in 1878–9 and made a single Test appearance. Sandford was a Cambridge blue whose first-class career with Lancashire covered the years from 1876–85.

A rather unique England cap was earned by **Reg Wood**, who was born in Woodchurch in 1860. Reg was an amateur with Lancashire from 1880–4 before emigrating to Australia. He was regarded as a useful all-rounder and actually played as a professional for Victoria in Australia. However, during the England tour to Australia in 1886 injuries so depleted the side that Reg Wood was called into the team and received his one and only England cap in the Second Test at Sydney in 1886.

A more enduring England international was wicketkeeper **George Duckworth**, born in Warrington in 1901. George was an aggressive batsman and a fine wicketkeeper, who would have made far more than his 24 appearances for England if the country had not been blessed with the outstanding Leslie Ames. Nevertheless George, who played for one season with Cheshire in the Minor Counties league, had a sparkling career. Capped for England against Australia, South Africa, the West Indies, India and New Zealand, he was also a vital part of the very powerful Lancashire side that won the County Championship five times between 1926–34. His first-class career lasted from 1923–47 and he followed that by writing and broadcasting about the game. He then managed the Commonwealth Touring Team on three trips to India from 1949–54. George died in 1966.

Another fine cricketer from that era was **Len Hopwood**, who was born in Hyde in 1903 and whose first-class career, lasting from 1923–39, was cut short by ill health. Len was regarded as a fine all-rounder in the great Lancashire side and did the double in the 1934–5 season which saw him win his two caps against Australia. Despite retiring from the game in 1939, Len actually lived to the age of 82, dying in 1985.

Norman Oldfield, born in Dukenfield, was an excellent, stylish right-hand bat whose career was curtailed by the outbreak of World War Two. In his only England Test match against the West Indies in 1939 he scored 99 runs. After the war Norman played for Northamptonshire and in 1949 he toured India with the Commonwealth side, scoring three successive hundreds in the series.

Northwich-born **Len Wilkinson** was another of this rich era whose first-class career from 1937–47 cut across the war years. He took 151 wickets for Lancashire in 1938 with his right-arm leg breaks and reached the peak of his career by topping the bowling averages in his three appearances for the MCC against South Africa in South Africa in 1938. Sadly he was unable to maintain this level of performance and finished his first-class career with a total of 282 wickets.

Born in Hyde in 1925, **Nigel Howard** was a good right-hand bat who played for Lancashire from 1946–54. In fact Nigel captained Lancashire from 1947–53 and went on to play for and captain England against India in four Tests in 1951. Sadly his playing contribution was a modest 86 runs. However, he did captain the 1951–2 MCC touring side to India, Pakistan and Ceylon (as it was then, now Sri Lanka). Howard retired from playing the game in 1954 but gave Lancashire great service, before passing away at the tragically young age of 54 in 1979.

Although **Ken Cranston** was born in Aigburth, Liverpool, it is Neston with which he is most associated. Ken was a good all-rounder who spent only a short time in first-class cricket before devoting his time to his dentistry business. He earned eight England caps playing against South Africa and the West Indies in 1947 and against Australia in 1948. Like a number of Cestrians Ken had the distinction of captaining Lancashire and England.

Paul Allott, born in Altrincham in 1956, went to Altrincham Grammar School and played for Cheshire in 1976. From there he graduated to the Lancashire team and thence to England. A good right-arm fast bowler Paul played for England in 13 tests against Australia, the West Indies, India and Sri Lanka from 1981–5 and gave Lancashire good service from 1978–91. Following his retirement from the playing side of the game, Paul went into broadcasting and is now a much-respected commentator for Sky Television. He fronted the World Cup commentary team in the 2003 One Day World Championship from South Africa.

Warrington-born **Neil Fairbrother** gave Lancashire great service for 20 years, playing for the county from 1982 until his retirement in

Altrincham lad Paul Allott went on to represent Lancashire and England. Now he is a cricket commentator for Sky. Lancashire CC

2002. A forceful, attacking left-hand bat, Fairbrother played many fine matches for Lancashire, establishing a number of records. He made 10 test appearances for England against New Zealand, Pakistan, India and Sri Lanka from 1987–1992. England never saw the best of Neil as a Test player but he was far more successful when playing for England in the one-day internationals which were more suited to his aggressive style. Neil was yet another Cestrian to captain Lancashire.

Frank Hayes was another who had all the promise and the attributes to make a first-class Test player. Indeed he made a century on his Test debut against the West Indies, but his talent

Lancashire and England batsman, Warrington-born Neil Fairbrother. Allsports/Ben Hadford

should have brought him more than nine Test caps. Although he was born in Preston his creative and formative years were spent in Marple where he grew up and showed great promise as a schoolboy. Promise did mature into reality and in a first-class career with Lancashire which spanned the years from 1970–84, Frank captained the county as well as appearing for England. After retiring he took to journalism, writing and broadcasting about the game.

Lancashire stalwart **Barry Wood**, who was capped 12 times by England, once played for Cheshire, as did England Ladies captain **Carole Ann Hodges**.

A number of Cestrians went on to play for England without playing for Lancashire. **Hugh**

Richard Bromley Davenport from Chelford played for Cheshire and Middlesex before earning his four England caps.

Maurice Tremlett, born in Stockport in 1923, had a first-class career from 1947–60 playing with Somerset. Powerfully built, Tremlett was a hard-hitting straight driver of the ball who made over 1,000 runs in a season 10 times. From 1956–9 he was Somerset's first professional captain. He played for England on three occasions and toured South Africa with the MCC. Maurice Tremlett died in 1984.

John Morris played in Crewe Cricket Club's first team at the age of 14 and scored a century for them at the age of 15. He played for Cheshire and England Boys before joining Derbyshire CC, where he eventually became vice-captain in 1992. One of the highlights of his career was being selected for the Australian/New Zealand touring party in 1990–1. However during that tour and after scoring a century against Queensland, he went up in a Tiger Moth aircraft with David Gower and 'buzzed' the ground in celebration. The authorities took a dim view of the incident and, despite having made 63 not out in a one-day international against New Zealand, he never played for England again. John, who played for Derbyshire, Nottinghamshire and Durham throughout a distinguished career, played in three Test matches for England against India in 1990 and finished his career with a respectable first-class career batting average.

Jonathan Agnew, born in Macclesfield in 1960, was a tall rangy fast bowler whose first-class career with Leicestershire covered the years from 1978–90. Agnew, who played in three tests against the West Indies, Australia and Sri Lanka in the period from 1984–5, has made an extremely successful conversion to the commentary side and is currently the BBC cricket correspondent for Radio 4 and Test Match Special and travels the world following the game he loves. It was 'Aggers' who, when working with the late Brian Johnston, featured in the now legendary live radio giggling sequence when referring to the 'Botham leg over' incident which has been consigned to the annals of BBC misdemeanours. Both men were reduced to helpless laughter while trying to continue with the commentary. Johnston was pleading 'Stop it Aggers' – it was a wonderful moment of human frailty.

Cheshire has provided the England team with four captains: **Nigel Howard**, born in Hyde; **Carole Ann Hodges**, who once played for Cheshire and captained England Ladies; and perhaps the most famous of all – **A.N. Hornby**. The fourth Cestrian to captain England was the legendary **Ian Botham**.

A.N. Hornby, one-time England cricket captain. Lancashire CC

Albert Nielson Hornby was born in Blackburn in 1847 but moved to Nantwich, Cheshire with his family in 1861. Hornby most famously captained England against Australia at the Oval in 1882 when England's shock defeat started the whole of the 'Ashes' tradition, which continues 120 years later. England, with Hornby and W.G. Grace in the side, were not expected to lose, and the defeat, although only by seven runs, was dubbed 'the death of English cricket'. The infamous obituary was published in *The Sporting Times*, affectionately remembering English cricket and deeply lamenting its death. It says that the body will be cremated and the ashes taken to Australia. That match started it all. Although prominently featuring in this historic incident, Hornby's fame and abilities extended far beyond that one occasion.

Hornby was the quintessential English Victorian gentleman, a real *Boy's Own* character, a Corinthian. Despite his height, about 5ft 6in, he was a true sporting giant in an era of giants. For example, in 1882 he became the first and only person to captain England at cricket and rugby and for good measure that year he scored a goal playing for Blackburn Rovers against Sheffield in the FA Cup! In true Corinthian style he ran and won a road race in Chester in order to settle a dispute, and was also a competent boxer. As a boy of 14 he played for Harrow at cricket against Eton and was regarded as the smallest boy ever to play in the fixture. He was nicknamed 'Monkey', a name which was to stay with him all his life. Undoubtedly, as the son of an MP whose considerable family wealth was based on cotton and railways, he did live a privileged life, able to indulge his love of sport, hunting, riding and shooting. Nevertheless he was renowned for his sense of fair play, his honesty, sense of justice and the ability to lead and make decisions. He married

Nantwich Cricket Club, once home to England and Lancashire cricketer A.N. Hornby.

in 1876, moving to Church Minshull, and then in 1885 seeking a larger house he returned to Nantwich, the town which he loved and served with such distinction.

His first cricket match for Lancashire was in 1867 and his last some 32 years later, when at the age of 51 he scored 53. During this time Lancashire were County Champions three times and in 1881 Hornby topped the national batting averages, outscoring the legendary W.G. Grace! His eldest son **A.H. Hornby** played for Lancashire with his father and also captained the county, while Hornby himself became President in 1894 and held the post for 20 years. As well as the notorious England game in 1882 Hornby's international career was marked by his courage and sense of fair play. In 1878 while touring Australia with Lord Harris's team Hornby forcibly defended Lord Harris, who was attacked on the pitch by a thug, an action which was repeated when he left the pitch to restrain a

The Ashes Urn from 1882.

hooligan who was causing damage in another match. Incidentally in that touring team to Australia in 1878 were two other Cheshire men, **Revd Vernon Royle** from Brooklands, and **Sandford Schultz (Storey)** from Birkenhead.

Hornby, despite his high national profile, was very active in his service and devotion to Nantwich and its community. Nantwich Cricket Club had been founded in 1848 and he took an active interest in it. In 1885 he brought Lancashire to play Nantwich, a tradition which lasted until the 1930s, and Hornby personally paid each local player to compensate for lost wages. The matches were grand occasions, with huge crowds flocking to watch the stars of the day. People walked many miles, travelled by train, pony and trap or horse-drawn vehicles, bringing hampers and carrying blankets or seating. Spectators added to the glamour of the event with Victorian men attired in blazers, straw boaters, suits, waistcoats and bowler hats, and ladies in long flowing flowery dresses or all in white, with large wide-brimmed hats, laced up boots and dainty parasols. It was an occasion, a place to be seen in your Sunday best. It certainly put Nantwich on the map. Hornby became President of Nantwich CC in 1887 and held the post for more than 20 years. Whenever he could he would play cricket for the club and also soccer for Nantwich FC, of which he was also President, knowing that his very presence would increase the crowds to two or three thousand.

Nevertheless, his services to the community transcended sport. At various times he was a captain in the Cheshire Militia, a Cheshire magistrate, First County Councillor, and Chairman of Nantwich Conservative Association, in addition to his own business activities. As his active sporting life came to a end he devoted more time to hunting, shooting and riding. Indeed he terminated his rugby career by turning down an invitation to play against Scotland in 1884 as he had a shooting engagement. This remarkable man did indeed have an amazing career, and he actually had a poem written about him. Penned by the respected English poet Francis Thompson, and strangely entitled *At Lord's*, the poem features the anguished line 'O my Hornby and my Barlow long ago'. Hornby the amateur was an aggressive, hard-hitting batsman, always on the move, while

The gravestone of Hornby in Acton churchyard, Nantwich. He captained England at the start of the Ashes controversy.

An England cricket blazer and cap.

his very famous professional partner Richard Barlow was a patient, careful methodical run-getter. Theirs was a formidable partnership and the poet was inspired by their deeds. He repeats the line 'It is little I repair to the match of the Southern folk' several times then underlines his feelings by restating 'O my Hornby and my Barlow long ago'.

Hornby died in Nantwich on 17 December 1925 aged 78 and the whole area was plunged into mourning. All the many organisations with which he had been involved in his life sent their condolences and he was buried in the church at Acton on the outskirts of Nantwich. Fittingly, the grave is marked by a marble tombstone on which are carved wickets, a bat and a ball, and Hornby's signature is at the foot of it. Hornby was a true Victorian, a product of the time and a legend of the 19th century, and although he was born in Blackburn he was a Cestrian through and through.

Intriguingly, if Cheshire can lay claim to a 19th-century cricketing legend it can also lay claim to a 20th-century cricketing legend: **I.T. Botham.** Botham, who was born in Heswall on 24 November 1955, is undoubtedly the finest all-round cricketer ever produced by this country and is arguably one of the greatest all-rounders of the 20th century. Botham not only captained England but actually appeared in 102 Test matches from

I.T. Botham – a cricket legend.

1977–92 scoring 5,200 runs and taking 383 wickets. He captured the hearts and minds of the vast majority of cricket fans with his arrogant, swashbuckling, reckless but always exciting and entertaining style. Written forever into cricket's hall of fame is that magical, unbelievable 1981 third Test against Australia at Headingley, often referred to as 'Botham's match'.

Australia made 401 in their first innings and dismissed England for 174. England were asked to follow on, still 227 behind. They fared no better in the second innings and were soon 135

for 7, 92 runs behind the Aussies with only three wickets left. Both teams apparently booked out of their hotel rooms believing the result to be a foregone conclusion. Botham, however, ably assisted by Dilley and then Chris Old, went on to make 149 not out, one of the greatest fight backs in Test match history. Typically Bothamesque, it was not a backs to the wall scratch for survival. Botham took the fight to the Aussies and finished with 25 fours and 1 six – one of the greatest ever Test innings. Australia still only required 130 to win but were undone by a magnificent display of fast bowling from Bob Willis, who took 8–43 as the Aussies finished 19 short. Although Willis deserved a great deal of the credit it should be noted that in Australia's first innings Botham took 6 wickets for 95 runs and contributed 50 runs to England's meagre first innings total of 174.

In the early 1980s Botham renewed his relationship with Cheshire when he became involved with Tim Hudson, who proposed to turn Botham into a Hollywood-style icon, promoting fashionable English-style blazers and jaunty head gear. Hudson, who was born in Manchester, had made a fortune in America in property and was a well-connected DJ. He saw in Botham an ideal foil for changing the face of cricket. Hudson and his wife Maxi lived in an old country house just outside Macclesfield at Birtles, where he had created his own cricket ground which he called the Birtles Bowl. Celebrity cricket matches were the order of the day and many an exotic name travelled the Cheshire lanes to play in those matches. However, the partnership lasted no more than two years before the final parting of the ways. Nevertheless, while it lasted it brought much colour to an otherwise quiet part of the Cheshire countryside.

Plagued by controversy, headlines followed Botham around, sometimes obscuring the selfless work he did for charity, particularly with his series of sponsored walks. Although he left Cheshire when he was an infant the county is proud to claim him as a Cestrian.

Cheshire continues to feed Lancashire with quality young players, with Poynton's promising all-rounder **Mark Currie** scoring an unbeaten 48 in his first-class debut against the touring West Indies 'A' team in 2002. At the age of 23 Mark looks set to embark on a first-class career. In addition the Lancashire County Cricket Club Academy, founded in December 2002 to improve and nurture talented young players aged 13–18 from Lancashire and Cheshire, has two young players from Cheshire. **Chris Ashling**, born in November 1988, from Timperley, is a right-arm medium-fast bowler who has captained the Cheshire under-11's and under-13's, while **Daniel Berry** from Hyde is a promising 15-year-old all-rounder who has played with the England under-14's team and is currently a member of the England under-15's squad.

16-year-old **Warren Goodwin** from Chester Boughton Hall, who was actually born in South Africa, has already made a century playing for Cheshire's under-17's and has also joined the Academy.

Although Cheshire is not regarded, in the playing sense, to be in the mainstream of our national game, its overall contribution to this great game of ours is nothing short of first class.

Athletes – Olympians and International Champions

On 25 July 2002 the north-west hosted the XVII Commonwealth Games in Manchester and welcomed more than 4,000 competitors from 72 nations from around the world. Cathi Freeman of Australia, the legendary Aussie swimming sensation Ian Thorpe, the world dominating Kenyan middle-distance runners, the powerful Caribbean sprinters, and rugby's awesome Jonah Lomu provided entertainment and spectacle to satisfy the most demanding. In this remarkable gathering Cheshire was well represented, as indeed it has been in past Commonwealth and Olympic events. For any athlete or sportsperson the prime objective is to represent their country and the ultimate pinnacle is to achieve Olympic selection, with a gold medal win being the stuff of dreams. Those dreams have been realised for six of Cheshire's sportspeople who have brought home gold medals from Olympic Games around the world.

The success of Cheshire athletes goes back to the Olympic Games of 1908 in Paris. **Willie Dod** from Bebington became the first, and to date the only, Englishman to win an archery gold medal. At the same games the remarkable **Lottie Dod**, the Wimbledon tennis icon from Bebington, Willie's sister, made it a memorable day by winning a silver medal for England, also in the archery.

Another gold medal came Cheshire's way in the 1920 Antwerp Olympics when sporting legend **Max Woosnam** won the Men's Tennis Doubles gold partnering Noel Turnbull.

In 1952, Cheshire had a most underrated Olympic gold medal winner. Nantwich farmer **Wilf White**, riding Nizefella, won an equestrian show jumping team gold medal. However, Harry Llewellyn riding Foxhunter was lauded for clinching the gold for Britain by jumping clear in the last round, although White had the best scores in the team over the two days. Without his consistency Llewellyn's last round would have been irrelevant. Wilf went on to win a bronze at the 1956 Olympics and was eventually honoured with an OBE for his service to the sport.

In 1984 **Sean Kerly**, playing hockey for Britain,

won a bronze medal at the Los Angeles Olympics, but he achieved the revered gold at the next games in Seoul in 1988. Sean is not Cheshire-born, but spent his formative years in Macclesfield. He attended Ivy Bank School, where he came under the influence of games master Alan Capper. It was Alan, Sean claimed, whose teachings on positional play and tactics during soccer coaching gave him the taste and the enthusiasm to apply the same principles to hockey. Alan must have been a very good teacher as Sean played 190 games for England and Great Britain and was awarded the MBE for his services to the sport following his retirement.

While Scan was playing for England in the 1980s another young man was racing through the winding leafy lanes of Cheshire in a furious attempt to perfect his art. Those leafy lanes were the practice grounds of one of the best athletes ever produced by Cheshire and Great Britain, Hoylake's **Chris Boardman**. However, Chris didn't see much of those picturesque leafy lanes as he was driving himself in relentless training routines which would eventually stand him in good stead. In 1986 he had his first real success when he won a bronze at the Commonwealth Games in Edinburgh, followed frustratingly by two more bronze medal wins in the 1990 Commonwealth Games in New Zealand. However, he finally achieved the major break-through which his talent had promised when, riding a sleek, all-black machine in the Barcelona Olympics in 1992, he became the first British cyclist for 72 years to win a cycling gold in the 4,000 metres pursuit. In 1994 he became double world champion and won a bronze medal in the 1996 Atlanta Olympics in the individual time trial. Chris won more honours in the gruelling, ruthless, highly competitive Tour de France, including the yellow jersey, and became the last

Barcelona Olympic gold medal cyclist Chris Boardman in 1992. Paul Wright

man to beat the one-hour world record held by the legendary Eddy Merck. Sadly the years of tough competition and injuries led to the announcement of his retirement in 2001. After Chris brought home his Olympic gold he became determined to do something positive for the sport and set about starting a cycling group for dedicated ambitious cyclists. The group called itself North Wirral Velo-Kodak and within four years its riders had achieved 15 British titles between them, had won the silver medal at the 1994 Commonwealth Games for the four-man team time trial, and had seven of its nine riders called into the British Olympic squad for the Atlanta Olympics in 1996.

Matt Stephens, who used to cycle every day from his home in Crewe to work in Chester, raced in the 1996 Olympics but sadly lost the chance of a medal when he crashed.

The latest Cheshire-born gold medal winner is **Ben Ainslie**, who triumphed in the Sydney 2000 Olympics by winning the Laser Class yachting gold medal. Ben, who was born in Macclesfield, left the town at the age of nine and developed his love for sailing at Holmes Chapel. At the age of 19 in 1996 he won an Olympic silver medal at the Atlanta games. Since the Sydney Olympics, Ben has switched to the bigger Finn class, and in 2003 won the European and World titles. He is currently training very hard with Britain's successful sailing squad to ensure success in the 2004 Olympics in Athens. However, towards the end of 2003 there was intense press speculation that he was being considered for the prestigious position of helmsman for Team New Zealand for the 2007 America's Cup – recognition indeed.

The 2002 Commonwealth Games was not only a resounding success for Manchester, the north-west and for Britain, it was also an excellent success for Cheshire athletes. The county doubled its number of Commonwealth gold medal winners from five to ten.

A gold medal winner in the 1958 games was the 14-year-old Stockport sensation, **Diana Wilkinson**. As a 13-year-old Diana became the first British woman to swim 100 yards in under 60 seconds, achieving 59.3 – an incredible feat. In the final of the women's 4 x 100 yards medley relay in 1958 on the last leg she held off the

Diana Wilkinson (now Bishop) of Poynton, first left, in the 1958 Empire games Gold team. Other from left are Judy Grinham, Christine Gosden and Anita Lonsbrough.

legendary Australian world champion, Dawn Fraser, to clinch the gold for England in a world record time. Diana went on to represent Great Britain in the 1960 Olympics in Rome and in Tokyo in 1964. In a distinguished career she also became the *Daily Express* Sports Personality of the Year for 1957, won a European silver medal in 1962, was seven times British Champion and was at one time ranked number two in the world. However later in life further honours came her way. After a teaching and lecturing career, marriage and a family, Diana returned to the sport and to Cheshire. As **Diana Bishop** from Poynton, she is now the Director of Development for the ASA (Amateur Swimming Association) for

Diana Bishop receiving the IOC Women and Sport Achievement Award from HRH Princess Anne in 2003. Diana Bishop

the whole of the UK and in 2003 was nominated by the British Olympic Committee to receive the 2002 International Olympic Committee Women and Sport Achievement Award for her dedication to the sport, which she received from Princess Anne.

An amazing and perplexing athlete won a marathon gold in 1974 in the fastest time ever recorded. **Ian Thompson**, born in Birkenhead, entered and won his first-ever marathon in 1973 and three months later won the gold at the Commonwealth Games. The amazing start to his

athletics career continued when he won the European marathon title a short time later. He was undisputed the best marathon runner in the world at the time, but sadly and inexplicably his great talent just seemed to evaporate and the enormous promise faded away.

Shirley Strong from Northwich, victorious with an Olympic silver medal at the 1984 games. Tony Vickers

A top-class athlete with proven ability was the glamorous blonde **Shirley Strong** from Northwich. Born in 1958, Shirley became Britain's greatest short hurdler, winning her first major medal, a silver, in the 1978 Commonwealth Games. She followed that with gold in the 1982 games and underlined her class with a magnificent silver in the 1984 Los Angeles Olympics. She won the UK Championship in 1979, 1980 and 1983, setting five British records.

The 1986 Games produced a gold medal for Sale lad **Andy Ashurst**. Andy started his athletic career as an 11-year-old runner with Sale Harriers. Quite by chance he was asked to try pole-vaulting and several years of dedication brought him the first of several UK Championship titles in 1985 followed by the Commonwealth gold.

Swimming provided a Commonwealth gold when world-class athlete **James 'Dolphin Boy' Hickman** from Stockport became champion in 1998. James has been world class for several years and has a stack of medals from European, Commonwealth and World championships, but sadly an Olympic medal has so far proved to be elusive. James has held the world record for short course butterfly on several occasions and in winning nine gold medals has broken world records and games records at all the major events

in which he has competed. He had the honour of captaining the English swim team at the Manchester Games but unfortunately on that occasion he had to rely on the 4 x 100 medley relay for his only medal, a silver.

Nevertheless, five Cestrians won gold medals in Manchester to cap a wonderful games in front of stadiums packed to capacity with enthusiastic fans. I attended the opening ceremony, and having been to the Sydney Olympics I was extremely proud of the organisation and the response from the spectators. Many say that Sydney was the best-ever Olympics, with which I would agree, and many others have said that Manchester was the best-ever Commonwealth Games. I have been lucky to have witnessed both.

James Goddard, also from Stockport, who won gold in the 200 metres backstroke, compensated for the disappointment of **James Hickman**

Swimmer James Hickman of Stockport. Speedo

Stockport swimmer James Goddard with his Commonwealth gold and bronze medals at Manchester in 2002.

gymnast **Elizabeth (Beth) Tweddle** from Bunbury in the asymmetric bars. South African-born Beth returned to this country with her English parents as a one-year-old and settled in Bunbury. Educated at Queen's School, Chester, Beth's gymnastic interest was fostered at the Crewe and Nantwich Gymnastic Club before she moved clubs to join the City of Liverpool GC in 1997. She is arguably the finest gymnast this country has produced. She has represented Great Britain on numerous occasions and won several major championships. Beth trains in Liverpool with her coach Amanda Kirby and shows immense promise for the future. Already, besides Commonwealth gold, she has won a European bronze, the first by a British athlete, and finished fourth in the world in Hungary in 2002. Her

missing out on gold. He later won a bronze as well.

Macclesfield's **Michael Dabbs** picked up the gold with his partner Neil Day in the rifle prone pairs, which was held at Bisley, the Wembley of shooting. Proving his quality, Michael also collected a silver in the individual prone rifle competition. In 2003 Michael, a financial advisor by profession, won the three major trophies at the British Championships at the National Shooting Centre at Bisley, including the Champion of Champions, and has been selected for the British team at the 2004 Olympic Games in Athens. Michael finished 24th representing Britain at the 2000 Olympics in Sydney and is hoping to win a medal this time.

A superb gold medal was won by 17-year-old

Beth Tweddle, Commonwealth Gold winner in 2002. Rowena Pearce

efforts were recognized when she was chosen as the OCS Young Sportsperson of 2002 for her contribution to her sport and her dedication and determination to maintain her studies during her arduous training sessions. In March 2003 she continued her progress, with a third place finish on the asymmetric bars in the Visa America Cup in the US, her first competition of 2003. Beth was also in the British Senior Squad training for the 2004 Olympic Games. However, in August 2003 as British Champion she was part of the British ladies' team which competed in the World Championships, which was also the qualifying competition to decide those nations that would go forward to compete in the 2004 Olympics. Beth had an outstanding competition, winning a place in the asymmetric bars final and denying Olympic champion Svetlana Khorkina the chance to compete in the final. In the final Beth performed superbly to achieve the bronze medal and helped the British team to an overall ninth position, thus ensuring their place in the 2004 Olympics. In an international tournament in October 2003 Beth won the gold medal on the asymmetric bars and became the first British gymnast to have won World and European medals. It is also worthy of mention that Beth's older brother, **James Tweddle**, has represented England at hockey.

A much-deserved gold went to Runcorn's **Alan Condon** who trains with Sale Harriers. Alan, usually a 200-metre specialist, won his medal with England's victorious 4 x 100 metre relay team.

Without question the star of the games was Northwich's **Paula Radcliffe**, who has already become an icon. At the games Paula, who captained the English ladies and also captains the Great Britain ladies team, literally romped away with the 5,000 metres gold to maintain an unbelievable run of success. She is the world cross

country champion, London Marathon champion, Commonwealth gold medallist and the European 10,000 metres champion, and when she won the Chicago Marathon in the autumn of 2002 she

Paula Radcliffe, an athletics icon from Northwich. Mark Shearman

once again broke the world record. It therefore came as no surprise when she was elected BBC Sports Personality of the Year.

It has been a remarkable turnaround for an athlete who has frequently finished out of the medals, her stamina deserting her late in races as opponents passed her in the last few yards. She won the hearts of the whole athletics world when racing in the World Championships in Seville in 1999 in the gruelling 10,000 metres. Paula typically led all the way in searing, blistering heat, her head rolling from side to side in familiar fashion. Mile after mile she led, with the pack trying desperately to keep in touch with her. A massive global audience watched with bated breath as one runner gradually started to catch her and cruelly, with only 200 metres to go, passed her. This was to happen time and again, and she finished fourth in the Sydney Olympics. The change in her fortunes has been remarkable. She is dedicated and determined and has won many friends throughout the world with her outspoken and uncompromising approach to drugs in athletics. Her honesty and modesty has endeared her to all and she certainly is the golden girl of British athletics, with sponsors queuing up to jump on the band wagon. Nike has signed her to a four-year contract and she has signed with a sports management agency, Octagon. Quite clearly Paula, with her success, her popularity and wholesome appealing personality, should not be very difficult to promote! Experts have projected that her earnings should exceed £3 million by the year 2006, a figure which at first seemed enormous. However, by winning the 2003 London Marathon on 13 April and breaking her own world record by an unbelievable 1 minute 53 seconds she is said to have earned over £600,000 in prize money, appearance money, bonus and kit sponsorship fees from Nike. Not bad for a modest, likeable Cheshire girl!

For many athletes of course just being selected for the Olympics was a priceless achievement. **Neil McKechnie** from Wallasey was a 1950s British swimming champion who competed in the Olympics of 1956 but had to wait until the British

Empire Games (as the Commonwealth Games used to be called) of 1958 to gain a team bronze medal. Macclesfield's **Steve Mellor** and Alsager's **Mark Stevens** both made the British Olympic swimming teams, without the extra joy of a medal.

Unlucky **Margaret Edwards** from Heston, a world-class backstroke swimmer, had the misfortune to be around at the same time as the great world champion Judy Grinham. In the 1956 Olympics it was gold to Judy and bronze to Margaret; in the Empire Games of 1958, gold to Grinham, silver to Edwards, with the same result in the European Championship. Margaret Edwards held the world record for 110 yards on two occasions.

A world-class athlete and sports icon who should have won Olympic gold if the circumstances had been different was the incredible **Reg Harris**, who was Britain's best-ever cycling track racer. Born in Bury in March 1920, Reg died in Macclesfield in 1992, the year that other fabulous Cheshire cyclist, Chris Boardman, won his Olympic gold. Reg was the World Amateur Champion in 1947 and red-hot favourite for the Olympic gold in 1948. However, a broken arm disrupted his training and he could only manage a silver in the individual and a silver in the tandem.

Statue of Reg Harris, Britain's greatest-ever cycle racer, in Manchester Velodrome.

Inside the Manchester Velodrome.

This represented failure for Reg. He turned professional and was the World Sprint Champion from 1949–52, breaking the world kilometre record five times. He won the Sportsman of the Year award twice and was Britain's most recognised sportsman. In 1956 he came second in the world championship and decided to retire. Reg was awarded the OBE for his services to the sport and to Britain. He moved to the Macclesfield area and lived there until his death in 1992. However, what gives Cheshire a stake in the great man's career is the incredible fact that in 1974, 17 years after retirement, Reg Harris, at the age of 54, decided to make a comeback! Not only did he resume his career, but he also won the British Sprint Championship. That old truism, 'form is temporary, class is permanent' has never been more apt. Fittingly, Reg's achievements have been formally recognised for posterity in the form of a statue of him erected at the Manchester Velodrome, the National Cycling Centre. Not only would Reg have been pleased with the statue, he would have been delighted by the magnificent facilities at the Velodrome which are encouraging future cyclists. He is buried in the grounds of Chelford church

Harris's headstone in Chelford churchyard.

and his headstone lists his many considerable achievements. Reg Harris was unquestionably an athlete of world class.

Richard Stanhope from Chester and the Royal Chester Rowing Club won a silver medal at stroke in the 1980 Olympics.

Another Olympian from Nantwich who had a very distinguished career was **Norman Hughes,** who played hockey for England and Great Britain. Norman made over 100 appearances, captaining the side on occasions and winning an Olympic bronze in 1984 in Los Angeles in the same team as Sean Kerly.

A man who perhaps should have won Olympic gold was Winsford-born **Richard Fox.** He had won five world titles in the canoe slalom class and was the hot favourite at the Barcelona Olympics in 1992 but sadly it was not meant to be.

A Cestrian not to be argued with is Runcorn-born **Robin Reid,** who won an Olympic bronze in the 1992 Olympics in Barcelona, boxing at light-middleweight. Reid certainly attained his potential when he turned professional and won the world WBF title, which he still holds in 2003.

Ann Williams had the honour of running for Great Britain in the Barcelona Olympics in 1992 at 800 metres but finished outside the medals. Another first-class Cheshire athlete who was unfortunate not to collect more honours is Middlewich's runner **Bev Nicholson.** Yorkshire-born Bev started as an 11-year-old with the Crewe and Nantwich club and developed into one of our most versatile runners. At one time uniquely UK Champion, WAAA and WAAA Indoor Champion in the same year, Bev went on to represent England and Great Britain on many occasions. In 1989 she was ranked No.7 in the world and won a bronze medal at the 1990 Commonwealth Games in New Zealand Her long career culminated in her appearance at the Manchester Games

in 2002, where she ran the marathon for England. She had in her career competed at every distance from 800 metres to the marathon.

Another regular for Great Britain in one of the toughest sports of all is Crewe triathlete **Carole Billington.** Carole was born in Crewe and educated in the town before moving on to Bedford College and thence to Loughborough University, where she obtained a training qualification. A true athlete, she was selected at junior and senior level for Cheshire in swimming and running. Presumably this gave her the taste for the triathlon, which at Olympic level demands cycling for 40 kilometres, 10 kilometres of running and a 1.5 kilometre swim. Carole has represented Great Britain on several occasions all over the world, at the World Championships in America in 1990, Australia in 1991, Canada in 1992 and the European Championships in Switzerland in 1991. Training is demanding over several disciplines, but despite the world competition Carole still found time to work as a local teacher.

Dominic Bradley, born in Stockport, is a young athlete with great promise. Educated at All Hallows in Macclesfield, Dominic combines his job as a PE teacher with his ambition to further progress his athletics career. He has represented Great Britain at Under-21 and Under-23 levels and in 2000 became the UK 110 metres hurdle champion before an injury interrupted his progress.

If potential is realised then Great Britain has another Steve Redgrave or Matthew Pinsent waiting to continue the great British tradition in rowing. **Matthew Langridge,** a Northwich lad born in 1983 and educated at Hartford High School, joined the Northwich Rowing Club. It was realised very quickly that here was a special talent. In 2001 in Germany he became the World Junior Champion at single sculls, winning the gold medal, a feat which neither Redgrave nor

Langridge competed for Great Britain in the 2003 World Rowing Championships and ensured qualification for the 2004 Olympics. John Buckley, Northwich Guardian

Pinsent managed in their early careers. Matthew is now with the Leander Rowing Club in Henley and in August 2003 was selected to represent Great Britain in the quadruple sculls in the 2003 World Championships held in Milan. The team had to do well in order to qualify for the Athens Olympics in 2004. In the final race, with qualification in doubt, the quad sculls were last with 400 metres to go. Newspaper reports stated that

Matthew Langridge, world junior single sculls champion in 2001. John Buckley, Northwich Guardian

it was Matt Langridge who lifted and inspired the team to a third-place finish, which guaranteed their place for Athens in 2004.

Another young athlete who has shown tremendous talent and great promise for the future is gymnast **Rebecca Mason**. Born in Northwich on 1 April 1986, Rebecca is a member of Sandbach Gymnastic Club. Her early career was sprinkled with honours: British Champion in 1995 age group 9, also 1996 and 1997, and in 1998 she represented Great Britain Juniors against Sweden, Finland and Holland. More international appearances followed in 1999 and she trained with the British Olympic Camp in Florida. In 2000 she was installed as the British Junior Champion in the 14/15 age group and in an international competition of eight nations trying out their Olympic hopefuls for 2004, Rebecca won an individual gold! Tragedy struck when she sustained a bad injury in October 2000 and she spent 20 months on the sidelines, causing her to miss the Commonwealth Games. In her first major competition after returning from injury she achieved a commendable fourth place overall in the British Junior Championships and a silver medal in the bars. She got a great boost from being nominated for the Great Britain Olympic games squad of 15 for the 2004 games. In 2003 she won the English Women's Artistic Gymnastic Championship and in a Great Britain v Russia match Becky was fourth overall but best British performer in a team which included **Beth Tweddle**. Becky and Beth have been friends and rivals for much of their young lives and Britain is indeed fortunate to have produced two such fine gymnasts. Did I say Britain – I meant Cheshire!

The two girls united in August 2003 at the World Championships in California and helped Britain to achieve ninth place, guaranteeing qualification for the 2004 Olympic games. Peter

Becky Mason of Sandbach gymnastic club and Great Britain.

Aldous, Rebecca's coach, is also one of the national team coaches supporting the national Olympic effort and was confident that Britain, with the quality of Beth and Becky, would qualify.

Sale Harriers have produced a number of high-quality athletes, some of whom are not Cheshire-born, but who were attracted by the facilities, the expertise available and the club's reputation. **Diane Edwards** (later **Modahl**) was born in Manchester but joined Sale Harriers as a youngster and went on to win British titles as well as Commonwealth gold and silver. She appeared in four Olympic games in a first-class career before being overtaken by drug charges. The allegations made in 1994 prevented Diane from defending her Commonwealth title when she was sent home in disgrace from the games. She received massive support from the public and from people within the sport who could not accept the charges. Diane was later completely vindicated and cleared of all blame. She did come back to win a bronze medal at the 1998 Commonwealth games before retiring and turning to sports journalism for newspaper, TV and radio. It must have given her enormous pleasure to return to her home town, Manchester, to commentate on the 2002 games. She has recently appeared on ITV's popular show *I'm A Celebrity ... Get Me Out of Here!*.

Darren Campbell, a high-class sprinter, already has European, Commonwealth gold and silver and Olympic silver medals to his credit, but alas! he is Manchester born, although he trains at Sale. In the World Championships in Paris in August 2003 Darren completed a unique record of achieving medals in all the world's four major athletic meetings when he won a bronze in the 100 metres and a silver in the 4 x 100 British relay team. He is a top-quality athlete who has never failed to produce his best whenever the pressure is on.

Meriting recognition in any Cestrian athletics chronicle is Tarporley's **Marshall Brooks**, born in 1855 and the second son of the 1st Baron Crawshaw. While at Oxford University Marshall became the first athlete in the world to clear the high jump at 6ft. He followed this jump three weeks later by clearing 6ft 2in, a world record which lasted for a remarkable 44 years! Regrettably his talent pre-dated the modern Olympics and by the time they restarted in 1908 he was too old.

Another promising athlete from Alderley Edge eventually got to the Olympics but by a different route. Nevertheless Cheshire Mile Champion **David Coleman** left his mark on British sport by becoming one of its finest commentators.

Cheshire can certainly be proud of its contribution to Commonwealth, European and Olympic Games, supplying champions at all the various games in addition to numerous other medal winners and athletes who have been honoured to represent their country. However, there are many other sports and events outside the major athletics meetings at which Cheshire has enjoyed much success.

Motor cycling

Born in Wallasey on 14 September 1911, **Les Graham** became a war hero when, in December 1944, he won the DFC while piloting a Lancaster Bomber. However, in British sport he made his name when he became the first Briton to be acclaimed as 500cc World Champion in 1949. During that year he won Grands Prix in Austria and Ulster. Tragically he was killed while riding for MV Augusta in the Isle of Man TT on 12 June 1953. Graham was popular and respected by all for his good humour and modesty, and at the time of his death he had won five Grands Prix championships.

Another world champion was **Bill Smith** from Chester, who won the World Formula 3 Motorcycle title in 1979. Daughter Claire has kept the family name well to the fore as she graces our television screens as a popular presenter.

Horse racing

Warrington born **Steve Donoghue** was the darling of the racing public and was the Frankie Dettori of his day. A true sporting icon, he was 10 times between 1914–23 named Champion Jockey, and he dominated the 'sport of kings' for a time in the 1920s. For five years he managed 100 wins per year and in 1920 rode 143 winners. He retired in 1937 with a career record that included 14 classic wins, six of them Derby winners. Following his retirement he spent some time as a trainer before his death in 1947.

Show jumping

Following in the tradition set by Olympic gold medal winner **Wilf White**, Cheshire produced another international jumper. **Paul Cook** from Malpas has represented Great Britain in competi-

Nantwich's Wilf White on Nizefella and Pat Smythe on Flanagan in 1956.

tions all over the world, helping to win the Nations Cup for Great Britain in Norway in 1989. He has featured regularly in the Horse of the Year Show, international events and, not forgetting his roots, supports local competitions.

Shooting

The gold medal for **Michael Dabbs** at the 2002 Manchester games underlines the tradition that the sport has. Perhaps it is something to do with our ancient past and hunting. A Cheshire lady, **Denise Eyre**, from Marple, became in 1984 at the age of 24, the youngest woman ever to become World Clay Pigeon Shooting Champion. Not only did she win it again, but during her career she was also English, British, European and World champion. She represented Great Britain in international competitions and established her own shooting ground business in Glossop.

Another lady who represented Great Britain in a shooting discipline was **Tracy Fitzsimmons** from Sandbach. Educated at Sandbach High School, Tracy developed a liking for full bore rifle shooting and was selected at the age of 26 in 1989 to represent Great Britain in the Kolapore Cup, a major Commonwealth event.

Wrestling

A real character, but also a superb athlete, who enjoyed enormous success, was Crewe-born **Geoffrey Condliffe**. Born in 1923, he was a natural sportsman and in 1939 won a gold medal in the National Cyclist Thousand Yard Sprint competition and won the prestigious Carless Cup. As part of his fitness regime he started working with weights and eventually started to wrestle. In 1939, fighting as **Jeff Conda**, he had his first professional bout against the reigning World Flyweight Champion and despite his weight advantage he lost. However, the valuable experience was put to good use. The war interrupted his career and yet at the same time allowed him to gain considerable experience. It was during his time in the army that his wrestling really took off. He was virtually unbeatable and came home with the South East Asia Gold Belt, the Victory Belt and the Malayan Heavyweight Championship title.

Just after the war, in 1946, he adopted his world-famous alter ego, the masked **Count Bartelli**, and embarked on a hugely successful career. He was 16 times Commonwealth Heavyweight Champion and it wasn't until 1966 that he suffered his first defeat and was unmasked. That single defeat was merely a blip and the following year he won the Commonwealth Heavyweight Championship in Australia, which earned him the silver belt. It was the first time in 30 years that the title had left the southern hemisphere. He successfully defended the title on many occasions. His dominance was such that he was allowed to keep the silver belt. When Count Bartelli retired in 1986 after having

over 9,000 professional fights in a 47-year career, the sport lost a larger than life character.

Hockey

A truly unique sporting lady was born and grew up in a Cheshire pub and later became the landlady. **Kathleen Harrison** was born in the Red Lion at Barnton, near Northwich, on 29 October 1913 and went on to play more than 50 times for England Ladies as goalkeeper. She played for the Winnington Park Hockey Club for more than 20 years, kept goal for Cheshire and played for England 54 times between 1936–52. In fact her international caps would have been more numerous if she had not had to decline one or two tours because of her commitment to her business at the Red Lion. Her first appearance for England

'Paddy' Dale, the England Ladies hockey goalkeeper and landlady of a pub near Northwich. Roger Stubbs

was against Ireland and after she married Alf Dale she became better known in England's goals as **Paddy Dale**. Paddy enjoyed it all: touring America, tournaments in Europe, 60,000 crowds at Wembley, winning a world hockey tournament with England, giving talks around the country and broadcasting about her beloved sport. However, Paddy was a true all-rounder, and she played soccer for England as well, scoring twice in a win over Belgium. She also played cricket for Cheshire and the North of England and played tennis for Winnington Park. Kath 'Paddy' Dale died at the age of 71 and her nephew **Roger Stubbs**, a former rally driver of some renown, donated a trophy in his aunt's memory to the All England Hockey Association for the country's top under-18 team. Sadly Kath has gone and so has the Red Lion, but her record will live on in the annals of British Ladies hockey.

Paddy Dale (extreme left, back row) with the England team before an international against Holland c.1948. *Amsterdam Company*

Other sports

Jayne Roberts from Chester won a gold medal in the 1986 Commonwealth Fencing Federation team event.

British Ice Dancing Champions, **Paul Askham** from Blackpool and **Sharon Jones** from Altrincham, were dominant in the sport in the 1980s and at one point were ranked 13 in the world.

A young lady from Sale who went to school in Ashton on Mersey and started figure skating at the age of seven changed her discipline to speed skating. It certainly paid off when in 1989 **Alyson Birch** became the British Ladies short track speed skating champion.

Ian Griswold from Marple, educated at Marple Grammar School, was in 1989 the British and European Barefoot Water Skiing Champion. Not only that, he captained the team and represented Britain in three world championships and five European competitions.

Although she was born in Woolwich, **Lucy Macswirey** moved to Cheshire when she was six. Lucy, from Tarvin, entered the 1990 World Paragliding Championship in Austria as a virtual novice. Incredibly, from a field of 126 competitors from 26 countries, including a 12-strong British team, she won!

Jane Clague from Sandiway became a champion windsurfer in 1994 when she won the European Ladies Racing Board title.

Lisa Eyre of the Royal Chester Rowing Club was stroke to the first British women's open weight crew to win an international gold when guiding the coxless fours to their win in the 1997 World Championships in France.

Although no championship was at stake and he had the assistance of others, nevertheless a sporting feat worthy of record is that of **Keith Moore** of Altrincham. Keith paid around £25,000 to compete in the 2000 BT Global Challenge Round the World Yacht Race. They sailed the wrong way round the world (east to west), against the tides and currents and prevailing winds. He spent 10 months at sea in a 72-foot yacht with 17 others, sailing a distance of over 30,000 miles. He thus became a member of the select band of 400 or so people to have completed this unique feat.

Cheshire, or Alderley Edge to be precise, is home to Britain's leading female rally driver. **Natalie Barratt**, a former pupil at Mount Carmel School, has represented Britain in the World Rally Championships and in 2003 the 28-year-old driver agreed to appear in a televised documentary showing the pressures behind the scenes before one of Britain's biggest car racing events, the Seat Cupra Championships.

Macclesfield's **Rob Jones** is one of the country's leading kick boxers. In April 2003 he beat the favourite to take the WKA North-West Title and has been selected for the England squad to travel to Ireland for the WKA world championships.

Macclesfield also has a promising junior water-skiing champion. **Will Morrison**, who was educated at Fallibroome High School, is a member of the British squad and was selected as part of a four-man team to represent England against Germany in August 2003. Will, aged 17, has only been skiing for four years, so his progress has been nothing short of phenomenal. Certainly one for the future.

Boxing

Cheshire has supplied the country with a respectable number of British champions and actually has a reigning World Boxing Champion in **Robin Reid** from Runcorn. Robin is the current World Boxing Federation super-middleweight champion and has a hard-hitting style which many experts believe could see him achieve much more. Born in 1971, Reid boxed as a boy at Runcorn Boys' Boxing Club and harboured dreams of one day becoming a world champion. Even while studying at Brookvale Comprehensive he maintained a regime of training which eventually bore

fruit when he won a bronze medal for Britain at the Barcelona Olympics in 1992. A mere four years later he was the World Boxing Council (WBC) World super-middleweight champion in a surprise victory when he stopped the world champion Nardiello of Italy in the seventh. He successfully defended his world title three times but then unexpectedly lost it to Sugar Boy Malinga.

In 1999, in a fight all the pundits were waiting to see and in which Reid's opponent Joe Calzaghue was the hot favourite, the tough bout ended with a split decision in favour of Calzaghue, who retained his World Boxing Organisation (WBO) title. Despite the closeness of the fight Reid had a poor 2000 and actually took a six-month break, and many thought that perhaps he was finished with boxing. However, he came back to challenge for and win the WBF super-middleweight title by a knock-out in the first round and has since that day, 19 December 2000, successfully defended it six times against all comers. The 'Reaperman', as he is known, looks set for even greater success in the future.

The county also had a recent British Champion in Birkenhead's **Jamie McKeever**, who won the featherweight title on 6 February 2003 when he beat Tony Mulholland of Liverpool. However, he

Runcorn's Robin Reid, a WBC Super Middleweight Champion, successfully defending his title against Hassine Cherfi of France in Widnes on 11 September 1997. Runcorn Weekly News

lost the title in his first defence later in the year but will no doubt be challenging once again.

Birkenhead, as one might expect, has supplied the greatest number of British champions. The harsh conditions of dockland work, the ship-building at Cammel Laird and the deprivation after World War Two left few other opportunities for young men with ambition who did not wish to spend 40 years of their lives with little prospect of bettering themselves. Many out of work men, or those just disillusioned with their lot, took themselves off to the boxing gyms hoping for a short cut to wealth and fame. Several made it, many didn't.

One of the talented survivors of the Birkenhead school was **Wally Thom**, born in the town on 14 June 1926. Thom boxed professionally from 1949–56 and won 42 fights, drew 1 and lost 11. A superb stylist, he won the British welterweight title in 1951–2 and again in 1953, holding it until 1956. He was also the British Empire welterweight champion from 1951–2 and the European Champion in 1954–5.

Boxing in the same era and from the same town was **Pat McAteer**, born on 17 March 1932. His career spanned 1952–8, involving 57 fights, of which he won 49, lost 6 and had 2 draws. In the course of his very successful career he won the British middleweight title in 1955 and held it undefeated until 1958. During this period he was also the British Empire champion.

Another Birkenhead-born fighter to win a British title was **Tommy Malloy**, born in the town on 2 February 1934. He fought professionally from 1955–63, during which time he was British welterweight champion from 1958–60. He had 34 wins, 6 losses, 2 draws and a no contest in his career.

The Birkenhead conveyor belt continued with the arrival of **Les McAteer**, born on 19 August 1945, whose professional career spanned the years 1965–79. Les never quite lived up to his potential, but he was British and Empire middleweight champion 1969–70. In his career he won 27 bouts, lost 10 and drew 2.

Chester-born **Jimmy Walsh** was British lightweight champion from 1936–8. Born in 1913, Walsh's career was interrupted by World War Two just as he was approaching his peak. His 89 contests embraced 67 wins, 19 defeats, 2 draws and 1 no contest. He died in 1964 at the tragically early age of 51.

One of the most intriguing of Cheshire fighters was heavyweight **Ray Wilding**, who was born in Weaverham, Northwich, on 6 September 1929. Ray started boxing at the local Weaverham Boxing Club and as he moved on he quickly came to the notice of the experts as his hard-hitting style began to take its toll on opponents. A good heavyweight, he was unlucky to be around at the same time as

Ray Wilding of Northwich, heavyweight boxer who made the New Jersey Boxing Hall of Fame. Mrs Yvonne Bagshaw

Weaverham Boxing Club, a theatre of dreams. Now closed, it launched Ray Wilding on to the world's boxing stage.

Bruce Woodcock, Jack Gardner and Don Cockell. He turned professional in 1947 and although he never did win the British title he did win the British Northern and Central Area titles. However, what transformed his life and got him entered into the New Jersey Boxing Hall of Fame in America, which was praise indeed, was the visit of American heavyweight boxing champion Lee Savold to Britain. Savold's manager took a shine to Wilding, believing him to have potential. Wilding went to the States and had 12 fights there, winning 11. He had the distinction of fighting in that most hallowed of all boxing theatres, Madison Square Gardens. However, it is not clear why his career did not take off from such a good start. Perhaps it was the fact that he met his wife to be, Cathy, just after arriving in the States, because within two years he married her in 1950. He retired from boxing in 1956 at the age of 28 and, staying in America, set up a waterproofing business which is still run by his son and son-in-law. However, Ray never lost his love for Cheshire and made frequent trips home to visit his friends and younger sister Yvonne Bagshawe and her husband Noel in their Northwich home. He even, Yvonne told me, once made a trip from the States just to watch his beloved Northwich Victoria in the non-League FA Cup Final at Wembley. Ray retired from business

in 1993 and sadly died in May 1995. A memorial service was held for him on 7 June at a crowded St Helen's Church, Northwich. Ray never forgot Northwich and Northwich remembers with affection a favourite son. The old building housing the Weaverham Boxing Club, in which he set out for fame and glory, still stands on the corner of Fern Way and Forest Street, Weaverham. It no longer echoes to the grunts and groans and the thud of leather on leather or leather on flesh as it stands empty and forlorn. Once a house of dreams, it did lead a local boy across the Atlantic to America and into the New Jersey Boxing Hall of Fame. At one time, according to the American ratings, Wilding was ranked 11th heavyweight in the world at a time when there were a number of great fighters. His entry into the Hall of Fame perhaps was assisted by the fact that when he was boxing in the States he was believed to have sparred 65 rounds with Rocky Marciano; and to have trained, sparred and boxed with Cassius Clay, Ezzard Charles, Joe Louis, Joe Baksi, Lee Savold and Gus Lesnevich – a veritable parade of legends of the boxing world. Perhaps Ray realised that after sparring with such an outstanding array of talent that he would best be served away from the sport. That

Boxer Ray Wilding (right) back in England to watch Northwich Victoria in the Cup. Accompanying him are from left to right: Bob Roberts, his old trainer, Mrs Talbot-Butler and her children Mark and Nick. Mike Talbot-Butler

makes him an intelligent human being. His own fight record shows a respectable 53 fights, 47 wins, 4 losses, 1 draw and 1 no contest.

Boxing continues to thrive and give hope to young men wanting to get away from an impoverished childhood. Although conditions today are not as severe as those pre- and post-war days, boxing is still seen as a way to short-term success.

Rugby

The twin codes of rugby league and union have both flourished over the years and have produced great characters whose deeds have placed them at the very highest level of the game, both nationally and internationally. In rugby league the flag for Cheshire has been carried by Widnes and in rugby union Sale, or Sale Sharks as they are now known, is the dominant club. However, from the 1880s until the 1920s Birkenhead Park was the dominant force in Cheshire rugby union and during this period more than 20 of their players were capped by England. Since the end of World War Two, Sale has come to the fore and has had nine players capped by England since the 1990s. The most recent, Hodgson and Sanderson, appeared in the Six Nations Tournament in 2003.

However, a more permanent fixture for England is the speedy full-back **Jason Robinson**, who can electrify a crowd with just one run. Robinson, who was born in Leeds and lives in Lancashire, cannot really be classified as a Cestrian. Yet since joining Sale in 2000 he has sprung into prominence. Ever-present in England's all-conquering team, Jason was selected for the Rugby World Cup in Australia in 2003 and scored England's only try in the final against Australia as they became World Champions for the first time. They were welcomed home to tumultuous acclaim from a grateful nation. Sale,

pushing hard to appear in the European Cup, moved to their new ground in Stockport at the start of the 2003 season.

Two Cestrians have the right to be considered as outstanding English rugby union greats. Warrington's **Wade Dooley**, a man of massive frame at 6ft 8in, and tough and uncompromising, was a fixture in the England team from his first cap in 1985 until his retirement in 1993. A policeman, Dooley was capped 55 times by England, making him the most capped lock in British rugby. He played his club rugby for Fylde and Preston Grasshoppers and by the time of his retirement had achieved virtually all the game had to offer, playing in the World Cup in 1987 and on the Lions Tour in 1989. **Steve Smith**, born in Stockport and educated at King's School, Macclesfield, played for England 28 times and

Stockport-born Steve Smith leading out England at Twickenham.

Smith now co-owns Cotton Traders in Altrincham with Fran Cotton.

had the distinction of captaining his country. He was part of England's Grand Slam-winning team of 1980, and toured New Zealand with the British Lions side in 1983. Steve still lives in Cheshire and runs a highly successful business in Altrincham, Cotton Traders, with another English rugby legend, Fran Cotton. In November 2003 he was part of the television team that commentated on England's amazing World Cup triumph.

Rugby league has also produced outstanding players, none more so than the legendary **Vince Karalius**. Born in Widnes in 1932, his nickname 'Wild Bull of the Pampas' gives a graphic indication of the style of his game. Fierce and tough, even the Australians had a healthy respect for Karalius, whose forward play was direct and to the point. He played as an amateur before signing for St Helens and led them to a Challenge Cup win in 1961. Transferring to his home town,

Widnes, he then led them to a Challenge Cup win in 1964. However, he really came to the fore when touring Australia with Great Britain, when his fierce tackling and never-say-die spirit inspired the team to memorable victories. At the end of his playing days he turned to coaching, enjoying spells with Widnes and Wigan.

Another who deserves recognition in any rugby hall of fame is another son of Widnes, **Alan Prescott**. Alan, born in 1927, played for Great Britain 28 times and captained the side on 17 occasions. He started his career with St Helens in 1951 and guided them to the Challenge Cup triumph in 1956. He was perhaps the best prop forward of his day and an inspirational leader. An indication of the example he set and the quality of the man was best illustrated during the 1958 tour international in Australia, when Prescott played for 76 minutes with a broken arm to ensure that the victory was achieved. The injury necessitated the insertion of steel plates into the arm, which culminated in his retirement. However, he retained contact with the game by taking up coaching duties with St Helens.

Cheshire continues to produce good quality players and in both codes the game has moved on and is now much more professional. Large transfer fees have featured in rugby league, and rugby union has taken a more commercial stance. No doubt Sale Sharks, Widnes and the rest of the Cheshire clubs will continue to produce internationals, although the legends of the past are a hard act to follow.

Soccer

Although Cheshire does not have a Premier League side, it is a dormitory for many of the star names of Manchester City, Manchester United and Everton, who enjoy the benefits of large houses in small, elegant country towns with easy access to their places of work. Many of these players cannot be considered Cestrians as they are on short-term contracts and are very often unable to put down roots. There are, however, exceptions, who could be classified as Cestrians because their success has happened while they have resided in Cheshire and they have elected to make the county their home long after retiring from the great game. Indeed several have started and maintained successful businesses and have become part of the fabric of the region. Examples are stalwarts of the game like the mercurial **Paddy Crerand**, who owned a pub in Altrincham and has remained in the area long after retirement, working with radio and the *Manchester Evening News*. Another great United player who shared in many great triumphs with Crerand, winning the FA Cup, European Cup and League, is Republic of Ireland international **Tony Dunne**. Tony lives in Sale and looks after his golf driving range in Altrincham, a business which he set up after retiring from soccer.

Francis Lee, the controversial former Manchester City striker, still lives in South Manchester and has built on his business success with a stud farm near Wilmslow. At one point he did take over the chairmanship at Manchester City in an effort to regenerate the club.

Mark Hughes, the former United striker, has only just retired from playing and has recently and successfully taken over as the team manager for Wales while remaining in South Manchester. There are several more players who have chosen to stay in the county but it would be wrong to claim them all as Cestrians. However, Cheshire has certainly got a claim on two of the greatest of all the Football League managers. The late Sir **Matt Busby**, who I was most fortunate to meet on several occasions and got to know well, joined Manchester United in 1945 when the ground was nothing but a bombed-out shell. At the time of his death in 1994 it had become one of the greatest football clubs in the world. He won all the major honors and was known as the 'father of English football'. It was his vision which was largely responsible for the hugely successful European Championship.

In 1957 the English FA tried to discourage United, as English champions, from entering the new European Cup. Busby, seeing the benefits, ignored their protestations and the European League is now a major success. It was while returning from a European game against Red Star Belgrade that United's plane crashed in the snow of Munich in 1958. Eight players died and two were so badly injured that they never played again. Busby himself was ill for many weeks and it was feared that he would never recover. Yet recover he did, and he rebuilt United, who went on to win the European Cup in 1968. He was knighted in 1969.

In 1985 I hosted a dinner for him in Manchester to celebrate the 40th anniversary of his arrival in the city in 1945 and several of the players from the three great United sides that Busby built – 1948, 1958 and 1968 – were present to honour him. It was abundantly clear that the man was still much respected and loved.

Author Bob Burrows is second left, presenting an award to Sir Matt Busby in Manchester in 1985. Bobby Charlton is first left.

Matt lived in Sale and spent almost 50 years in Cheshire, and achieved all of his success in the county that he called home.

By the same token, but perhaps not with the same longevity as Sir Matt Busby, another Scot has taken over the mantle at Old Trafford and deserves in terms of success, to be ranked with the greatest managers in the history of the game of soccer. **Sir Alex Ferguson** has surpassed the great man's trophy wins since arriving from Aberdeen in 1987. Since winning the FA Cup in 1990 he drove United on to dominate the Premier League throughout the

Manchester United manager Alex Ferguson holds the Premier League Trophy in 1993. To his left are author Bob Burrows and Brian Kidd. Now Sir Alex Ferguson lives in Wilmslow.

1990s, culminating in the nigh impossible treble in 1999, when United won the FA Cup, the Premier League and the European Cup. United are now a highly successful business, and are arguably the best-run soccer club in the world. Their merchandise enjoys a worldwide market and the success demanded and sought by Alex Ferguson keeps this great club at the forefront of world soccer. Sir Alex Ferguson lives in the Wilmslow area, which is of course convenient for Old Trafford.

If we turn now to soccer players, Cheshire has a claim on one of the game's all time legends, **Sir Bobby Charlton**. Although Bobby was born in the small mining village of Ashington, Northumberland, on 11 October 1937, he has lived in Cheshire for more than 40 years since signing for United as a schoolboy. His success as a footballer came during his years spent in Cheshire. The young Charlton had blonde hair, which glinted and flowed as he moved at pace, and to watch Charlton move at pace was a sight to behold. A packed Old Trafford would hush with expectation as he collected the ball and then suddenly, without any apparent effort, he would surge at the heart of the defence and with a sudden explosion he would detonate a shot at goal – left or right foot, it didn't matter – the ball moving like a high-velocity shell as it burst into the net. The crowd would erupt, ecstatic to see a God in action. Little did I know, as I watched him perform alongside Denis Law and George Best, that one day I would work with him as he embarked on the Bobby Charlton Soccer School concept. For many years Charlton has been one of Britain's finest ambassadors, recognised throughout the world not only for his ability, but also for his sportsmanship. Capped 106 times for England, he scored 49 goals, which is still the record for an England player. He has won everything that the game has to offer. FA Cup, League Championships, World Cup, European Cup, Football Writers' Player of the Year, European Footballer of the Year, and many more. He was knighted in 1994, still lives in Cheshire, has business interests in the county and is now on the board at Manchester United. Fame has not fazed him in the slightest – he has always kept his feet firmly on the ground... usually at Old Trafford.

A modern legend also qualifies for Cheshire on the same grounds as Sir Bobby, but not alas with the same longevity, since he transferred to Real Madrid in June 2003. **David Beckham**, born in Leytonstone on 2 May 1975, moved into the area when he joined

United in 1991 as a young trainee. Already Beckham has been festooned with honours: FA Cup, League Cup, Premier League, European Cup, England caps and the England captaincy. He has been sent off in a World Cup match and single-handedly got England into the 2002 World Cup with one of his exquisite trademark free kicks with virtually the last kick of the game against Greece. Despite one or two early mishaps he has handled his celebrity lifestyle with commendable restraint. The adulation heaped upon him and the constant harassment by the tabloids pursuing him and wife Victoria (Posh Spice) is a phenomenon that Bobby Charlton did not have to cope with. Nevertheless his good nature has endeared him to many and he can often be seen driving in the area of Wilmslow and Alderley where the Beckhams have a house. David Beckham is a good role model for young people and, like Charlton, is a first-class ambassador for Cheshire. It remains to be seen whether he retains his house in the county.

Beckham is regarded by many as England's finest footballer, but if he has a rival then it is a true Cestrian, **Michael Owen** of Liverpool and England. Michael exploded onto the Premiership stage, scoring on his debut in 1997 and finishing his first season with an astonishing 30 goals. He then became the youngest player ever to play for England at the age of 18 and 2 months when picked against Chile. Michael's father had been a professional footballer, enjoying spells with Everton and Chester, so it was no surprise when Michael showed an aptitude for the game as a young boy. Although he was born at the Countess of Chester Hospital on 14 December 1979, Michael was raised just over the border in Hawarden, Wales. He broke goalscoring records in the Deeside Primary Schools League Under-11's and went to Hawarden High School before signing as a YTS apprentice at Liverpool Football Club. Not yet 20, he had a thrilling 1998 World Cup and set the country alight with a fabulous goal, fashioned out of

nothing against Argentina. At the end of the year he was voted BBC Sports Personality of the Year. Injuries interrupted his progress but highlights still abounded, such as a memorable hat-trick against Germany in Munich in a vital World Cup qualifier in 2001 and then helping England reach the World Cup quarter-finals in 2002, scoring twice in the tournament.

As a player he has also won the FA Cup, UEFA Cup, FA Charity Shield and European Super Cup and in 2003 his career record included almost 300 games for Liverpool, with 133 goals. At 23 he was the youngest player ever to have appeared in 50 games for England. In his 50th game in June 2003, he not only captained England, but also scored both goals as the team beat Slovakia in a European qualifying game, thereby bringing his total goals scored for England to 22. This is an absolutely amazing record for a player not yet considered to be at his peak. It looks at this stage in his career as if Michael Owen could break all the records in the books. Appearances for England and goals scored are well within his grasp. The England goalscoring record is held by that other legendary Cestrian, Bobby Charlton, with 49 goals.

Despite his amazing success Michael Owen is also an excellent role model and he has not allowed fame and celebrity to change him. A large close family, who all live in the same street in Hawarden in a house bought by Michael to keep the family together, helps keep him focussed. He has since bought a very fine house in Cheshire which he shares with his childhood girlfriend (they met at primary school) Louise Bonsall, and they had their first child, Gemma, in May 2003. It is a clear indication of the level-headed way in which Michael has accepted the adulation heaped upon him that he described the birth of his daughter as the happiest day of his life. England look set to enjoy a golden period, driven on by two of Cheshire's best.

Another player who has had a distinguished career which ended with his retirement in 2002 is Arsenal's **Lee Dixon**. Lee was born in Manchester on 17 March 1964 but moved to Styal at the age of eight. He was educated at Wilmslow Grammar School and then moved on to Macclesfield College of Further Education where he studied economics. He played for six years in the local Macclesfield League with Priory County FC before being spotted by talent scouts and signing professional forms for Arsenal in 1983. While he was an apprentice Lee spent two seasons, 1983–5, playing with Chester City. However, he remained a one-club man and spent almost 20 years with Arsenal in a career which yielded several League and FA Cup wins, including the Double and a European Cup Winners win as well as 22 England caps. A fast attacking full-back with a sound instinct for defence, his fitness and dedication resulted in him playing at the very highest level in the Premier League until the age of 38, a remarkable achievement in modern-day sport. Since his retirement he has taken a new direction, commentating on and summarising football league matches. Although he lives in the south, Lee is a frequent visitor to Cheshire as his wife's family live in Knutsford and Congleton.

Soccer legend Dixie Dean.
Tony Tighe

Dipping a little further back into soccer history Cheshire can compile a soccer hall of fame to compare with any national institution. **William Ralph Dean**, born in Birkenhead in 1907, known throughout his life as 'Dixie', was, in terms of the ratio of goals to games played, the greatest and most prolific goalscorer the British game has known. Tough, strong, a no-nonsense centre-forward with a powerful shot, Dixie was a supreme header of the ball who scored 473 goals for Everton in 502 games between 1925–38. He still holds the record for the most goals scored in an English season: 60 in 39 matches in 1927–8. In his 16 games for England he scored 18 goals, a ratio still unmatched today. During his career, as well as England caps, he won a League Championship medal and an FA Cup winners medal, before eventually retiring to run a pub in Chester. This hugely popular man died in 1980 at Goodison Park, the home of his beloved Everton, watching Everton play deadly rivals Liverpool. An appropriate way to go for such a footballing legend. Wayne Rooney, the current great hope of Everton, could not have a better role model.

Two other fabulous Cheshire soccer characters knew each other very well, and both enjoyed immense success as players and after their playing days ended. **Stan Cullis**, born in

Ellesmere Port in 1916, and **Joe Mercer**, born in 1914 also in Ellesmere Port, first played together for Cheshire Schools. Later Cullis, a strong determined centre-half, signed for Wolves, while Mercer, a wiry, tricky wing-half, signed for Everton. They played together for England and would have played many more times for their country if World War Two had not intervened. After the war Mercer transferred to Arsenal and won FA Cup and League Championship medals. He was honoured to receive the Footballer of the Year award in 1950. Stan Cullis remained at Wolves, where besides his England caps he received an FA Cup runners-up medal. Cullis actually

Stan Cullis and Joe Mercer. They played together for Cheshire boys and later England.

enjoyed more success as a manager when he took over at Wolverhampton. During his 16-year tenure, Wolves won the FA Cup twice and the League Championship three times! Joe Mercer also went into management and achieved his greatest success with Manchester City, when, along with the flamboyant Malcolm Allison, they produced a marvellous side whose swashbuckling, attacking football swept all aside in the 1970s. A great team, it included Summerbee, Corrigan, Lee, Oakes and Bell, who all became household names as they won the FA Cup, League Championship and the European Cup Winners Cup. Joe Mercer received the ultimate accolade when for a short spell he was appointed England manager. Popular and genial, it was the perfect end to an illustrious career.

Two men who played soccer together at school and who remained friends for life became legends in their own lifetimes and sporting icons for all time. Crewe-born **Ronnie Cope** played for Crewe Boys and then England Schoolboys before joining Manchester United as a professional in 1951 at the age of 17. After the tragic Munich air disaster, when United lost more than half of their players, Cope stepped up into the first team and played more than 100 games as United's centre-half, including the losing 1958 Cup Final at Wembley. During his time at United he played with some of the game's great players: Charlton, Quixall, Viollet, Gregg and Setters. After leaving United he played for Luton Town before retiring from league football at the age of 29 and returning to Cheshire to join Northwich Victoria, with whom he played as an amateur well into his 40s. Another native of Crewe, **Frank Blunstone**, was born within shouting distance of Crewe Alexandra's ground. Educated at Bedford Street School, he signed for Crewe after leaving school, having played for England Schoolboys. After impressive performances on the left wing, he

An international soccer programme which has Cullis and Mercer lining up for England against Scotland.

signed for Chelsea in 1953 aged 18 for a transfer fee of £7,500. He was a member of the Chelsea side which won the First Division title in 1954–5 and was capped five times by England as a dashing left winger. In a piece of excruciating irony he was made captain for the day when Chelsea and Crewe were drawn together in the 1960 third round of the PHA Cup. In a typical cup shock Crewe knocked out Chelsea 2-1, though Blunstone did score Chelsea's goal. Frank had a number of injuries which blighted his career and cost him dearly in terms of England caps, but when he retired he stayed on at Chelsea as a coach before moving to Manchester United as deputy to Tommy Docherty. A move to Derby as deputy was followed by an overseas coaching

post, but Frank has now returned to live in the Crewe area. Frank was inducted into the Crewe and Nantwich Sporting Roll of Honour in 1993.

A man who never received an England cap, much to the dismay of virtually every sports pundit in the land, was **Alan Oakes**. Born in Winsford on 7 September 1942, it is mystifying why this powerful, attacking wing-half was never selected for England despite being included in the full England squad on three occasions and selected to represent the Football League team against the Scottish League at Hampden Park in 1969. Although he was never awarded an England cap, Oakes won many honours after making his debut for Manchester City in November 1959. He became a permanent fixture in the great Manchester City side of the 1960s, which was managed by another great Cestrian, Joe Mercer. City won the Second Division title in 1965–6, the First Division League Championship in 1967–8, the FA Cup in 1968–9, the League Cup in 1969–70 and again in 1975–6, and topped everything by winning the European Cup Winners' Cup in 1969–70. After leaving Manchester City, where he played more than 560 games, a club record, Oakes joined Chester where he became player-manager. In 1983 he joined Port Vale as coach but actually played in a league game at the age of 41. His appointment wasn't the happiest of times and Alan eventually resigned. His son became a professional player and today Alan has no official capacity in the game and confines his interest to following the fortunes of his son. I can testify personally to Alan Oakes's ability. I was a hopeful young wing-half playing with Stockport County A against Manchester City A at Cale Green, sometime in 1958. I remember being up against Neil Young and Alan Oakes, who were both attacking my section of the pitch as I was a right-half and they were both on

City's left. We won 3-1, which was memorable for us, as before the game we were told that City had one or two youngsters who were expected to make it at the very highest level. They certainly did, but not that day.

Another great player from that superb Manchester City side is **Joe Corrigan**, arguably one of the unluckiest of players. Joe was a first-class goalkeeper who had the misfortune to be around in an era when England had its truly great 'keepers. His competitors for the England jersey were Ray Clemence and Peter Shilton. It is certain that if only one of them, or indeed neither of them, had been in the frame, then Joe would have gained far more than the nine England caps that he won. Although Joe was born in Manchester in 1948, he was raised in Sale, attending Sale Grammar School, and spent virtually all of his life in Cheshire. He signed for Manchester City from Sale Amateurs in 1966 and during a long career, which finished after injury in 1985, he won domestic honours and a European Cup Winners' Cup medal. After a spell in America Joe returned to this country and started to train goalkeepers for Football League sides. Today he has helped develop a National Diploma for the coaching of goalkeepers and has spent almost 10 years at Anfield, Liverpool, where he is a valuable full-time member of the coaching and backroom team. Joe and his family moved to live in Macclesfield in 1986, where they still reside today.

Another player who went on to distinguish himself in the game is Southport-born goalkeeper **Tony Waiters**. Born in 1937, Tony was a young fellow at Loughborough College when Macclesfield Town, then playing in the Cheshire League, gave the young amateur a few games and an opportunity to impress. Blackpool spotted his potential and he signed for the Seasiders in 1959. After making his debut at Christmas 1959 he never looked back. He was selected for the

Football League against the League of Ireland in 1963 and was capped five times by England, including an appearance against Pelé and Brazil. He played more than 250 games for Blackpool and proved to be a first-class buy. It must be said that as he was an amateur, Macclesfield were not entitled to a fee, but it is believed that Blackpool paid a small fee anyway. They certainly got a bargain. After retirement he had one or two appointments in the game, including an unexpected spell with Burnley as a goalkeeper before becoming England Youth Team Coach. He now lives in Canada.

In the unreal world of modern football, no current Cestrian can be classed as an icon. Beckham is certainly moving in that direction, but there are a couple who in terms of transfer values are ranked in the 'millions' bracket and play in the Premier League. **Jason McAteer**, who was born in Birkenhead, is currently playing for Sunderland. He has played 34 times for the Republic of Ireland, including the World Cup, and during his career has been involved in transfer deals from Bolton–Liverpool–Everton–Sunderland amounting to more than £10 million. Chester-born **Danny Murphy**, following his transfer from Crewe to Liverpool, has experienced enormous success. Not only has he been capped by England, but he has also won FA Cup, Football League Cup and UEFA European Cup medals. However, the one black spot on an otherwise excellent career to date was the sustaining of an injury while training with the England World Cup team in Japan, which necessitated his return home before the tournament actually started. Nevertheless, judging by the way he is playing, other opportunities will no doubt come his way.

Modern football does not compare to the old game – it is now very much big business. Hall of fame, legendary players or no, the present-day players earn more in a week than Dean, Cullis and Mercer did in a lifetime. Such is progress, but it can never detract from the memories left behind by these great players. Can any other county match Cheshire's soccer hall of fame?

Tennis

An English summer conjures visions of racing at Ascot, rowing at Henley, cricket at Lord's, golf at the Belfry and strawberries and cream at Wimbledon. Its manicured lawns, immaculate hedges, ivy-covered walls and traditional All England Club pedigree grass courts, once a theatre of dreams, have now become, for British tennis fans, a theatre of tears. A glass of Pimms and a bowl of strawberries necessitate the taking out of a second mortgage, and a blazered Sir Cliff Richard can be found lurking, willing, nay insisting, on breaking into song at the slightest hint of damp in the air. The atmosphere is now exacerbated by 'Henmania'. Tim Henman, the best British player since World War Two, continues to pursue his annual quest for the Holy Grail, the All England Club Championship Men's Singles title. Sadly, however, Henman's performances have flattered to deceive. Victories over the top-seeded players have been regularly followed by semi-final defeats against lesser opponents. Nevertheless, his popularity remains undiminished, as he seeks to become the first British male to win the singles title since 1936. Once again, as June arrives, Wimbledon fever will grip the entire nation for two weeks as Henman's quest continues, despite the fact that our players are clearly second best. It was not always so of course, and Britain did once have an excellent record at Wimbledon. Indeed an intriguing trivia question would be, which county in Britain has

the best record at Wimbledon in terms of champions and performance? Any idea? The answer is Cheshire, yes Cheshire!

Britain's last male winner at Wimbledon was a true sporting icon. **Frederick John Perry**, born in Stockport on 18 May 1909, was indisputably the best player in the world, winning the singles title at Wimbledon in 1934, 1935 and 1936. In an era of Don Budge, Jack Crawford and Jean Borotra, the mercurial Frenchman, Perry also won the US Open in 1933, 1934 and 1936, the French Open in 1935 and the Australian Open in 1934, becoming the first man to win the world's four major titles. Despite the frenzy and hero-worship Tim Henman has yet to win a major tournament. Britain won the Davis Cup four times under the leadership of Fred

Three-times Wimbledon champion Fred Perry, pictured in his prime.

Perry. This amazing athlete also won the World Table Tennis singles title in 1929. In 1936 he turned professional, but unfortunately, in 1941, had to retire through injury. Sadly, he became disenchanted with Britain, and in 1940 became a US citizen, serving with their forces in World War Two. During his time in the States he ran the Beverley Hills Tennis Club, befriending Charlie Chaplin, Errol Flynn and David Niven. In time his regular visits to this country led to the relationship being restored and he became a popular and much-respected commentator for the BBC. In 1950 he set up the Fred Perry Sportswear business, which still thrives to this day, and he was delighted when the All England Club erected a statue of him on the lawns at Wimbledon, to commemorate the 50th anniversary of his first title win. He died while attending the Australian Tennis Championships in 1995. World tennis champion, world table-tennis champion, successful businessman, former beau of Hollywood legend Marlene Dietrich – the man was a sporting legend. Not bad for a Stockport lad.

Fred's record is superb, but surely one man, good as he was, doesn't make Cheshire the greatest achiever in Wimbledon history, does he? No, but what about a lady with an even better record than Fred Perry's? A lady who won the Ladies Singles title at Wimbledon six times, and indeed was never beaten there. **Lottie (Charlotte) Dod**, born in Bebington in 1871, has the distinction of being the youngest-ever Wimbledon champion when she won her first title at the age of 15 years 8 months, in 1887. Subsequent titles in 1888–91, and again in 1893, gave her another record which has never been matched. She was never defeated in a singles match at Wimbledon during the championships. When she retired at the age of 21, she had lost only five matches in her career. A wonderfully gifted sportswoman, she turned her talents to other sports, playing hockey

Perry's birthplace, complete with blue plaque, on Carmmiton Street, Stockport.

for England, winning the British Open Women's Golf Championship in 1904 and winning a silver medal for archery in the 1908 Olympic Games. She died in 1960 at the age of 89.

Cheshire can be proud of its record at Wimbledon: both of its champions can truly claim to be icons – not just champions or out-standing athletes, but people who rewrote the history books, setting new standards for their art.

One man who did rewrite the history books was **Max Woosnam**. Liverpool-born Max was a sporting hero, a gifted athlete who excelled at soccer. He captained England at amateur and professional levels, captained Manchester City, scored 144 for The Public Schools' XI against the MCC at Lord's and was a scratch golfer! However it is as a tennis player that he features in this section. After World War One Max returned north to join Manchester City in 1919 and, determined to improve his tennis, he joined Didsbury Lawn Tennis Club. Quickly he began to impress and was selected for the Great Britain Olympic team for Antwerp in 1920 where, in partnership with Noel Turnbull, he won the gold medal for the doubles. In the same year he became the youngest-ever playing member to captain the British Davis Cup team against France, winning the doubles. The following year he won the Wimbledon Doubles Championship with Randolph Lycett. He also appeared against the US and Australia in the Davis Cup but still found time to play in the Cheshire county league tennis matches. Woosnam was a very popular figure and much respected in Cheshire tennis circles. He became employment manager for Brunner, Mond in Northwich, which in 1926 merged with ICI, and in 1940 he moved to London to take up a board position. Although he was not Cheshire-born, his tennis years were certainly spent in Cheshire and for over 20 years he was an adopted Cestrian. He died in London in 1965 at the age of 72.

The Cheshire County Lawn Tennis Association, founded in 1895, has continued to produce good quality tennis players, but sadly those halcyon days have never been equalled. How could they be? In the days when tennis was an amateur sport the ultimate achievement and acknowledgement of outstanding excellence was to be accepted for the All England Championship at Wimbledon. A number of Cheshire players attained their lifetime ambition, including **Richard Fontes** and **Nancy Fontes**, a highly regarded doubles partnership who appeared several times at Wimbledon in the 1930s. **A.M. Wedd** had the rare distinction of playing the defending champion, Sydney Wood, on the Centre Court in 1932. Although, as expected, he lost, he nevertheless gave a good account of himself. **Barbara Beazley** from Heswall appeared several times at Wimbledon in the 1930s and

reached the third round of the Ladies Doubles with Mrs Tew in 1934. She qualified for the All England Championships again in 1935, 1938 and again in 1939, when she played an excellent match against the reigning American champion Alice Marbee. Another excellent player from Heswall was **J.D. Anderson**, who also qualified for Wimbledon, but his highly promising career came to a tragic end when he was killed in World War Two. **Mrs J. Kemsley-Bourne** was the Cheshire Ladies captain and champion and appeared at Wimbledon in 1955.

The 1970s produced two very good Cheshire ladies and a promising young man of whom great things were expected. **Anne Hobbs,** born in Nottingham in 1959, came to Cheshire and as an infant lived in Cheadle Hulme. She attended Hollies Convent Grammar School in Didsbury and the family moved to Wilmslow before finally settling down in Alderley Edge. Anne first started to play tennis at the age of seven. Her natural ability attracted attention and at the age of 17 she became in 1977 the British Junior No.1. Her potential promised much, particularly when, in 1981, she reached the last 16 at Wimbledon by defeating the former champion and British legend Virginia Wade. In 1982 she was ranked in the top 30 players in the world and won singles and doubles titles in New Zealand and at the British Championships. Her athleticism stood her in good stead when she won a BBC Superstars contest from a group which also contained Mary Rand. In 1986 Anne, who was ranked No.3 in Britain and had represented the country in the Wightman Cup and the Federation Cup, was in the top echelon of Britain's female tennis players and well ranked in the world ratings. Among her many renowned victims were Cathy Jordan, Betty Stove, Virginia Wade, Sue Barker, Bettina Bunge and Rosemary Casals. Despite her talent Anne, unlucky at crucial times with injuries, was never able to win one of the major titles, but nevertheless performed at the highest level. At the end of her playing career she moved to America and embarked on a coaching career.

In 1976 **Belinda Thompson** appeared in the world rankings and was also accepted to play at Wimbledon and other major tournaments. At Under-21 level she represented Great Britain in international competition but found it difficult to break into the highest strata.

One young man who did have all the qualities for the highest level of tennis was **Nick Brown**. Born in Warrington in 1961, he turned professional after a string of successes at junior level, including the British Championship and representing Great Britain in the Under-21 Davis Cup. Selection for the King's Cup Team, a British ranking of No.9 and the title of British Indoor Doubles Champion represented steady progress. However, he really made the headlines when playing with David Felgate at Wimbledon in the doubles in 1985, when they beat the then World Doubles Champions, Seguso and Flach. More success followed, albeit joint. When playing with Jeremy Bates against Austria in the 1991 Davis Cup Team he won an exciting four-set match. Undoubtedly his most memorable individual performance, which made all the national headlines in 1990, was his victory over the formidable Goran Ivanisevic at Wimbledon, which was followed by defeat in the next round by the not-so-formidable Thierry Champion. Brown clearly had the ability but could not sustain a level of play to compete with the very best day in, day out. The Ivanisevic match was the pinnacle of Brown's career and it wasn't long before he accepted the offer of a coaching role with the LTA. Over the past few years he has assisted several young players, including a certain Tim Henman. Nick is still very much involved in tennis and is still working for the LTA.

For Cheshire's male tennis players, or indeed any male tennis player, Fred Perry's achievements would be extremely difficult to emulate. Nevertheless the county has produced good players, some of whom showed great promise but were unable to make the breakthrough into world class. One young man who it seemed had all the potential to make it right to the top was Stockport-born **Simon Dickson**. As a junior Simon was unquestionably world class. He was a member of the Great Britain Junior team which won the World Junior Championship in Tokyo in 1995 and in that competition, as a 13-year-old, he defeated a certain Lleyton Hewitt. He beat Hewitt on a subsequent occasion and also defeated Roger Federer. Hewitt is currently the World No.1 ranked tennis player and Federer is ranked No.4. Sadly Simon has yet to transfer his enormous potential to the senior stage. However, his younger brother Scott, aged 13, is showing tremendous potential and is the UK Under-14 Masters Champion. He has also won an Under-16 Grand Prix Tournament in Spain. Let us hope that he continues to develop.

Of the present-day players, 22-year-old **Mark Hilton** from Chester is currently ranked No.7 in Britain and 396 in the world. He was called into the Davis Cup squad in 1992 to sample the atmosphere and to gain experience of the big occasion. Let us hope that Mark's potential is fully realised in the years to come. Cheshire needs British champions once again.

Credit must also be given to the administrators of the Cheshire county LTA, many of whom, over the years, have given their time and by virtue of their quality have been recognized at national level. **Arnold Herschell**, a founder member of Cheshire LTA, was honoured for his outstanding work in 1953 by being appointed honorary life vice-president of the LTA, the highest honour that the LTA could bestow on an individual. Another stalwart, **John White**, became Chairman of the Lawn Tennis Association in 1975 and was also rewarded with the life vice-president honour. Malcolm Booth was elected a member of the All England Club in 1982 and in 1994 became a member of the management committee of the Wimbledon Championship, which is universally acknowledged as the biggest and the best in the world of tennis.

Mention must also been made of the late **R.H. Gill**, who as a member of the British Tennis Umpires Association officiated at many of Wimbledon's finest matches. Another who has also officiated at many of Wimbledon's matches over several years is **Michael John Nevett**, whose qualifications as an umpire have involved him in a myriad of tournaments and appointments all over the country.

An interesting curiosity in Cheshire's tennis history occurred in the 1923 Cheshire County Tournament. That year a precocious 13-year-old girl had reached the final and was up against the much older, much larger figure of the captain of the Cheshire team, who as expected drove her young opponent all over the court. However the youngster refused to give in and, fighting hard to the end, lost a three-set final and impressed the watching Cheshire selectors. Taken with her resolve, ability and tenacity, they wrote to the girl's parents offering to give her a series of coaching lessons. Sadly they were too late as the young girl had agreed to embark on a teaching career. Nevertheless, it was not the last that the world would hear of this young lady. Resolve, tenacity and a refusal to give in were all characteristics which at times would infuriate people and yet in others inspire admiration. Mary Whitehouse, who died in November 2001, became the self-appointed watchdog against permissiveness on television, but she might have become Cheshire tennis champion and a Wimbledon icon!

Golf

Cheshire has an abundance of high quality golf clubs set in picturesque surroundings. There are more than 100 golf clubs in the county and the sport is thriving. Several clubs are more than 100 years old and more recently several new courses have been built. Municipal and pay-as-you-play courses provide a healthy alternative to the many 'members only' golf clubs.

The elegance of Mere, the exclusivity of Prestbury, the spectacular scenery of Macclesfield, the quality of Wilmslow, Knutsford, Delamere Forest, Portal, Sandiway, Styal, Alderley; the list is endless for the fortunate Cheshire golfing enthusiast. For many years the jewel in Cheshire's crown was Royal Liverpool Hoylake, founded in 1864 and Cheshire's oldest club. This wonderful old seaside course played host to the British Open on 10 occasions from 1897 to 1967. Some of the true legends of the sport – Bobby Jones, Walter Hagen, Peter Thomson and Roberto de Vicenzo who beat Jack Nicklaus – are recorded on the clubhouse honours board. Sadly the modern day Open outgrew the facilities of Hoylake, but the course still hosts the Walker Cup and the Curtis Cup.

In the 1980s a splendid new club at Tytherington, Macclesfield, was established. It became, for a number of years, the headquarters of the Women's Professional Golfers Tour and hosted the Ladies English Open. Cheshire country houses, such as Shrigley Hall and Mottram Hall, have added superb golf courses to their hotel complexes.

Over the years Cheshire has produced some excellent amateur golfers. One of the greatest was

John Ball who was born within a decent 5 iron distance of Royal Liverpool Hoylake in 1861. He grew up watching the club being developed and at the age of 17, in 1878, he finished fourth in the British Open. In 1890 he became the first amateur to win it and was the British Amateur Champion eight times. When he won the British Open and the British Amateur Championship in the same year, he joined an exclusive club of two; the legendary American Bobby Jones was the other winner. Despite his success it is obvious that John Ball would have created even more records were it not for the intervention of the Boer War and World War One. This remarkable golfer died in 1940.

Another top class amateur to follow John Ball was Wallasey's Ronnie White who was born in 1921. Just after World War Two White represented his country five times against the US in the Walker Cup from 1947–53. He lost only three of the 10 matches he played. He won the English Amateur Open in 1949 and then the English Open Stroke Play title in 1950 and 1951.

Cheshire ladies have also been good quality amateurs in the national game. Lottie (Charlotte) Dod, born in Bebington in 1871, was the consummate sportswoman. She won Wimbledon five times and was never beaten there. She played hockey for England, was an excellent ice skater and in 1908 won a silver medal for archery in the Paris Olympic Games. After retiring from tennis at the age of 21 she turned to golf and in 1904 won the British Women's golf championship at Troon. This remarkable lady died in 1960 aged 89.

Bramhall's Elizabeth Chadwick (Mrs E. Pook) was five times Cheshire champion, North England champion and on two occasions won the British Women's Open Championship. As an amateur golfer she attained the ultimate goal when she was selected to represent Britain against the US in the 1967 Curtis Cup.

The amateur game is thriving, but it is the explosion of the professional game that has made golf a global sport. Tournaments are held all over the world throughout the year and there is a constant touring professional circuit in both the men's and ladies' game. It seems strange to think that only a few years ago more affluent members of clubs regarded a professional golfer with disdain. Some professionals were actually barred from the clubhouse.

One of the legends of the sport constantly fought this early prejudice and through his own efforts to help and support young golfers, helped establish the Golf Foundation. Many experts insist that despite Nick Faldo's superb record, he remains Britain's second best ever golfer, behind Sir Henry Cotton, born in Holmes Chapel in 1907, arguably the finest golfer ever produced by these islands. In an era of great golfers, Cotton was truly outstanding. He won the British Open in 1934, 1937 and in 1948 and the Matchplay championship three times. In addition he won several titles in Europe and played for Britain on several occasions in the Ryder Cup against America. In 1953 he captained the British Ryder Cup team. After retiring he became a golf teacher, author and architect and was familiar with a number of Cheshire clubs. Henry Cotton was the first well-known British golf professional and was, for his time, a superstar. If the war years had not intervened he would undoubtedly have rewritten golf's history books. Sadly he died in 1987 just days before his knighthood was announced. No Cheshire golfer since has been able to match the standard set by Sir Henry Cotton.

David Gilford, born in Crewe in 1965, has to date had a very creditable career in professional golf. David turned professional in 1986 and is still on the PGA (Professional Golfers Association) European Tour. Although still achieving excellent results

Gilford perhaps reached his peak in the 1990s. He represented England in the Dunhill Cup in 1992–93 but achieved the dream of all professional golfers when he was selected to represent Europe in the Ryder Cup. He played in the notorious contest at Kiawah Island, US, when the Americans unsportingly, arrogantly and prematurely celebrated their one point victory. Gilford, playing with Nick Faldo, lost his match. However, in 1995 he helped Europe to win back the Ryder Cup in Rochester, US. David personally played brilliantly; playing with Ballesteros and then with Langer, they won their doubles matches and then in the head-to-head singles, Gilford defeated Brad Faxon. As a professional he has had six European Tour victories and from 1988 until 1999 he was in the world's top 100 players. Although still playing on the European Tour David may never again achieve such a level of personal satisfaction as that victory in the Ryder Cup.

Stretford-born **Andrew Murry** learned his trade as assistant professional at Bramhall as a 16-year-old before eventually joining the European tour. During a distinguished career this popular professional achieved a memorable win in 1989. Andrew beat Sam Torrance, Ian Woosnam and several others when he won the Panasonic European title at Walton Heath. Andrew has his own business, P.A. Golf, at Northwich. In 2003, together with fellow professional Nigel Preston, Andrew helped raise more than £3,000 for Marie Curie Cancer Care in a televised golf challenge. The challenge was to break a record established in 1921 for driving a golf ball five miles across open country from Buxton Road, Macclesfield, to the Cat & Fiddle pub. Nigel finished the task in 34 strokes but Andrew finished in an astonishing 33. The previous record holders from Prestbury Golf Club had managed 83 and 64 strokes.

Macclesfield is the present base for a golfer enjoying something of an 'Indian summer' in his career. **Dennis Durman** is a professional whose career highlights were representing his country in the World Cup and the Dunhill Cup in 1989. He is now enjoying great success in the Seniors Professional Golf Tour, a competition restricted to those golfers in the 50+ age group. It is now worldwide with Tom Watson, Jack Nicklaus, Gary Player and Sam Torrance being just a few of the great players of the game involved. Dennis, who was born in 1950, won the Scottish Seniors' Open and finished in the top 10 in the Senior British Open. In the tour league table he was lying second at one stage and in 2003 finished fifth. His career earnings are estimated to be more than £700,000 and his latest recognition is selection for the European Warburg Cup. He is currently attached to Styal Golf Club where he trains and practices, particularly in the winter months.

Another young Macclesfield professional just settling into the PGA European Tour, and hoping to make a name for himself is **Jamie Donaldson**. Born in Wales in 1975, Jamie moved with his family to Macclesfield where he perfected his skills. As an amateur he played for Great Britain in the Eisenhower Cup in 2000 before turning professional. In his first tour he won the Russian Open and the Grand Prix in Sweden before venturing on to the European PGA Tour. In only three years on the tour it is estimated that he has won more than £400,000. Several finishes in the top 10 of tournaments with his highest in the Dutch Open earned him 53rd place in the tour's Order of Merit. All indications are that Jamie will have an excellent golf career.

Several Cheshire ladies joined the professional golf circuit and a number joined the LPGA, the Ladies Professional Golf Association. **Suzanne Strudwick** from Knutsford won the British Junior Championship before enjoying considerable success after turning professional. **Julie Stratham**, born in 1959, from Wilmslow, was Cheshire girls champion and then a Cheshire county player before turning professional and becoming PGA qualified in 1983. She spent 10 years on the European Tour with some success before becoming a teaching professional at Portal Golf Club, Tarporley.

Linda Percival, who is now head teaching professional at Hartford Golf Club, had a successful amateur career playing for England before joining the professional ranks in 1987. After several years on the circuit she turned her attention to teaching. Cheshire's most successful lady golfer is undoubtedly **Joanne Morley**. Joanne, born in Sale in 1966, won the English Strokeplay championship in 1992 before turning professional in 1993 and joining the European Tour. She won the German Open in 1996 and in the same year achieved the pinnacle desired by all lady professional golfers by being selected to play for Europe against America in the Solheim Cup (the ladies equivalent of the Ryder Cup). She again won the German Open in 2000 and finished third in the Hawaiian Open and with eight top 20 finishes firmly established herself in the top flight of the ladies professional game. Sale Golf Club has an annual competition for the Joanne Morley Trophy and Joanne trains and practices at the club.

Does Cheshire have any budding Henry Cottons? Judging by recent developments there may well be one or two likely candidates. **Daniel Wardrop**, raised in Stockport, has developed into a young golfer of great promise. He has honed his skills at Didsbury Golf Club where his parents are the hosts. He played for England Boys and then England Youths before gaining his first full international cap against Spain in 2003. England nurtured his promise when he was brought into the Elite England Squad and benefited from specialised training. This young man recently turned professional and at the time of writing had just returned from a tournament in South Africa.

Cheshire is fortunate in that several young men: **Paul Grannell** from Sandiway, **Mark Pilling**, Astbury, who won the British Boys Championship and also represented Great Britain boys against Europe, **Scott Jackson**, Bramhall and **Paul Waring**, Bromborough have all been recognised by England. Paul Waring not only captained England and represented his country in the World Junior Championships in Japan, but he also won the award for the longest drive in the tournament.

To support this bright picture of future potential **Ian Winstanley** from Warrington was recently crowned England Boys Under 16 champion.

Golf titbits

- Wallasey Golf Club member **Dr Stableford** devised a method of scoring to even players' abilities in competition, which is now accepted and used worldwide.
- Sale Golf Club. Professional **Dick Burton** won the last British Open championship at St Andrews in 1939 just before the outbreak of war.
- Prenton Golf Club, Wirral. **Peter Dutton** became President of the English Golf Union in 1990.
- Heswall Golf Club. **Fred Caroe**, former treasurer of Cheshire Union of Golf Clubs, is President elect of the English Golf Union for 2005.

CHAPTER 5

Scientists, Academics, Clergy

CHESHIRE scientists have been prominent in various fields of science, making significant contributions to aeronautics, computers, radar, radioactivity and supplying leading figures in medical research in genetics, stem cell research and gene therapy. One Cestrian received the Nobel Prize for physics and a number of academics have been acknowledged on the world scene.

One of the very early scientists to make a name for himself nationally was **John Whitehurst**, who was born in Congleton in 1713. Although Whitehurst entered the family business of horology, he moved to Derby and began to expand his horizons into engineering and mechanics. His expertise in pneumatics and hydraulics gained him a wide reputation and soon he was the accepted authority in Derbyshire and surrounding counties. He moved to London to continue his research and his home became a centre for scientists and philosophers of a similar bent. In 1778 Whitehurst published *Inquiry Into The Original State and Formation Of The Earth*, which among other things considered the issue of valuable minerals below the surface of the earth. He was elected a member of the Royal Society in 1779 and continued to research scientific theories, particularly in regard to the measurement of time. He died in Fleet Street, London, in 1788.

Sir Joseph Whitworth was born in Stockport in 1803, and was an engineer, scientist and inventor. Innovative and imaginative, he took advantage of the ground-breaking Great Exhibition of 1851 to display and demonstrate tools and machines that he had made. In 1859 he invented a gun of compressed steel with a spiral polygonal bore, and later founded the Whitworth Scholarship, which encouraged engineering science. He was knighted for his services to scientific engineering and was honoured when the standard screw thread was named after him. He died in 1887.

Although **Sir John Allen Harker** OBE, FRS was born in Cumberland, he was educated at Stockport Grammar School and Manchester University. After a number of posts and appointments he came to national prominence when named as Britain's representative at the International Petroleum Congress in Vienna in 1912. Harker was a Doctor of Science and a Fellow of the Royal Society and served on several government committees. During World War One he was Director of Research at the Ministry of Munitions, a post he held from 1916–21. In fact he had a narrow escape when the Cunard liner that he was travelling on was torpedoed off the coast of Ireland. He travelled to the US on several occasions to represent the British government and produced a number of scientific journals before his death in 1923 at the early age of 53.

Another prominent scientific Stopfordian was **Sir Horace Lamb** D.Sc, FRS. Born in Stockport in 1849 and educated at Stockport Grammar School, he later went to Cambridge where he won the Smith's Prize and became a maths tutor. After three years in the post he moved to Australia, becoming Professor of Mathematics at Adelaide University before returning to Manchester after 10 years to take up the Beyer Chair of Mathematics. Lamb published a number of works, perhaps the most famous of which was *Hydrodynamics*, which really established his reputation. Other works, *Dynamic Theory of Sound Statics* and the *Science of Aeronautics*, made him the leading scientist in his field and an expert in the effect of stress on propellers created by the flow of air around them. He received many honours, including a knighthood, for his services to science. He was a Fellow of the Royal Society, won the Royal Medal in 1902, the Copley Medal (the highest honour) in 1924, and in 1931 was appointed President of the British Association. When he died in 1934 Sir Horace Lamb was acknowledged to have been the greatest mathematician and physicist of his time.

Cheshire-born **Sir Ernest Barker**, who was one of the country's leading political scientists, was educated at Manchester Grammar School before moving on to Oxford. He was the Principal at King's College, London, from 1920–27, before taking up the post of Professor of Political Science and fellow of Peterhouse, Cambridge from 1928–39. His works included books: *National Character* in 1927, *Reflections On Government* in 1942 and *Principles of Social and Political Theory* in 1951. Barker actually came out of retirement to take up the post of Professor of Political Science in war-ravaged Cologne in 1947.

He published his autobiography, *Age and Youth*, in 1953, and died in 1960 at the age of 86.

Another old boy of Stockport Grammar School to attain international recognition was born in Romiley on 26 June 1911. Professor **Sir Frederick Calland Williams** was an electrical engineer who during World War Two did valuable research into radar. His work culminated in him inventing an automatic radar system suitable for use in fighter aircraft for which he was awarded the OBE in 1946. It was in 1946 while he was Professor of Electrical Engineering at Manchester University that he developed a data memory device based on cathode ray tubes. Williams did in fact build the world's first-ever electronic random access memory (RAM) for a computer. His achievement created worldwide interest and he became, in 1956, the first recipient of the Benjamin Franklin Medal of the Royal Society of Arts. He also received the Hughes Medal of the Royal Society. He was created CBE in 1961 and was knighted in 1976. Sir Frederick Williams died in Prestbury in 1977.

Another Cestrian renowned worldwide was **Sir James Chadwick**, born in 1891 in Bollington near Macclesfield. Chadwick studied at Manchester University, Cambridge and Berlin before moving into the research field. Chadwick worked on radioactivity with Ernest Rutherford in the 1930s and was awarded the Hughes Medal of the Royal Society in 1932. However, as his work progressed in radioactivity and magnestism, he discovered the neutron, which Rutherford, who was awarded the Nobel Prize for Chemistry in 1908, had predicted existed. Chadwick's discovery of the neutron made the groundwork possible for the release of energy from the atom and received worldwide acclaim. He was awarded the 1935 Nobel Prize for Physics, the highest award a scientist can achieve. He went on to build Britain's first

Sir James Chadwick from Bollington, who won the Nobel Prize for Physics, worked on the development of the atomic bomb. University of Liverpool Library

Cyclotron in 1935, the same year that he was appointed Professor of Liverpool University, a post he held until 1948. He published *Radioactivity and Radioactive Substances* and *The Existence of A Neutron*. During World War Two Chadwick was invited to America to work on the Manhattan Project – the atomic bomb – for which he was awarded the US Medal of Merit in 1946. Further awards, a knighthood in 1945 and the Franklin Medal in 1951, served to underline this great scientist's work in a specialist field. He died in 1974, his place in history assured.

Although Professor **Leslie John Witts** was not strictly a Cestrian when he was born in Warrington in 1898, he was a Cestrian when he died in 1982. He was educated at Botelar Grammar School, Warrington, and Manchester University, and worked for a time in Manchester, New York and Prague before being appointed physician at Guy's Hospital. Research into blood cells, anaemia and haematemesis became his life's work. In 1937 he published a definitive work, *Ritual Purgation In Modern Medicine*, which put a stop to the outdated and barbaric practice of purgation on severely ill patients, which was featured in the *Lancet*. In 1938 he became the first Nuffield professor of clinical medicine at Oxford, which was followed by several other appointments, book publications, lecture tours and appointments as honorary fellow in America and Canada. A much respected Professor of Medicine, Witts was made President of the Association of Physicians and died in 1982.

Macclesfield-born **Alexander Stokes** was the first scientist to discover that the DNA molecule was probably helical in shape. Born in 1919, he was educated at Cheadle Hulme School, then Manchester Grammar, and went on to Cambridge, where he graduated with a First in Natural Sciences. He worked at the university in the field of X-ray crystallography and in 1947 joined John Randall's King's College, London team studying the molecular structure of biological molecules. Stokes worked in this field for

DNA pioneers from 1953, from left to right: Raymond Gosling, Herbert Wilson, Maurice Wilkins and Macclesfield's Dr Alex Stokes. King's College, London

more than 20 years, examining evidence of the complex structure of DNA from X-ray diffraction patterns. He also had to understand the specialised mathematics involved. Maurice Wilkins, who with James Watson and Francis Crick received the 1962 Nobel Prize for discovering the structure of DNA, consulted Stokes in 1950, asking him to calculate mathematically the pattern that a helical molecular structure might make. Overnight Stokes produced the diagram which helped confirm their findings, which were published to great acclaim a few years later. It was said by many, including James Watson but not the modest Stokes, that he should have shared in the honour of the Nobel Prize. Alexander Stokes was chairman of the College Board of Studies in Physics for several years before retiring in 1982. During his lifetime he wrote several books including *The Principles of Atomic and Nuclear Physics* and *The Theory of the Optical Properties of Inhomogeneous Materials*. In 1993 a plaque was installed at King's College, London, listing the names of those, including Stokes, who had been involved in the 1953 project of the X-ray study of DNA structure. Alexander Stokes died on 5 February 2003 at the age of 83.

Professor **Mike Dexter** from Adlington has risen through the ranks from laboratory technician to Director of Christie's Paterson Institute for Cancer Research after 27 years of service. He has a worldwide reputation. In 1998 his ability was recognised when he moved to London to take on the position of Director of the Wellcome Trust, the world's largest biomedical research charity. It is arguably one of the most prestigious posts in British science. Professor Dexter is largely responsible for a world first, a major breakthrough in instigating a new treatment for leukaemia through gene therapy. Called the 'Dexter Bone Marrow System' the technique involves growing bone marrow stem cells in the laboratory which are able to destroy leukaemia cells, enabling the surviving cells to be restored to the patient. Professor Dexter's system is now accepted world wide and he is acknowledged as a world expert in experimental haematology stem cell transportation. A Fellow of the Royal Society, it seems certain that many more awards will come his way.

The medical world is further graced by two more Cestrians. Professor **Francis Richard Ellis**, born in Halebarns on 3 March 1936 and educated at Altrincham Grammar School, Manchester University and Leeds University, is an acknowledged expert in the field of anaesthesia. Professor of Anaesthesia at Leeds University, he is also a fellow of the Royal College of Anaesthetists and has written papers and books including *Inherited Disease and Anaesthesia* and *Neuroanaesthesia*. Professor **Stephen Kevin Smith**, born on 8 March 1951 in Birkenhead, attended Birkenhead School, London University and then Cambridge before embarking on his medical career. He is Professor of Obstetrics and Gynaecology at the University of Cambridge and has written various articles and books on his specialist subject.

An interesting scientific figure who was very much in the national and international spotlight in the 1960s as the race into space took place is Professor **Sir Bernard Lovell**, of Jodrell Bank renown. Professor Lovell was born in Gloucestershire on 31 August 1913, but has spent almost 60 years in Cheshire. As his creative years were spent in the county, he qualifies as a Cestrian. He was educated at Kingswood Grammar School, Bristol, and then the University of Bristol, before embarking on his life's work as a scientist and radio astronomer. In 1945 he founded the Nuffield Radio Astronomy Laboratory at Jodrell Bank, becoming the resi-

Professor Sir Bernard Lovell of Jodrell Bank. University of Manchester.

dent Professor of Radio Astronomy. In 1981 the name was changed to the Jodrell Bank Observatory and it is well known throughout the world. During this time he also became Professor of Radio Astronomy at Manchester University, a position which he held from 1951–80. Respected throughout the world for his experience and knowledge, Professor Lovell and Jodrell Bank have become known as a centre of expertise and have hosted visitors from all over the world. In 1969 during the successful moon landing of the Apollo 11 mission it was Jodrell Bank which helped track the 239,000-mile journey, giving the Americans valuable support. Indeed, for many years Jodrell Bank, situated in Cheshire's leafy country lanes, was the largest radio telescope in the world and was called upon to assist with countless space missions. In 2003 it is assisting with the Beagle II mission to Mars. Professor Lovell, an acknowledged world expert in his field, has written many books – *The Story of Jodrell Bank* in 1968, *In The Centre of Immensities* in 1975, *Emerging Cosmology* in 1981, *The Jodrell Bank Telescope* in 1985, *Voice Of The Universe* in 1987, *Astronomer By Chance* in 1990 and *Echoes of War* in 1991 – which have been popular throughout the world. Honours and awards have been bestowed on him from all over the globe and are far too numerous to mention,

but the volume reflects the esteem in which this scientist is held by his peers. He has received the OBE and a knighthood in Britain, among several other honours. He was President of the Royal Astronomical Society from 1969–71 and held numerous posts, both national and international, and still lives in the peace and solitude of Swettenham, very close to his beloved Jodrell Bank Observatory and the renamed Lovell telescope.

Another hugely popular Cheshire space scientist is Dr **Heather Anita Couper,** who was born in Wallasey on 2 June 1949. Heather began observing the heavens as a very young child, not because she was particularly interested in the stars, but because she was always trying to catch

Space scientist and broadcaster Doctor Heather Anita Couper, born in Wallasey. David Higham

a glimpse of her father, who was a pilot. It was her father who nurtured her early interest. Educated at St Mary's Grammar School, Leicester University and Oxford, she worked as a trainee with Peter Robinson Ltd for two years before becoming a technician at a basic level at the

Cambridge observatories. However, her ambitions were fired by her PhD research into galaxies at Oxford and in 1977 she became a lecturer at the Greenwich Planetarium, a position which she held until 1983.

It was at about this time that her knowledge, experience and presentation skills propelled her into the media world and she embarked on a whole new career as a broadcaster, writer and presenter on astronomy and science. Her own star was in the ascendancy and in 1984 she was elected President of the British Astronomical Association. After her term of office ended in 1986, she was appointed President of the Junior Astronomical Association, a body established to encourage beginners into the world of science and astronomy. She was very popular on television and radio chat shows and launched a whole series of television shows commencing with a children's programme, *Heaven's Above*, in 1985, followed by an adult programme, *The Planets*. In 1988 she became a director of Pioneer Film and TV Productions and after that was never off the nation's television screens or the radio. Programmes like *The Stars, Avalanche, Raging Planet, Killer Earth, Stormforce, Universe, A Close Encounter of The Second Kind, Neptune Encounter, ET Please Phone Earth, Space Shuttle, Wonders Of Weather, Electric Skies, On Jupiter* and *Black Holes* have enhanced her reputation as a scientist and astronomer.

In addition to her film-making she wrote a regular column on astronomy for *The Independent* and was appointed Gresham Professor of Astronomy from 1993–6. As a writer she has been no less prolific, turning out more than 30 publications, such as *The Universe, The Stars, The Planets, Black Holes* and, in 2001, *Mars, The Inside Story of the Red Planet* and *Extreme Universe*. Dr Heather Couper is unquestionably a world-respected space scientist who is able to communicate her knowledge to a wide audience.

Academics

One man who did a great service to the education system of this country was **Richard Sutton**, who was the co-founder of Brasenose College, Oxford, regarded for many years as the greatest college in Britain. He was knighted for his services to the country and died in 1524. There is a memorial to him in Gawsworth Church, near Macclesfield.

Sir Maurice Powicke MA, FBA was born in Alnwick in 1879 but was educated at Stockport Grammar School while his father was the minister at Hatherlow, Stockport. Powicke went to Oxford and after graduating embarked on a brilliant academic career. Appointments followed rapidly: Professor of Modern History, Queen's Belfast; Professor of Mediaeval History, Manchester; Regius Professor of Modern History, Oxford; and seven universities including Oxford gave him doctor's degrees. Further honours followed. He became a Fellow of the British Academy in 1927, a Fellow of the Mediaeval Academy of America in 1929, and President of the Royal Historical Society from 1933–7. He also published several books and papers, ensuring that he was regarded as the greatest mediaeval scholar in the English-speaking world and a first-rate historian. His books included *Mediaeval England* in 1931, *The Christian Life In The Middle Ages* in 1935, *Reformation In England* in 1941 and *The Thirteenth Century* in 1953.

Professor **Sir Edward Anthony (Tony) Wrigley** was born in Chorlton, near Manchester, but spent his formative years at King's School, Macclesfield, before moving on to Cambridge. He lectured at Cambridge where he became Master of Corpus Christi College and as Professor of Populations and Economic History he went on to obtain numerous appointments at various universities. He wrote many papers and a number of books on population and wealth: *Industrial Growth and Population Change* in 1961, *English Historical Demography*, *Population and History*, *People, Cities and Wealth* and *Continuity Chance and Change*. He was knighted in 1996.

Widnes-born Professor **Peter Doyle** was acknowledged as the leader in the field of marketing, certainly in Europe if not the world. Born on 23 June 1943, he was educated at West Park Grammar School, St Helens, and Manchester University, where he obtained a First in Economics before moving on to America where he obtained a MSc and an PhD in Pittsburg. His early career was as an economist, and he then became a senior research fellow at the London Business School and had a time as a lecturer in marketing. From 1973 until 1985 Doyle was Professor of Marketing at Bradford University, where he taught retail and marketing strategy, working closely with many of the leading retailers: Asda, Boots, Tesco and Marks and Spencer to name just a few. His reputation was such that he was personally sought by the country's leading businesses. British Airways, British Telecom, Mars, Shell and Unilever were just a few of the major companies that sought his advice on strategy and understanding their markets. He also acted as a consultant to several of the advertising agencies as well as the CBI, the DTI and on occasions the Cabinet Office. He was highly regarded in America and was awarded the Gold Medal of the American Marketing Association, a very rare honour. He was much sought after by other universities and regularly visited America, France and Hawaii as a visiting professor. At the time of his death in March 2003 at the age of 59, he was the Professor of Mar-keting and Strategic Management at Warwick Business School, a post which he had held from 1985. The Business School under his guidance had grown from 45 staff to over 400 and is now regarded as one of the best in the country. Doyle's skills have been encapsulated and handed down for students in a series of articles and books, including *Marketing Management and Strategy* in 1994, and his last book was completed in 2000 and entitled *Value-based Marketing*.

The village of Poynton was delighted when one of its long-term residents, Professor **Sir Robert Boyd**, was knighted in the 2004 New Year's Honours List for his dedication and work in the field of medicine. In an illustrious career Robert Boyd had spent over 30 years as a consultant children's doctor, mostly at Booth Hall Hospital, Manchester, and St Mary's Children's Hospital, before becoming one of the highest earning academics in Britain when appointed to the post of principal of St George's Hospital Medical School in London. At the same time he became Pro-vice Chancellor of Medicine at London University, which gave him full responsibility for all the medical schools in the capital. Highly respected in the profession, he had also been chairman of the Council of UK Heads of Medical Schools, had acted as an advisor to a range of medical charities and had sat on the London Modernisation Board. His knighthood at the age of 65 came just as he retired from his distinguished career, but his service to public life continues with his acceptance of the post of chairman of Lloyds TSB Trust, which supports charities that help the disabled and deserving to participate in the community. Sir Robert accepted the honour modestly, remarking that although he was pleased, the honour reflected the hard work of many others. A true Cestrian, Sir Robert still lives in Poynton, and his three children were all educated at Poynton High School. His wife Meriel is studying at Manchester University in pursuit of a Masters degree in Art History.

Clergy

Over the centuries the clergy has played a powerful and influential role, not only in the history of this island, but also in society. That influence is not perhaps as strong today as it was in the past, but for many, the church is still an important part of modern life.

One of the very early Cheshire priests mentioned in history was **Archbishop Plegmund**. It is not known when or where he was born, but he was living as a hermit on an island five miles north-east of Chester when he was summoned in AD 890 to the court of King Alfred. He was made Archbishop of Canterbury and crowned Alfred's son Edward at Kingston. It is believed that an 18th-century tomb in Plemstall may well be the site of his original hermitage. He clearly made his mark as his name was given to copies of the *Anglo-Saxon Chronicle*, and a 'Plegmund edition' is in Corpus Christi College. On his death in 914 he was buried in Canterbury.

Another ancient clergyman of note was **Ranulf** or **Randall Higden**, who was a Benedictine monk in the community of St Werburgh's, near Chester. Ranulf was a writer, historian and playwright. He took on a prodigious work, *Polychronicon*, finished in 1350, which purported to be the history of the world from its formation to until Ranulf's time. The original manuscript is believed to have survived and is in Chester Cathedral, together with a copy printed out by Caxton's assistant.

Preacher **Dr Ralph Shaa**, brother of **Sir Edmond Shaa**, was a clergyman whose reputation was somewhat tarnished by his notorious sermon at St Paul's Cross in London on 22 June 1483, when he questioned the validity of Edward IV's marriage and his right to rule. The sermon was seen as being orchestrated by Richard III, who wanted the throne for himself. Shaa never lived down the shame and the infamy and died in 1484 with his name besmirched. The Shaa family originated from Dukenfield and Ralph became a much acclaimed preacher. He was uniquely appointed chaplain to Edward IV and later to Richard III. Ralph and Edmond Shaa's parents are buried in the church of St Mary in Stockport.

Reginald Heber, best known as the Bishop of Calcutta, was born in Malpas in 1783 and educated at Whitchurch Grammar School and then Oxford. He inherited the estate at Hodnet from his mother and appointed himself rector and lord of the manor. In 1815 he was a lecturer at Oxford and in 1822 became a preacher at Lincoln's Inn before being offered the See of Calcutta. Heber wrote several books on religion, poems and hymns, of which *From Greenlands Icy Mountains* and *Holy, Holy, Holy, Lord God Almighty* are still sung today. They stand as a living testimony to him, as does the Bishop Heber High School, Malpas, which was founded by him. He died at Trichinopoli in India in 1826 aged 43.

Born in the rectory in Alderley in 1815, **Arthur Penrhyn Stanley** left his mark on the church. Educated at Seaforth, Rugby and Oxford, he was ordained as deacon in 1839, priest in 1843 and in 1856 was appointed Chair of Ecclesiastical History at Oxford. In 1854 he was appointed Dean of Westminster and introduced an open and independent style, inviting English and Scottish Nonconformists to preach in the abbey. Stanley was himself a great preacher and usually performed to packed congregations. He set about a restoration programme for the fabric of Westminster Abbey and wrote several books, the best of which was *Life of Arnold*. He died in 1881 having, it is said, never recovered from the death of his wife, Lady Augusta Bruce.

In more modern times a unique clergyman created a stir and attracted a great deal of controversy. Born in Macclesfield in 1874, **Hewlett Johnson** was educated at King's School, Macclesfield, Manchester University and Oxford. He set out in life as an apprentice engineer but soon found himself performing welfare work in the Manchester slums. Stirred by the poverty and deprivation Johnson joined the Independent Labour Party, which set him on the way to political controversy. He was ordained in 1905, became the Dean of Manchester in 1924 and from 1931–63 he was Dean of Canterbury. A visit to the Soviet Union in 1938 sparked his 'treasonable' embrace of Marxism and an enthusiasm for the social and political system of communism in the Soviet Union. Johnson published *The Socialist Sixth of the World* and, although he never joined the communist party, he received the Stalin Peace Prize in 1951. Further publications *Christians and Communism* in 1956 and his *Autobiography – Searching For Light,* published in 1968, after his death in 1966, ensured that his nickname 'The Red Dean' followed him to the grave.

A more conventional clergyman attracted worldwide headlines in the late 1980s in far more difficult circumstances. **Terence Hardy Waite,** born in Bollington, near Macclesfield, on 31 May 1939, was raised in Styal and attended Wilmslow School. At the age of 14 he moved with his family to Thelwall, where at the age of 16 he started work in Warrington. In 1956 aged 17 he joined the army but was quickly discharged due to ill health. He married in 1964, the year in which he received his first appointment as lay education adviser to the Anglican bishop of Bristol. He started his global travels

Terry Waite. Cheshire Life

when he moved with his family to Uganda to work with the Anglican Archbishop of Uganda, Rwanda and Burundi. In 1972 he was working in Rome, which was followed by several years of world travel before returning to London in 1978. In 1980 he was appointed assistant to the Archbishop of Canterbury and as his special envoy was called in to negotiate the release of three hostages taken in Iran in 1981. Waite was successful and was awarded the MBE for his efforts. Towards the end of 1984 he was again called upon to negotiate with Colonel Gadhafi the release of four more hostages taken in Libya. It was in 1987, while representing the Archbishop of Canterbury, Robert Runcie, in the Lebanon, in secret negotiations to obtain the release of more European hostages, that he was himself taken hostage in Beirut by Islamic fundamentalists. Despite diplomatic attempts to free him he was held captive in trying circumstances until released on 8 November 1991 after almost five years as a hostage. Terry Waite acted with great dignity throughout his ordeal, which he recalled in his best-selling book *Taken on Trust*. Other publications followed and his latest *Travels With A Primate* has also sold very well. Today he is still writing and campaigning, supporting charities and working with the homeless.

A much-respected Cheshire clergyman passed away in December 2002 aged 84. Canon **Maurice Ridgway** spent more than 34 years as a preacher and pastor in two Cheshire parishes. Born in Stockport, Maurice's family later moved to Tarvin, near Chester, and Maurice went to King's School, Chester, then to St David's College, Lampeter, before completing his training in holy orders at Westcott House, Cambridge. After being ordained at Chester Cathedral he went as curate to Grappenhall, Warrington, then moved to Hale for five years, and then to Bunbury. His final move was to Bowden, where he was the vicar from 1962–83.

Apart from his long service to his communities and the Church, what made Canon Ridgway unique was his interests: restoring church buildings, the Church's music, mediaeval stained glass and especially Cheshire silver, a subject on which he was an expert. He was so expert in fact that the silver gallery in Chester Museum, which was opened in 1997 by the Prince of Wales, was named the Ridgway Gallery in his honour. He published a number of works, several on Chester goldsmiths, contributed to *Jackson's Silver and Gold Marks* and wrote a book on Church plate. Ridgway was unique in a number of ways and his personal style – he always tried to visit each home in his parishes during the year – was complemented by his scholarly interests and his sense of history.

History has shown that the clergy performed a valuable function in communities, bringing balance and comfort and support during troubled and turbulent times. Despite the modern view that the church is becoming less influential, it was interesting to see that following the 11 September tragedy in America, and during the Iraq war, people flocked back to their churches. Comfort, support and balance are exactly what humanity requires.

CHAPTER 6

Literature, Poetry, the Arts

Literature

Although Cheshire has made a significant contribution to the literary archives of the British Isles, its links to Britain's – and arguably the world's – greatest playwright, **William Shakespeare**, continue to intrigue historians. There is no doubt whatsoever that Shakespeare was extremely familiar with Cheshire and many of its characters appear in his works. The long line of his links to the county goes back to his very birth.

He was christened on 26 April 1564 in Stratford-upon-Avon, by the Revd John Bracegirdle, who left the Cheshire village of Great Budworth in 1561. In his student days it is thought that he came into contact with another Cestrian, **John Brownsherd**, who was an accomplished grammarian and Latin poet who taught at the King's School, Macclesfield. Brownsherd, who was born in 1540, eventually left Macclesfield to teach in Stratford-upon-Avon, but he later returned to the area, where he died in 1589. There is a tablet to his memory in the Macclesfield Parish Church. In 2002, the King's School at Macclesfield set up a research project in response to speculation that Shakespeare might himself, at some stage, have been taught at the school.

Many historians also believe that Shakespeare may have had an affair with Mary Fitton, who

William Shakespeare. Shakespeare Birthplace Trust

was a maid of honour to Elizabeth I. It is thought that Mary, the daughter of Sir Edward Fitton of Gawsworth, may be the 'dark lady' of Shakespeare's famous sonnets.

What is unquestionably accepted is that Shakespeare relied heavily on the work of **Ralph (Raphael) Holinshed**, who was born in Sutton, near Macclesfield. Holinshed wrote *The Chronicles of England, Scotland and Ireland*, which Shakespeare used as the source for 14 of his plays.

At the time of his death in around 1580, Holinshed was working on a history of the world, and because of the genius of Shakespeare, his work will never be forgotten. It is also known that while on one of his visits to Cheshire, Shakespeare wrote part of *Richard II* while staying at Holt Castle. The great playwright clearly had an affinity with Cheshire but sadly his life ended tragically early at the age of 52 in 1616, although he left behind a legacy of written works which enjoy worldwide acclaim.

Another writer who left a recognisable mark was Nantwich's **John Gerard**, who was born in 1545. Gerard was a gardener and expert on herbs, which he used as the basis of his work as an apothecary. When in 1597 he wrote his work, *Herball and General Historie of Plantes* it was the first published work to classify many British and some imported plants and trees. He died in 1607 but his much-respected work has survived.

John Speed, born in Farndon in 1552, made a very useful contribution to the culture of these islands when in 1610 he produced an atlas of the counties of England. Although Speed was a tailor by trade he quickly became known as the best cartographer of the 17th century and followed up his 1610 publication with a pocket atlas of England and Wales in 1627. Just before his death in 1629 he published a book, *Theatre of the Empire of Great Britain*.

One of the excellent contributors to the rich vein of Victorian literature of the 19th century was **Charles Lutwidge Dodgson** better known to the world as **Lewis Carroll**. Born in Daresbury in 1832, his father was the vicar of Daresbury and his grandfather was an old boy of King's School, Macclesfield. Dodgson went on to study at Oxford, where he eventually became a maths tutor. It was during a day out on the river with three young daughters of the Dean of Christ

The stained glass window dedicated to Lewis Carrroll in All Saints' church, Daresbury. He was born Charles Ludwidge Dodson there in 1832. The window depicts scenes from *Alice in Wonderland*.

Church College, Oxford, that the seed of the idea for *Alice In Wonderland* was first sown. Alice was one of the young daughters and asked Charles at the end of the day to tell them a story about what they had seen during the trip along the river. His fertile imagination took over and a literary icon was born. *Alice in Wonderland, Alice Through The Looking Glass* and other writings became compulsive reading at the time and indeed for many years after. Films, plays and television have ensured that those classic stories are never forgotten. At the time of his death in 1898, Dodgson was also regarded as a leading pioneer in photography. In the village of Daresbury All Saints' Church has a stained-glass window which shows Lewis Carroll with Alice. Many of the characters from the books are also featured, giving enjoyment to the many tourists who flock to the village.

Although **Thomas Hughes**, author of *Tom Brown's Schooldays*, was not Cheshire-born, he worked and lived in Cheshire for many years. He had a magnificent house built overlooking the

Plaque recording the 150th anniversary of Mrs Gaskell's birth.

River Dee in Chester, which he named Uffington House (Tom Brown was brought up in Uffington), and he lived there for more than 15 years before he moved to Brighton shortly before his death in 1896. In the early part of the 1880s Hughes was made a county court judge of the Chester circuit and worked throughout the area.

Another writer who was not born in Cheshire but is Cheshire through and through and cannot be mistaken for anything else is **Mrs Elizabeth**

Mrs Gaskell's house in Knutsford.

The tower erected
to the memory of
Elizabeth Gaskell.

Cleghorn Gaskell, who was born in Chelsea in 1810. Her father was a Unitarian minister and her mother came from a Cheshire family. The family moved to Knutsford, where Elizabeth spent her childhood, and she grew up and married there. Her love for the town and for Cheshire is very evident in her writing. Arguably her best work, *Cranford* is a classic story of a small town with an established society and intrinsic values. Her last book, *Wives and Daughters,* is also about her beloved Knutsford. When she died in 1865 at the early age of 55 she was buried in the Unitarian Chapel in the town which has a campanile memorial to her.

A highly-successful novelist born in Runcorn in 1853 trained to become an architect before spending a year as secretary to Dante Gabriel Rossetti in 1881. **Sir Thomas Henry Hall Caine** later wrote an account of his time with Rossetti, before embarking on a prolific series of popular novels, many of which were set in the Isle of Man. *The Shadow of a Crime, The Deemster, The Bondsman, The Scapegoat, The Manxman, The Eternal City* and the last one, in 1904, *The Prodigal Son,* were followed by a *Life of Christ* and his autobiography *My Story.* Sir Thomas died in 1931 after a hugely successful career as a novelist with a regular following.

Dramatist **Stanley Houghton** was born in 1881 and educated at Stockport Grammar School, where he won the English Prize. After leaving school he worked in his father's warehouse selling cloth and spending what little spare time he had writing drama. Success came quickly and readily to this gifted writer, with *The Dear Departed, Independent Means, The Younger Generation, Master of the House* and *Fancy Free.* However, his masterpiece *Hindle Wakes* was a huge success in both the UK and the US. His success meant leaving the warehouse and he lived for a time in Manchester, moving to London in 1912 and Paris in 1913. Tragedy struck on a trip to Venice where he caught a fatal disease and died on his return home in December 1913. He was just 32 – a great talent cut down at the very moment when his skills were being rewarded.

Cheshire-born **Malcolm Lowry** was a novelist who was never fully appreciated during his short life. He left public school in a fit of restlessness and for a time became an alcoholic and a drifter, even becoming a deck hand and sailing for China at one point. This seemed to give him new focus, and on his return he went to Cambridge and secured a degree. His first work was *Ultramarine,* published in 1933, but it was 1947 before he produced the classic *Under The Volcano,* which bore more than a passing resemblance to his own life. It was about the last day of an alcoholic British consul and was uncomfortably prophetic. Lowry lived in Mexico with his first wife before settling in a shack in British Columbia with his second wife from 1940 until he choked to death in his sleep in 1957 aged 48. Like many other good writers some of his writings and letters were gathered together and published posthumously: *Lunar Caustic* in 1963, *Dark As The Grave Wherein My Friend Is Laid* in 1968 and *October Ferry To Gabriola* in 1970.

Another fine novelist, **Christopher William Bradshaw Isherwood,** was born in High Lane, Disley, in 1904. Educated at Repton and Cambridge, he became a medical student and then taught English in Berlin for a couple of years. On his return from Germany he worked on film scripts at British Gaumont and then enjoyed a period of work with MGM. He travelled extensively, especially with his friend, the poet W.H. Auden. He enjoyed his first real success with the publication in 1935 of *Mr Morris Changes Trains. Goodbye To Berlin* in 1939 was another great success, and was the basis for the huge musical hit *Cabaret. Down There On A Visit* in 1962 maintained his reputation as a fine writer, and he was awarded the Brandeis Medal for fiction in the US in 1975. Isherwood also wrote several plays in conjunction with Auden, including *On The Frontier* and *Ascent Of F6.* Again with Auden, he wrote several books on travel, exploiting his knowledge of visits to China and South America. Isherwood, who became a United States citizen in 1946, died on 4 January 1986.

The novelist **William Cooper** was born **Harry Summerfield Hoff** in Crewe in 1910. After studying at Corpus Christi College, Cambridge, he started life as a physics teacher and after World War Two, during which he served in the RAF, he commenced work at the Atomic Energy Authority. His talent for writing was starting to emerge, but it wasn't until after he had had published four novels under the name Hoff that a change of name to William Cooper coincided with his fifth book, *Scenes From Provincial Life,* becoming an overwhelming success in 1950. Indeed this book was the start of a trilogy, and *Scenes From Metropolitan Life,* which was actually written in 1951 but suppressed, due to fear of libel action, wasn't published until 1982. The final book, *Scenes From Married Life,* was published in 1961. The same character, a lower middle-class teacher trying to keep his girlfriend contented while trying to avoid being trapped into marriage, featured in the books, which demonstrated realism, and were the forerunner of the kitchen sink dramas that were to follow in the 1960s. Certainly at the time William Cooper had a following among several of the young writers of the time who would go on to later acclaim. Kingsley Amis, John Braine and Stan Barstow became admirers of Cooper's sardonic wit, and

telling prose. More books followed: *Disquiet and Peace* in 1956, *Young People* in 1958 about students in the 1930s, *Memoirs of A New Man* in 1966, *Scenes From Later Life* in 1983 and, more than 80 years after he was born, *Immortality At Any Price* in 1991.

Apart from his novels Cooper also wrote *C.P. Snow* in 1959 and revised it in 1971, and then in 1990 he wrote *From Early Life,* which was an autobiographical memoir. It is said by the experts that Cooper was appreciated not only for his literary merit but also because he was a catalyst in British fiction. He paved the way for other writers to produce outstanding fiction, portraying life as it really was, realistic without the glow of rose-tinted spectacles.

Alan Garner, born in Congleton on 17 October 1934, has enjoyed considerable acclaim as both a novelist and an author. Educated at Alderley Edge Primary School, Manchester Grammar School and then Oxford, where he came into contact with J.R.R. Tolkien and C.S. Lewis, Alan later worked as a researcher at Granada Television. He has written books, novels, dramas and children's books, utilising his knowledge of Cheshire. His work has been punctuated with awards reflecting the acclaim which his writings have deserved. His wonderful book *The Owl Service,* published in 1967, won the Guardian Award and the prestigious Carnegie Medal, and he became the first author to win both awards for a book. The Carnegie Medal was most satisfying as he had been runner-up in 1965 with his novel *Elidor.* In 1996 he won the Phoenix Award for *The Stone Book Quartet* which was first published in 1977 – they took a long time to appreciate it! Garner continued to collect awards, including a prize for his film, *Images,* which was entered in the Chicago International Film Festival. In 2001 he was awarded the OBE for his contribution to

British literature. Alan still lives in Cheshire with his wife and family.

Warrington-born **Pete McCarthy**'s first book *Macarthy's Bar* was an instant worldwide best-seller, achieving No.1 in the sales charts in the UK, Ireland and Australia. McCarthy, an excellent writer and performer in radio and television series such as *Desperately Seeking Something*, *X Marks The Spot* and *Travelog*, received the Newcomer of the Year award at the British Books Award for his first book. His second book, *The Road To McCarthy*, humourously describes his worldwide travels to trace members of the clan McCarthy, visiting Cork, Belfast, Gibraltar, Morocco, New York, Tasmania, Montserrat and Alaska. His background in stand-up comedy – he was resident compère at The Comedy Store and was nominated for the prestigious Perrier Award – stands him in good stead as a writer. Witty, sharp and vibrant, McCarthy performs all over the UK and abroad in literary festivals, pubs and theatres, happy to meet the public and conduct book signings.

Poetry

Thomas Ashe, born in 1836, was educated at Stockport Grammar School and then moved on to Cambridge where in 1859 he received his BA and founded *The Eagle* magazine, which sparked his interest in literature. His early days were spent in the church as a deacon and then priest, before he turned to teaching and then finally, in 1881, concentrated on literature. However, many of his better works were produced before 1881. His first published work was *Poems* in 1859, followed by *Dryope and other Poems* in 1861, *Pictures and other Poems* in 1865 and his best long piece, the poem *The Sorrows of Hypsipyle*, in 1867. In 1873 he went back to his roots with *Edith, Or Love and*

> ## Literary Titbit
> Although not herself a writer, **Lady Emma Hamilton** has been the subject of many books, articles and features over the years. Born Amy Lyon in Neston in the 1760s, to a simple working-class family, she grew up to be a striking beauty and eventually moved to London and then to Naples where her reputation and beauty caught the eye of Admiral Horatio Nelson, Britain's greatest naval hero. It is well documented that despite her marriage to Lord Hamilton she became Nelson's mistress, creating a most public scandal. For a time she enjoyed great wealth and influence but after his death at Trafalgar in 1805, life became very difficult for her and she died in Calais in 1815, alone and penniless.

Life In Cheshire, and in 1875 he published what many believe to be his best work, *Songs Now and Then*. After making the decision to concentrate on his literary pursuits he wrote *Songs Of A Year 1888* and then edited the works of Samuel Coleridge and produced a full edition of all of his own poems. Although his work was appreciated and respected he was not regarded as among the very best of the genre. Ashe died in 1889 in London, but is buried in Sutton, Macclesfield.

On the basis that qualification for *Cheshire's Famous* can include spending formative or creative years in the county, Cheshire does have a claim on Britain's fine war poet **Wilfred Owen**.

Owen was born in Oswestry in 1893, but moved with his family to Birkenhead in 1897, when his father obtained a job with the railways. Wilfred attended the Junior School of the Birkenhead Institute, where he quickly became recognised as a 'swot'. Even at such a young age it is believed that his talents for imagination and literature were easily recognisable. Encouraged by his mother, his talent for poetry revealed itself in 1903 when it is believed that he made his first attempts at constructive poetry. In 1907 the family moved to Shrewsbury and Owen's first recorded poem *To Poesy* was written in 1909. Using the old saying 'give me the boy at 7 and I'll show you the man' it could be claimed that Britain's greatest war poet was fashioned in Cheshire.

Eleven years after leaving Cheshire, Lieutenant Wilfred Owen MC, fighting with the Manchester Regiment, was killed in the last week of World War One. His often bitter but moving poetry was criticised by many as being anti-war but Owen did fight bravely for his country, earning the Military Cross for valour. Although he wrote more than 100 poems in his short life, it is his war poetry which is best remembered and is studied by students across the country. Cheshire can be proud that it nurtured, influenced and witnessed the blossoming of such a unique talent.

In more modern times Cheshire, and Britain and America, have enjoyed the skills of the multi-talented **Adrian Maurice Henri**. Born in Birkenhead in 1932, he was educated at St Asaph Grammar School, North Wales, and received a BA at the Department of Fine Art, King's College, Newcastle. For the next 10 years he worked on a Rhyl fairground and followed that with a spell of teaching in Manchester and Liverpool while leading a local rock band. In 1970 he turned to freelance work, embracing poetry, singing, song-writing, painting and lecturing and had the experience of a lecture tour of the US and Canada. As his reputation grew he enjoyed numerous appointments, ranging from resident writer at the Tattenhall Centre, Cheshire, to President of Liverpool Academy of Arts 1972–81 and Hon. Professor at Liverpool John Moores University in 1990. Henri was unquestionably a talented artist with a prolific output. He had many one-man shows throughout Britain, which were ample proof of his skill with the brush. He wrote novels, including *I Want*; plays like *The Wakefield Mysteries*; children's poems including *Eric, The Punk Cat*; prose for teenagers; anthologies; an autobiography; and television plays including *Yesterday's Girl* in 1973 and *The Husband, The Wife, The Stranger* in 1986. These are just examples – his output was immense. He wrote many poems for children but also some fine pieces of work which have stood the test of time: *Tonight At Noon* in 1968, *City* in 1969, *From The Loveless Motel* in 1980, *Wish You Were Here* in 1990 and *Not Fade Away* in 1994. Sadly this gifted artist passed away on 20 December 2000.

The Arts

Over the years Cheshire has acquired a reputation for producing sculptors. Perhaps the earliest known who received national recognition was **Thomas Thorneycroft**, who was born in Gawsworth in 1815. Thorneycroft was a skilled sculptor but was also a trained engineer. He left Cheshire to pursue his ambitions in London and at the time of his death in 1885 had achieved a national reputation for several of his works.

Tim Stead, born in Helsby in 1952, was a wood sculptor, craftsman and furniture maker who trained in Cheshire, Nottingham and the Glasgow Art School. He specialised in interiors

One of Britain's finest poets was of course **John Milton** (1608–1674). Milton wrote *Paradise Lost, Paradise Regained* and *Samson Agonistes* amongst several other fine works. It was, however, when he was 54, blind, lost spiritually and floundering that **Elizabeth Minshul**, a distant relative, came into his life. Elizabeth, born in Wells Green Farm and baptised at Wistaston, Cheshire in 1638, became Milton's third wife in 1662 at the age of 24. They settled down in Chalfont St Giles, Buckinghamshire. It is said that it was she who restored his confidence, brought order to his life and gave him purpose. When he died in 1674 he left her £600 in his will and she leased a farm in Brindley, but following the death of her brother she moved to Nantwich where she died in 1727.

early death in 2000 many of his best works were lodged in private collections, while several were owned by public and corporate bodies. I can recall on one occasion visiting the Tannery in Llanrwst on Anglesey, which was exhibiting some of Tim's work, and seeing a magnificent four-poster bed carved from yew which was for sale at £15,000.

Cheshire-born **Andy Goldsworthy** has achieved a national and international reputation as a sculptor making the best use of the environment. Born in 1956 he went to Bradford Art College and then from 1975–8 to Preston Polytechnic. A great lover of the environment, Goldsworthy, after his first one-man show in 1987, went in 1989 to Ellesmere Island, Canada and then on to the North Pole. Several of his works are easily recognisable: *Hazel Stick Throws* of 1980, *Slate Cone* of 1988 and *The Wall* of 1988–9 are all innovative pieces. Exhibitions and one-man shows throughout the UK, and in Paris and Chicago, together with his work being included in a respected reference work *Sculpture and Sculptors Drawings*, have enhanced his reputation. He delights in the unusual and several of his pieces for home and garden are new and refreshing. Recent works, such as *Cracked Stones*, are simple and uncomplicated and look great in a variety of settings, particularly in front of an open fire. *A Herd Of Arches* is a set of stones put together to form a series of arches set into a garden to form a very nice feature. Goldsworthy has many years of creative ideas ahead of him.

Another local sculptor with an international reputation is Stockport's **John Blakeley**. Although John was born in Salford in 1928, he came to Stockport at the age of five and has lived in the area and worked in his Stockport studios ever since. His work has been exhibited all over the

and distinctive wood features, accepting private and public commissions. After receiving a fellowship with the Scottish Development Agency Crafts, Tim concerned himself with protecting the environment. He devoted great efforts to replanting trees and encouraging community plantations along the Scottish Borders, which were the subject of a series of television programmes. Tim's work was exhibited in the UK, Europe and America following his first sculpture show in Glasgow in 1990. At the time of his

UK and Europe and he has achieved international recognition for his skill and realism. For one commission, *The Boy Jesus,* he actually visited Judea to ensure that his portrayal was accurate. One of his works, a marble bust of Joseph Smith, now stands in Salt Lake City, US, and another, *Mother And Child,* a 4ft bronze statue commissioned by East Germany, now stands in the British Chapel at the former Nazi prisoner of war camp Ravensbruck. Germany also has another commissioned work from Blakeley: *Soldier And Child.* John Blakeley also spent some considerable time in 1980 helping to restore St Mary's Parish Church, Stockport. He did superb work in remodelling the tops of pinnacles using a unique Italian method of reconstituting stone. It is warming to note that the skill of this Cestrian is appreciated and displayed around the world.

An artist, a painter, who ranks with the very best produced by this country is **Charles Frederick Tunnicliffe** OBE, RA. Born in the little village of Langley, near Macclesfield, in 1901, Charles grew up on the family farm in Sutton Lane Ends but his artistic ability was recognised at the Sutton village school, where the headmaster was instrumental in getting him a place at the Macclesfield School of Art at the age of 15. From there he moved on to the Manchester School of Art before winning a scholarship to the Royal College of Art in London. He spent some time teaching art and started producing etchings of farm animals and the country life with which he was so familiar back home. Tunnicliffe moved back to Macclesfield in 1928, following the death of his father, and started to establish a reputation for himself in the art world. His first notable work was with Henry Williamson, whose book *Tarka the Otter* was issued to great public demand and Tunnicliffe's wood engravings formed the basis of the illustrations. Williamson was very impressed

with his skill as an illustrator and they worked together on a number of publications. Tunnicliffe soon found himself in great demand by other writers and publishers and his illustrations embellished more than 100 works. He illustrated many Ladybird books and was responsible for *A Book of Birds, The Seasons and the Woodman, Both Sides of The Road* and *Green Tide* to name just a few. He also produced his own books: *My Country Book* in 1942, *Bird Portraiture* in 1945, *Mereside Chronicle* in 1948 (featuring Cheshire) and the very popular *Shorelands Summer Diary* in 1952, which was published after the Tunnicliffes left Macclesfield to live in Anglesey.

Tunnicliffe has perhaps no equal when drawing and painting birds. He was meticulous in his research and study and incredibly skilful in oil and watercolour. He provided many illustrations for the Royal Society for the Protection of Birds and for a whole variety of causes and was a frequent exhibitor at the Royal Academy. He died on Anglesey in 1979 and years later the Borough Council established a purpose-built gallery to house the collection left in his studio following his death. In 1996 Macclesfield refurbished its West Park Museum and established a permanent exhibition of Charles Tunnicliffe's works, etchings and oil paintings, which it had accumulated over the years, including many items gifted specifically to commemorate Tunnicliffe's art.

A painter who is enjoying something of a renaissance more than 40 years after his talent was first recognised is **William Turner**. Turner, who is enjoying unprecedented popularity in his eighties, is thankfully fit and well and able to enjoy it. Born in Manchester in 1920 he was in the 1960s recognised as an outstanding talent and then virtually forgotten. Cheshire has a claim on him as he lived and painted in the Stockport area for more than 30 years and 10 years ago moved

William Turner at home. On the right wall is the portrait of L.S. Lowry painted by Turner. Lowry sat for him in 1976, the year Lowry died.
Dave Gunning

to Congleton, where today, at the age of 83, he continues to paint. It was only three years ago that Turner acquired an agent, David Gunning of Todmorden Fine Art, who told me that since then he has sold more than 1,350 Turner paintings and the demand for his work continues unabated. A great friend of Turner's was the painter L.S. Lowry, who posed for him in a 1976 painting that hangs in Turner's house. Indeed their work has similarities, and they both relish painting northern industrial scenes. Turner has painted numerous Cheshire scenes, many of them dark, yet full of action – strong, powerful visions of Stockport, Ellesmere Port and so on – which are now selling for hundreds of pounds. His life and work were featured in an article in the *Sunday*

Telegraph in August 2003 and the media interest has been frenetic. Several other publications have featured him and there is soon to be a television programme on his work. In the meantime a very fit William Turner continues to paint and enjoy his 'Indian summer'. At the age of 83 he has a fanatical interest in cycling, a hobby which he has enjoyed all his life, and thinks nothing of a 30-mile bike ride around his beloved Cheshire lanes to refresh and fuel his imagination for his powerful works which are now highly collectable.

A great artist from a slightly different aspect of art is Cheshire-born **Ralph Steadman**. Steadman trained in London before joining the De Havilland aircraft company as an apprentice in 1952. It wasn't long, however, before his natural talent as a cartoonist came to the fore and he said goodbye to the aircraft industry and joined Kemsley (Thomson) Newspapers, where he worked from 1956–9. His reputation for cutting, satirical drawings led to him working successfully as a freelance throughout the 1960s, enjoying considerable success and exposure with *Punch* and *Private Eye*. He continued with political cartoons with the *New Statesman* from 1978–80 before retiring to embark on the work of writing the life story of Leonardo da Vinci. During his career Steadman was responsible for the illustrations in many books, including Lewis Carroll's *The Hunting of The Snark* in 1975 and Wolf Mankowitz's book *The Devil In Texas* in 1984. He wrote and illustrated his own books, *Sigmund Freud* in 1979 and *I Leonardo* in 1983, and several shows of his work at such venues as the National Theatre and The Royal Festival Hall have been held. He has received a number of awards for his art including the BBC Design Award for postage stamps in 1987. A first-class cartoonist, illustrator, writer and designer, he can literally turn his hand to anything.

Art of a similar nature but a slightly different genre has rewarded the skills of Hoylake artist **Dave Taylor**. Dave went to Hilbre Secondary School and then on to Birkenhead School of Art. In 2002, despite severe competition, he was commissioned by the powerful American company DC Comics to draw action scenes for *Batman and Robin*. The contract is set to run for 12 months and it is strange to think that as the popular comic hits the shops and major retailers and is read around the world that the illustrations have been done by a Cestrian.

Another popular Cheshire artist is **Paul Taggart**, who is highly respected for his very many paintings of Cheshire scenes. Not constrained by any specific discipline, Paul is skilled in watercolour, oils or pastels, but it is fair to say that he is better renowned in the county than nationally. That was until he started to write about painting. A couple of years ago Paul thought that people might welcome advice on how to paint in the various materials and styles and wrote *The Essential Painting Guide*. The book was a huge success worldwide and features dozens of Cheshire scenes as examples. Would-be artists around the world are now very familiar with Cheshire and hopefully are now better artists! Paul has written another book and has plans for several more.

Cheshire has another star in a slightly different branch of the arts, pottery design. Twenty-six-year-old designer **Emma Bossons**, born in Congleton, is already respected internationally in her field and has become the youngest living member to be elected a Fellow of the Royal Society of Arts. Emma was educated at Westlands High School, Congleton, and after leaving school joined a YTS scheme at Wedgewood and started painting pots at the Moorcroft Pottery in Burslem. She later moved on to design and such is her talent and skill that some of her designs can cost collectors several thousand pounds. Several items of her work are exhibited at the Moorcroft Museum.

CHAPTER 7
Politicians and Business Achievers

THE term politician is defined as anyone interested in the state or the affairs of the state. Someone who is sagacious, judicious, expedient and non-impulsive, according to the dictionary. Strangely hard-working, tenacious, honest, incorruptible and impervious to 'spin' are not qualities deemed to be essential! Perhaps we must assume, tongue in cheek, that these qualities are inherent in all politicians. Whatever the qualities needed, several Cheshire politicians have not only served their constituencies with great distinction but have also left their mark on British politics. Cestrians have attained the highest offices in the political structure of the British Isles: Foreign Secretary, Minister of State, Lord High Chancellor, Chancellor of the Exchequer, Speaker of the House of Commons, President of The Board of Trade, Deputy Leader of Liberal Democrats and Master of the Rolls to name just a few.

Politicians are not always fortunate enough to be able to serve the constituency in which they were born, but the politicians featured here are either Cheshire-born, or have served their Cheshire constituency for many years. **Sir Edmond Shaa,** the founder of Stockport Grammar School and brother of **Ralph Shaa** the clergyman, was one of the most skilful politicians of the past 600 years. The Shaas originally came from Dukenfield but Edmond Shaa is associated

Sir Edmond Shaa, founder of Stockport Grammar School. Stockport Grammar School

with Stockport. When he died in 1488 he left bequests to found the school and also bequests to St Mary's Church, Stockport, where his parents were buried. Edmond left Cheshire in 1462 for London, where he was appointed engraver to King Edward IV, responsible for all gold and silver coined in the Tower of London or in England or Calais. Very soon he became rich and powerful and in October 1482 he was made Mayor of London and of course held in esteem by the King. However, on the death of Edward IV the problems of the succession tested Edmond's political skills to the limit.

The right of Edward V to succeed to the throne was disgracefully contested by Ralph Shaa in his infamous sermon at the behest of Richard III, who was determined to take the throne for himself. Richard appointed Edmond as Privy Councillor and, just before his crowning ceremony, knighted him and gave him a prominent role in the procession. There is a painting showing Shaa on his knees offering the crown to Richard. At the banquet Edmond was honoured to act as the King's Cupbearer, a trusted and coveted role.

Despite his position Shaa was far from happy that the two princes, who had more right to the throne than Richard, had been detained in the Tower and were later murdered. Richard's enemies were determined to oust him and after the Battle of Bosworth Field in 1485, in which Richard was killed, Henry VII assumed the throne. Shaa was shrewd, clever and a well-regarded politician whose very existence depended on an entirely new regime in volatile and violent times. His skills stood him in good stead and soon he was enjoying the trust of Henry VII. He continued to benefit from royal favours until he died.

Sir Thomas Egerton, Baron Ellesmere and Viscount Brackley, son of Sir Richard Egerton of Ridley, was born in 1540. Educated at Oxford and Lincoln's Inn he was called to the bar in 1572 and became an MP in 1585 while he was Solicitor-General. He became a particular favourite of Elizabeth I and held a number of honoured political positions: Lord Chancellor of England, Master of the Rolls and Privy Councillor. He was knighted in 1593 and created Baron Egerton in 1603. Such was his fame that a sonnet was written about him. After his death in 1617 he was buried in Dodleston Church.

Another skilled political figure who was able to change sides during a war from the winning side to the losing side and still end up on the winning side was **Sir George Booth**, Baron Delamere of Dunham Massey, who was born in 1622. During the Civil Wars of the 1600s, Booth was at first a Cromwellian, serving in all the Protectorate parliaments and of course while Cheshire was split between Royalists and Parliamentarians, Booth was very much in support of the Parliamentarians. However, he later had a change of heart and in 1659 actually led the Cheshire rebellion as a Royalist. During the fighting he was taken prisoner and imprisoned in the Tower of London. After he was released he was instrumental in getting Charles II back to England and challenging once again for the throne. Sir George was rewarded for this and was created Baron in 1661 for his part in the Restoration of Charles II.

A highly controversial figure of this period, notorious even, was a politician who was remembered for sentencing a king to death. **Judge Bradshaw** was born in Wibbersley Hall, Stockport, in 1602 and was educated at Bunbury School, Middleton, and then Stockport Free School before embarking on a career as an attorney in Congleton. He was called to the Bar at Gray's Inn in 1627 and returned to Congleton, where he became Mayor in 1637. Ambitious and anxious to progress his career, he became Attorney General for Cheshire and Flint in 1637, a judge in 1640, High Sheriff for Lancashire in 1644, Chief Justice of Chester and North Wales in 1647 and a Sergeant at Law by order of Parliament in 1648. Rich and powerful, he allied himself with the Parliamentarians as the Civil War erupted. When Charles I was defeated he was placed on trial, accused of treason and murder. Bradshaw was Lord President of the Court, the presiding judge of England's highest court. Charles was found guilty and it was Bradshaw's signature and seal which was first on the death warrant. Charles I was beheaded on 27 January 1649. Bradshaw, of Marple Hall in Cheshire, went on to greater things. Shortly after Charles's execution Bradshaw was appointed to the highest position in the land, President of the Council of State, and in the same year became Chief Justice of Wales. The honours continued to flow and in 1650 he was made Chancellor of the Duchy of Lancaster and was given the Deanery of Westminster as a residence while gifts of land and money were bestowed upon him. He was elected MP for Cheshire in 1654 but for a time fell out of favour with Cromwell, who took away his highest office. However, after Cromwell's death in 1659, Bradshaw was re-appointed President of the Council of State. But after only a few months back in office Bradshaw died of an illness and a funeral of great style and ceremony took place at Westminster Abbey in November 1659. When Charles's son was restored to the throne in 1660, Judge Bradshaw's remains were disinterred and were ceremoniously hung by Charles II at Tyburn. His head was put on display at Westminster and his body flung into a hole at the foot of the gallows. His immense wealth and his estates were confiscated in a posthumous act of revenge. Whatever the final view of Bradshaw, he must have been a consummate politician of the highest order to have died of natural causes at such a

volatile time in English history, given his power, position and wealth.

Another Cestrian to hold high office was **Edward John Stanley**, 2nd Lord Stanley of Alderley. He entered Parliament as MP for North Cheshire in 1832, a position he held until 1841. Greatly respected, he quickly rose to be created Baron Eddisbury of Winnington in 1848, but his political career continued to soar. He became President of the Board of Trade from 1855–8 and was Postmaster General from 1860–6.

Cheshire can take a small credit for the formative years of **James Abercromby**, 1st Baron Dunfermline, who was born in 1776. Although he was not Cheshire-born, part of his education was at King's School, Macclesfield. Abercromby finished his education at the English Bar and worked as a steward on the Duke of Devonshire's estate before embarking on his political career. His successful career started when he was appointed MP for Midhurst, then Calne and finally Edinburgh. He became a Cabinet Member of Lord Grey's government and was later appointed Speaker of the House of Commons. He died in 1858.

A man of many talents who certainly left his mark was **Sir Joseph Leigh**, who was born in 1841. He was Mayor of Stockport four times and MP from 1892–5 and from 1900–6. He founded the Stockport Technical College, which is now the College of Further Education. His vision extended to a very keen support of the Manchester Ship Canal project, which was intended to turn Manchester into a seaport. Although he married the daughter of the instigator of the idea, Daniel Adamson, he was nevertheless a powerful supporter through difficult times and helped see the project through to completion in 1894. He was also considered to be one of the leading experts in Europe on the cotton trade and indeed was created a Chevalier of the Legion of Honour by the French in 1889. Knighted for his services, Sir Joseph Leigh died in 1908.

A true Cestrian received a multitude of political honours in a long and distinguished career. **Robert Offley Ashburton Crewe-Milnes**, Marquess of Crewe and Lord Crewe, was born in Milnes in 1858. Descended from John Crewe of Nantwich, the Manor of Crewe had been held in the family from the days of Sir Randolph Crewe at the time of James I. Crewe-Milnes was educated at Harrow and Cambridge and in 1885 was appointed Lord Houghton and later, as a prominent liberal, he held a series of vital positions. He was made Earl of Crewe while serving as Lord Lieutenant of Ireland from 1892–5, became Lord President of the Council in 1905, Leader of the Government in the House of Lords in 1908, Colonial Secretary in 1908–10, Indian Secretary in 1910–15 and he was appointed Lord President again from 1915–16. He was made Earl of Madeley and Marquess of Crewe in 1911 but sadly after the death of his sons the titles lapsed and the estate was sold to the Duchy of Lancaster. The last Lord Crewe died in 1945.

Another much-honoured Cheshire lord was born **Frederick Edwin Smith** in Birkenhead in 1872. He was educated at Birkenhead School, then went on to Oxford, where he became President of the Oxford Union, a much coveted office where presumably he honed his legendary skills as a debater. After Oxford he embarked on a political career as a Conservative and held a variety of offices: MP for Walton, Liverpool from 1906–19, Solicitor General 1915–16, Attorney General 1916–19, Lord High Chancellor 1919, and he was created Baron Birkenhead. He was involved in the very difficult times of the 1921 Irish Settlement and was Secretary for India from 1924–8. He was a great friend of Winston Churchill and lived in Bidston Hall, Bidston Hill, Birkenhead. Lord Birkenhead was only 58 when he died in 1930.

In more modern times, politics has become more difficult as today's media, newspapers and television, mull over every word and analyse every action. The advent of 'spin' and the influx of advisers and speech writers has helped the besieged politician to cope with the stress of modern politics. Therefore any of today's politicians who have not only survived in the modern era but have stood out from their colleagues deserve recognition.

One Cestrian who deserved the many accolades which came his way in a much decorated and distinguished career was Wirral-born **John Selwyn Lloyd**. Born in 1904, he was educated at Fettes College, Edinburgh, and Cambridge, where he studied law. He became a barrister in 1930 and opened his own practice in Liverpool. However, the lure of politics proved too strong and he stood, unsuccessfully, as a Liberal candidate for Macclesfield before deciding to join the Conservative Party in 1931. In 1936 he entered local government, becoming Chairman of Hoylake Urban District Council. World War Two put a halt to further aspirations but after the conflict he entered Parliament as Conservative MP for Wirral. He did, however, continue with his law practice and became a KC in 1947. A shrewd, intelligent and eloquent man, he started to rapidly climb the political ladder. In 1951 he became Minister of State and in 1954 was appointed Minister of Supply and then Minister of Defence. In 1955 he was given the vital post of Foreign Secretary when he was charged with defending Prime Minister Eden's decision to undertake the Suez War. Clearly a man of many gifts, he was in 1960 appointed Chancellor of the Exchequer but resigned the position in 1962. He continued to be recognised and was appointed Lord Privy Seal, Leader of the House in 1963 and from 1971–6 was Speaker of the House of Commons. Selwyn Lloyd was created a Life Peer in 1976 and died in 1978.

A contemporary of Selwyn Lloyd was a real character from a well-established old Cheshire family. Lieutenant-Colonel **Sir Walter Henry Bromley Davenport** was born at Capesthorne Hall, near Macclesfield, in 1903. He was educated at Malvern and later joined the Grenadier Guards. In 1933 he married Lenette, a lady from Philadelphia, and devoted much of his time to the county. Before the start of World War Two, he raised and commanded the 5th Battalion of the Cheshire Regiment. After the end of the war he turned his attention to politics and from 1945 until 1970 he was the Conservative MP for the Knutsford Division. He became the Conservative Party Whip from 1948 until 1951, a position he enforced with vigour. One famous story which did the rounds of the House of Commons was that in his enthusiasm to enforce the whip he kicked an MP down a flight of marble stairs. Sir Walter was an accomplished boxer, so perhaps he was an ideal choice to ensure orders were followed. For a time he served on the British Boxing Board of Control and before his death in 1989 he had served on numerous committees.

Lord Stanley Orme, who was born in Sale on 5 April 1923, has had a very distinguished career as a politician. After a modest elementary and part-time Technical School education he became a skilled engineer by trade and joined the Trade Union movement, an interest which he kept all his life. His first attempt in politics was contesting Stockport South in 1959, but it was in 1964 that he contested Salford West and entered Parliament. Boundary changes meant that in 1983 he was standing as MP for Salford East and once again he was successful. In fact Stanley Orme represented Salford as their MP from 1964–97, until becoming a Life Peer for his services to Parliament. Stanley Orme certainly made his mark in the Labour Party, attaining several prestigious positions. During his career he was Chairman of the Parliamentary Labour Party, and served in the Labour Government as Minister of State for Northern Ireland 1974–6, and was Minister for Social Security from 1976–9. Uniquely Lord Orme was born in Sale and still lives in Sale.

Another stalwart of the Labour Party is the Honourable **Mrs Gwyneth Patricia Dunwoody,** MP for Crewe and Nantwich. Mrs Dunwoody

Honourable Gwyneth Patricia Dunwoody, MP for Crewe & Nantwich. Cheshire Life

was born in Fulham in December 1930 and was educated at Fulham County Secondary before moving on to the Convent of Notre Dame. The daughter of Baroness Phillips, she started out as a career journalist with the local paper in Fulham and became a writer for radio. She entered Parliament as MP for Exeter from 1966–70 and later in 1974 was elected MP for Crewe, a position she held until 1983 when the constituency merged with Nantwich, when she became MP for the new constituency. Mrs Dunwoody has a reputation for a straight-talking, no-nonsense style which has earned her Parliamentary respect and several appointments to high office. She has been Parliamentary Secretary, Minister to Board of Trade 1967–70, a UK member of the European Parliament 1975–9, Chairman of NEC Local Government sub-committee 1981–90, Chairman of the Select Committee on Transport and Co-ordinator of Labour Party Campaigns from 1983–9.

Another highly-successful and much-respected Cheshire politician is **Lynda Chalker**, Baroness Chalker of Wallasey. Although not Cheshire-born, Mrs Chalker represented Wallasey as their Conservative MP from 1974–92. Born in 1942, she was educated at Roedean, the University of Heidelberg and London, and started out as a market researcher with Shell Mex and worked as a statistician with the Research Bureau Ltd before entering politics. Confident and lively, her career took off and she became Opposition spokesman on Social Services from 1976–9 and an under-secretary at the DHSS from 1979–82. However, when the Conservatives came to power she was appointed Minister of State for Transport from 1983–6 and became Minister for Overseas Development from 1989–97, a period in which she was responsible for the fifth-largest budget in the world. In 1997 Lynda Chalker took the deci-

sion to resign from politics and to carry on as an independent to continue the development of Africa, a project close to her heart. She was created a Life Peer in 1992.

It is extremely rare in modern day politics that a husband and wife can both enjoy active careers in what is a very demanding profession in terms of stress and time. Cheshire is fortunate in that it does possess such a husband and wife team who represent adjoining constituencies. Although not Cheshire-born, **Sir Nicholas Winterton** has repre-

Sir Nicholas Winterton, MP for Macclesfield. Brian Ollier Photography, Macclesfield

sented Macclesfield as a Conservative MP since winning a by-election in 1971. Born in March 1938 he was educated at Rugby and started out as a sales trainee with Shell Mex and was Sales/General Manager to Stevens & Hodgson Ltd from 1960–80. He married his wife Ann in 1960 and made his first attempt to get into

Parliament when standing unsuccessfully for Newcastle-under-Lyme in 1969. Throughout his time as Macclesfield MP, one of the longest periods of service in present day Parliament, Nicholas Winterton has been first-class in representing his constituency. His philosophy has been that he represents all constituents, not just Conservatives. In fact he attends a multitude of events in his constituency and is president, vice-president, patron or a member of virtually every organisation, sporting, social or cultural, throughout the area. Over the years he has been outspoken on all issues, even going against the party line and being called a maverick for defying party dictats. He has undoubtedly suffered in terms of career as a result but has been much in demand by the political system and has been much appreciated for his unbiased views, having graced numerous all-party Parliamentary committees. He has featured on committees covering virtually every aspect of the function of the House of Commons from procedures to transport, health, clothing and textiles and security, and has shown an interest in a variety of countries. He has been a member of the Speakers Panel, a member of the House of Commons Chairman Panel and was awarded a knighthood in 2002 for his services to the House of Commons and to British politics. He lives just outside Macclesfield at Astbury with his wife Ann.

The other half of the popular duo, **Ann Winterton**, came late to politics as she was busy raising her family. Ann, who was born in March 1941, was educated at Erdington Grammar School for Girls and married Nicholas in 1960. When the important task of setting four children on their varying ways in life was over she set out on a life in politics. Very much in the same mould as her husband – honest, straightforward and determined to represent her constituency – she

Lady Ann Winterton, MP for Congleton. Brian Ollier Photography, Macclesfield

entered Parliament as MP for Congleton in 1983. She was appointed Chairman of the all-party pro-life committee in 1991 and became a member of the Chairman's Panel in 1992–8. She was appointed Opposition frontbench spokesman for National Drug Strategy from 1998–2001. Her star really was in the ascendancy when in 2001 she was appointed Shadow Minister for Agriculture and Fisheries. Sadly this appointment did not last as she was sacked, it was said, following a joke that she allegedly made at a rugby club dinner in 2002. Most regarded the humour as being totally inoffensive but the powers that be took the headmasterish decision. Lady Ann Winterton will not be fazed by the incident and her career will continue to blossom and she will continue to speak her mind.

A true Cestrian, **Alan Beith**, born in Poynton on 20 April 1943, was educated at King's School,

Alan Beith MP, the Poynton-born Deputy Leader of the Liberal Democrats. Alan Beith

Glenda Jackson, MP for Hampstead & Highgate and former actress.

Macclesfield, before going on to Oxford where he achieved his BA. Very much a local lad, Alan did at one point act as sub-editor on the *Poynton Post*. However, his first appointment was as a lecturer at Newcastle University from 1966–73. During this time he had actively shown his determination to get into politics but was unsuccessful in contesting Berwick upon Tweed in the General Election of 1970, standing as a Liberal. In 1973 during a by-election he tried again and was successful and has represented the constituency ever since. From 1985–7 Alan was Liberal spokesman on foreign affairs and Chief Whip of the party from 1976–87. After the formation of the new party, the Liberal Democrats, Beith was appointed Chief Whip in 1992 and today is the Deputy Leader of the Liberal Democrat Party.

Glenda Jackson has been recognised in the Entertainers chapter for her outstanding contri-

bution to the British film, stage and theatre industry. Born in Birkenhead on 9 May 1936, she was educated at West Kirkby County Grammar School and then RADA. She gave up her acting career to embark on a political career and stood successfully as the Labour candidate for Hampstead and Highgate in the 1992 General Election. She has certainly made a mark on the political scene with her forthright comments, and has not been averse to crossing the party line whenever she has felt the need. She was particularly frank with regard to a number of aspects involving the Iraq war, and criticised the government with her outspoken views. In 1994 she was the Campaign Co-ordinator on Transport until 1996 and from 1997 until 1999 she was the Parliamentary under-Secretary of State for Environment and Transport. She was also a Labour Party nominee for the post of Mayor of

London, but was defeated by Frank Dobson in 1999–2000. In 2000 she was the appointed adviser on homelessness to the GLA. Glenda Jackson has successfully made the transition from idolised movie star to respected politician.

A man whose star shone brightly in the nation's and county's political sky before crashing to earth is **Neil Hamilton**. Born in Blackwood, Wales, in 1949, he was educated at the local grammar school before moving on to Aberystwyth and thence to Cambridge to study law. It was as an 18-year-old student that he first met his future wife **Christine Hamilton** at a students' conference in 1966. After qualifying he started to practise in London as a tax specialist. During this time he continued his relationship with Christine but also had an abiding ambition to make his mark in politics. He was given two opportunities to run for Parliament, both of which were no-hopers for a true blue Conservative: Abertillery in 1974 and Bradford North in 1979. Nevertheless the experience left him undaunted and when the new safe Tory seat of Tatton became available in 1983 he was nominated and entered Parliament. He had married Christine in 1982 and as he embarked on a full-time political career she worked as a private secretary in the House of Commons. They lived in the extremely affluent constituency, in a superb country house at Nether Alderley, and had an apartment in London. Confident, articulate, outspoken and with strong opinions, Neil Hamilton's brash, bouncy persona quickly established him as a man with a bright political future. Indeed he accepted posts as a Government Minister under Margaret Thatcher and John Major.

In 1987 he was appointed Chairman of the Treasury and Civil Service Select Committee; in 1990 he was Government Whip; in 1992 Corporate Affairs Minister at the Department of Trade and Industry, and he represented Britain at the European Council of Ministers and was the UK representative at the G7 Conference. His reputation as a speaker, particularly after-dinner speaking, enhanced his standing and he was much

Political Titbits

- Cheshire has a small claim on two of the country's Prime Ministers. **Harold Wilson,** born in Huddersfield in 1916, was educated at a council elementary school and then Huddersfield Secondary School before going to the Wirral Grammar School. Despite his modest background he thrived on the life at the Wirral Grammar School and was made Head Boy. This Cheshire school probably helped to shape the man who was British Prime Minister from 1964–70. **William Ewart Gladstone** (1809–1898), four times Liberal Prime Minister, was a student of Dr Turner and lived at the Rectory, Wilmslow in the 1820s before becoming an MP in 1832.

- **John Prescott,** MP for Kingston upon Hull and Deputy Prime Minister. Prescott, born in Prestatyn, was educated at Ellesmere Port Secondary Modern School before going on to Oxford and then to Hull University. He became Deputy Leader of the Labour Party in 1994 and is now second in command to Tony Blair.

in demand both as a speaker and as a writer of acidic, political articles for newspapers and magazines. *The Spectator* magazine awarded him their accolade of Parliamentary Wit of the Year. The future was set fair, Hamilton's political star was in the ascendancy, but then sadly it all came crashing down. Allegations that Mohamed al Fayed, the owner of Harrods, had given Neil Hamilton cash and favours, including a free holiday at the Paris Ritz, in exchange for Hamilton asking pertinent parliamentary questions on his behalf, were made public. The allegations caused an immense scandal and although they were strenuously denied and defended by the Hamiltons, Neil Hamilton resigned from the Government. In the 1997 General Election his Tatton constituency was taken over by the journalist Martin Bell, standing as an independent candidate against sleaze. In a memorable televised encounter, as the campaigning, white-suited Martin Bell was appearing in Tatton, he was ambushed by the Hamiltons and the media and was given a particularly hard time by Christine Hamilton.

In response to a 1997 television programme in which al Fayed claimed that the allegations of 'cash for questions' were in fact correct, the Hamiltons launched a libel action against him which came to court in December 1999. They lost the case and ruinous costs were awarded against them. They were facing financial ruin. Over the years the Hamiltons have continued to protest their innocence and have tried very hard to meet their financial obligations. They have both appeared on a whole variety of television programmes to try to earn a living and Neil has continued with his after-dinner speaking. The couple have even appeared in pantomime. Whatever the truth of the matter, the public has warmed to the couple and a spurious allegation of sexual abuse made against the couple in 2002, by

someone they had never met, earned them a great deal of public support. Neil Hamilton was the Conservative MP for Tatton from 1983–97 and lived in the county for more than 20 years until September 2003 when, after selling their house, the Hamiltons moved to London. It is very unlikely that Cheshire will easily forget the impact made by him and Christine.

Industrialists, Entrepreneurs, Achievers

This section is not about wealth but about recognition and achievement on a national and or international scale in business, industry, the professions and commerce. Cheshire is an affluent county, and its perceived wealth has been a source of speculation in the national

A scene depicting a silk-spinning wheel, set in the mid-17th century in Macclesfield.

press. Stories that Bramhall had the highest income per capita in Britain, that Poynton had the greatest number of millionaires in the country and the Macclesfield, Prestbury and Halebarns area being called 'Cheshire's Golden Triangle' have been compounded with stories of property prices booming on the same scale as the south-east.

I suppose it might be possible to produce a book on Cheshire's wealthy. The county certainly has many millionaires and is indeed the home, at

The site of the founding of the silk industry in Macclesfield by Charles Roe in Park Green in 1756.

Christ Church, Macclesfield, donated to the town by Charles Roe.

Eaton Park, of Britain's wealthiest citizen, the Duke of Westminster. Due to his vast holdings of land and particularly land and property in the heart of London, he is one of the richest men in the world with a fortune estimated at over £4 billion pounds. But this section is all about achievement. There will of course be a few millionaires, featured because achievement in businesses usually equates to financial achievement, but the qualification is national and or international recognition.

For more than 200 years Cheshire was renowned around the world for its production of silk, which at its peak was centred mainly in Macclesfield, Bollington and Congleton. A number of local companies featured prominently in the success story but perhaps two men, above all others, deserve recognition for the establishment and longevity of the industry. **Charles Roe**, born in Castleton in 1714, the son of a vicar, had intended to join the church but instead moved to Macclesfield where an older brother had become curate. He became a freeman of the borough at the age of 27 and stayed in Macclesfield for the rest of his life.

A natural entrepreneur, he was a manufacturer of buttons when he learnt of the process of silk throwing through water power, which John Lombe had discovered in Italy in 1718 and was using in Derby. Roe decided that the new process had potential and decided to develop the idea. At the time covering buttons in silk thread was largely a cottage industry and Roe saw the obvious benefits of manufacturing silk and taking the process further. He built his first silk factory between Mill Street and Park Green in Macclesfield close to the river at Dams Brook in 1743. Others joined in and within 30 years Macclesfield had seven silk factories and Cheshire had by far the greatest silk output in the country. Roe, having successfully created the industry, in 1760 diversified into copper, building a large works on the outskirts of town and eventually another in Liverpool. Although he is best known for creating the silk industry, Roe was a considerable industrialist of his time. He started to mine copper at Alderley Edge, the Lake District and Anglesey, and brought coal from Wrexham. At first his business was very successful but then the extraction and transport of the raw materials over great distances increased the costs dramatically. Macclesfield prospered for quite some time and the influence of Charles Roe, a rich generous man, is still apparent in the town in Roe Street, Charles Roe House and the magnificent Christ Church building which he founded in 1775 as a gift to the town. Although the church no longer holds services, it is still consecrated and is part of the Churches Conservation Trust. It remains a superb monument to the foresight and generosity of a shrewd industrialist. When Roe died in Macclesfield in 1781, the silk industry which he had kick started would, despite periods of depression, thrive for 200 years and make the town he had come to love renowned the world over.

Another prominent name in the Macclesfield silk story was that of **John Brocklehurst**, who was born in 1718 and joined the button manufacturer, Acton & Street, in 1748, embarking on a relationship which would keep the Brocklehurst name active in the silk industry for more than 200 years. John Brocklehurst quickly took over the company but it has not been established when he converted the company to silk production. What is known is that the company, Street & Co, was successfully exporting buttons and twist manufacturing all over Britain in 1787–9, and enjoyed an export trade with Holland, Russia, America and Scotland.

John Brocklehurst's son John, born in 1754, joined the business and is credited by some experts as having taken the decision to change over from pure button-making to silk throwing. Certainly by 1790 a document described Brocklehursts as manufacturers of silk. The family home was Pear Tree House, Jordangate, Macclesfield and still stands today as Jordangate House. However, it was the grandsons of the original John Brocklehurst who would put the family name and indeed the silk industry into the history books. **John** and **Thomas Brocklehurst**, John in particular, ensured that the dynasty would survive and thrive.

Born in 1788, John was a shrewd honest man who never forgot that the family fortune was built on the efforts of the people of Macclesfield. He was educated at King's School and eventually took an interest in politics and became, in 1832, MP for Macclesfield at the first-ever parliamentary borough election. He started out as a Whig politician before becoming a Liberal but served the town with great distinction for 32 years. The company was by now known as J. & T. Brocklehurst and on several occasions John Brocklehurst fought for the silk and textile industries in the House of Commons.

Over the years as industrialisation moved on and technology improved the industry suffered ups and downs, particularly when in 1860 Free Trade was introduced. Times were hard for some and many emigrated to America, where using their skill and expertise they helped found the American silk industry. Macclesfield continued to prosper because of the skill of the people and the fact that all processes in the silk manufacturing, production and design could be done in the town. In the mid-19th century John Brocklehurst had, as President of the Useful Knowledge Society, established to improve design training, pushed hard for better and more formal teaching. It led to the formation of the Macclesfield School of Art, which in 1888 was said to be one of the best in the country. John Brocklehurst died in 1870 aged 82.

Macclesfield continued to produce silk scarves, silk handkerchiefs and silk ties, which were exported to America, Japan, Australia and New Zealand. Brocklehursts amalgamated with another local company, William Whiston, to form BWA in 1929. It survived until 1992 when it closed its doors as the Macclesfield silk industry declined. The renown which Macclesfield enjoyed around the world was brought home to me when

I visited China in 1992. A local guide was showing a group of us round a silk factory in Chengde, northern China, when during his talk he paused and said that England had once produced the finest silk in a place called Macclesfield. He was astonished to learn that I was from Macclesfield. It was due largely to the foresight, the tenacity and the courage of men like Charles Roe and the several John Brocklehursts that Macclesfield and Cheshire became the centre of quality and expertise for the world's silk market.

A business encounter with George Stephenson of railways fame changed the fortune and shaped the life of **Thomas Brassey**. Born near Chester in 1805, Brassey was by profession a chartered surveyor, but after meeting and dealing with Stephenson he realised the enormous potential presented by the development of the railway system. His first contract was to build a rail viaduct in Staffordshire and then he had the good fortune to take over from Stephenson as engineer on the Grand Junction line. However, apparently influenced by his wife, he decided that the real money was to be made from contracting. He obtained a contract to build a railway line from Rouen to Le Havre, and in 1847 undertook a four-year contract, employing 6,000 men, to build the Great Northern railway. By this time his reputation was well established and he undertook further projects all over the world: Australia, Moldavia, India, Canada, Argentina and even in the Crimea, where he helped rescue British troops by building a rail track in record time. He even completed a project for the Austrians during their war with Prussia. However, his lasting memorial is surely the building of the Grand Trunk Railway in Canada. This was a huge task which Brassey controlled absolutely, from the building and supply of all the equipment from his base in Birkenhead, to hacking out almost 600 miles of

track across forest, plain and even across the St Lawrence River, which required a bridge that took several years to build. The stretch of rail is known today as the Canadian Pacific Railway and runs from Quebec to Toronto. Brassey completed many projects across Europe and it was sadly during the opening of the Mont Cenis route between Italy and France that he suffered a stroke and never really recovered. Thomas Brassey died in Sussex in 1870. Interestingly, he was featured in a *Sunday Times* survey which tried to estimate the wealth of the richest 200 people since 1066, using modern day inflation and cost of living adjustments. Thomas Brassey was 132nd on the list with his fortune estimated to be £3.2 million by today's standards. A successful man, indeed one of the century's great entrepreneurs, he was also said to be kind, modest and generous.

The Victorian era spawned a number of great industrialists as invention and commercialism took hold of the country as the spread of the railway network made communications quicker and easier. The explosion of invention and creativity in the Victorian era was typified by **Joseph Whitworth**, who was born in Stockport in 1803. Whitworth worked for a time as a clerk in a cotton mill before moving in 1825 to London where he commenced training as an engineer. He returned after a few years to Manchester, where in 1833 he established his own engineering company. However, Whitworth was not one to just build or operate others creations. He had the mind of a scientist and frequently built his own machines and devices. He is credited with having built a mechanical knitting machine and a horse-drawn sweeper. When the ground-breaking Great Exhibition of London was opened in 1851 Whitworth took the opportunity to display several of his new pieces and his reputation as an engineer of precision tools and machines was established. Like most engineers and inventors he had his failures. He invented a gun which was rejected by the British Government and yet accepted by the French and used by the Americans as a sniper rifle in the Civil War. However, he had more success when he built artillery pieces. Whitworth created the Whitworth Scholarship, which is dedicated to encouraging engineering science, and was knighted for his services to industry. A lasting legacy is that the Whitworth specifications for the screw thread are still regarded as the standard for the UK. He died in 1887.

One of the very first entrepreneurs to find a niche in a market and to make his name nationally associated with a product was **John Johnson**. In 1803, together with his brother, he saw the potential in a small undeveloped soap works in Runcorn and set about promoting and marketing what at the time was a product which could only be afforded by the wealthy. The brothers had turned their acquisition into the biggest soap producer in the UK by 1832 and for many years the Johnson Brothers brand name was synonymous with soap. At one point Runcorn produced 36% and Merseyside 50% of the entire British soap market. The Johnsons, fired by their earlier success, soon diversified into other products and added coal, chemicals and other tradeable goods to their portfolio.

William Hesketh Lever was a Victorian of vision – not just commercial vision, but social conscience – who balanced his drive for business and profit with care for his workforce. Born in Bolton in 1851, he worked for a time in his father's grocery shop before deciding to branch out into the soap making business in 1884. In 1886, together with his brother James, he leased a factory in Warrington and began making soap, changing the process by using vegetable oil

instead of tallow. Through a combination of business initiatives, bright packaging, scenting and colouring the soap and calling it 'Sunlight', and offering the workers a share in any profit, the business boomed and the brothers had to seek bigger premises. In 1888 they bought land on the southern banks of the Mersey, exploiting the river and excellent railway links, and started to develop not only a new factory, but also a new town, which they called Port Sunlight. As it grew it became a garden village housing the workers who worked in the soap factory. It was a brilliant experiment which gave the workers a bright healthy environment with good sanitation, so preventing the filth and disease so rife in many other industrial conurbations. In later years a public library, an art gallery and an outdoor heated swimming pool were added and by 1916 the village comprised about 1,000 cottages. William Lever, like so many other successful businessmen, stood for Parliament and was elected Labour MP for the Wirral Division for Cheshire in 1906.

Lever Brothers, with William as chairman, rapidly became a major worldwide business with a variety of companies, eventually changing their name to Unilever. During his lifetime William was honoured with the title 1st Viscount Lord Leverhulme, and by the time of his death in 1925 he had given Lancaster House to the nation and had endowed a school of tropical medicine at Liverpool University. The town of Port Sunlight still exists and today is a much sought-after place to live, without the qualification of having to work for Unilever. The buildings and houses are all Grade II listed and are a lasting and fitting monument to an industrialist with foresight and care for his fellow human beings.

Another gifted man who created his success in Cheshire was Liverpool-born **John Brunner**. Born in 1842, the son of a Swiss father, he set up business in Winnington, Northwich, with his partner Ludwig Mond, to produce alkali. Alkali was an important industrial product with a variety of uses. Produced mainly as soda ash or caustic soda, it formed the basic raw material for products such as aluminium, glass production and detergents. The business grew rapidly as the raw material had many uses in the growing industrial economy and by 1915 Brunner and Mond had a virtual monopoly in the soda ash market. World War One of course required vast amounts of explosives and needed Brunner's raw material in huge quantities. After the war the company was praised for its advice and help by the government. In 1926 in a major development Brunner Mond merged with Nobel Industries, British Dyestuffs and United Alkali to form a major new company which was launched on 1 January 1927 as Imperial Chemical Industries (ICI). Brunner was knighted for his contribution and from 1885 until shortly before his death in 1919 he was MP for Northwich. From that humble small factory in Northwich grew the global giant ICI which for very many years would compete and match the very best conglomerates in the world.

A Scotsman, **William Laird**, came to the Liverpool area as a young lad in 1810 and in 1824 he bought a piece of land at Wallasey Pool and started to develop a boiler and ironworks. So successful was he that within four years he received his first order to build an iron ship. Laird designed and built ships and within his first 10 years of business he had built 17 ships and was established as one of the leading shipbuilders in Britain. However, Laird needed a new site and in 1857 moved to a wider deep-water site near Victoria Dock, Birkenhead, where access to water and improving railway links were ideal for expansion of the business. Laird also had a vision to

establish a decent living environment for the workers close to the dock, and to create a thriving area around the shipbuilding site. By the time of his death in 1873 Laird's was established as the number one shipbuilder in Britain. The firm attracted the attention of **Charles Camell**, who merged his Sheffield business with Laird's to form the world-renowned company Camell Laird.

The company performed magnificently during World War Two, supplying 106 warships to the Royal Navy. After the war they built the Cunard liner *Mauretania* and the legendary aircraft carrier *Ark Royal*, which at the time and for many years, was the largest in the world. Increased competition and fluctuating fortunes led to a decline in the British shipbuilding industry. Cammel Laird continued in business over the ensuing years in various forms and resorted primarily to ship repairs in order to stay in business. This once-great company, with a global reputation started by a young Scotsman from a Cheshire base, still has ships traversing the world's oceans which were built in Cheshire.

A story of a somewhat different nature, about a very successful Cestrian who went into the people business, not chasing profit but from humanitarian concern, is about the triumph of entrepreneurial skills. Born in Chester in 1917 and educated at Stowe School and Oxford, **Leonard Cheshire** joined the RAF in 1942 and became at the age of 25 the youngest Group Captain to command a squadron. During the war he perfected a technique of low flying which marked targets more specifically and resulted in greater successes. He flew and incredibly survived more than 100 bombing missions, for which he was awarded the Victoria Cross. Such was the esteem in which he was held that he was selected to act as the British observer of the dropping of the atomic bomb on Nagasaki. Many believe that

Leonard Cheshire. Leonard Cheshire Archive Library

it was this incident which changed his life.

Acclaimed as a war hero, Cheshire turned his efforts to peace and actually joined the CND. However, it was after being asked to help an acquaintance who was terminally ill and offering to look after him in a house, Le Court in Hampshire, which Cheshire had bought from an aunt, that the seeds of caring for the needy were planted. Someone else needed help and Cheshire took her in. Very soon news spread of his generosity and within a few years, by 1948, the house was full of those needing help and those who were offering it to the terminally ill and disabled. The concept developed and soon the Cheshire Homes Foundation was launched and rapidly expanded in this country. In 1959 Cheshire married Sue Ryder, who had had plenty of experience in caring for the needy from her wartime role in Poland caring for concentration camp survivors. Together they were a formidable combination. Sue also set up the Sue Ryder Foundation to assist the sick and needy and for the rest of their lives the pair devoted all their time to those less fortunate. When Leonard Cheshire died from motor neurone disease in 1992 his Cheshire Homes Foundation had more than 200 facilities in more than 50 countries around the world and he had been created a Baron and had received from the Queen in 1981 the rarely bestowed Order of Merit.

Sue Ryder took over as president of the Cheshire Foundation and died Baroness Ryder in November 2000. The Leonard Cheshire legacy now embraces 250 services in 55 countries worldwide, offering skills training, day care, rehabilitation, self reliance programmes and a total support service for the needy and disabled. It relies heavily on voluntary donations.

Sebastian Ziani de Ferranti created a global giant from a modest company set up in London in 1889 before moving to Lancashire in 1896. Although he was a gifted engineer the company underwent a series of cash difficulties, unable to focus on a specific business goal. Their range was considerable, including radios, alternators, domestic appliances, power stations, televisions, air systems, armaments, guided missiles and electrical goods of all kinds. In 1949 Ferranti was responsible for producing the world's first commercially available computer, which was bought by Manchester University. Sadly the company, with a whole variety of off shoot companies, lurched from crisis to crisis and eventually passed out of the family's hands when the Department of Trade intervened in 1974–5. The principle of a family controlled, product-based business was sound in practice but finance was a

Peter Ellwood CBE, former Chief Executive of LLoyds TSB bank plc, and ex-King's School, Macclesfield.

problem. The last Ferranti to have a controlling interest was **Sebastian Basil Joseph Ziani de Ferranti**, who was born in Alderley Edge on 5 October 1927. Educated at Ampleforth, he went into the family business but was powerless, despite his long service, to save the company, parts of which survive in name only. At various times he was Managing Director of Ferranti plc from 1958–75, and Chairman of Ferranti plc from 1963–82. He also held a number of offices which reflected the respect he commanded: Director of GEC plc, Director of National Nucleur Corporation 1984–8, High Sheriff of Cheshire in 1988, commissioner for the Royal Commission for the Exhibition of 1851 and Chairman of the Hallé Concert Society. The beautiful old family house, Henbury Hall, at Henbury, is reputed to have been visited on a number of occasions by members of the royal family.

A man who spent his formative years in Cheshire went on to become the boss of Britain's and one of Europe's biggest banks. **Peter Brian Ellwood,** born in Manchester on 15 May 1943 but educated at King's School, Macclesfield, started his career by joining Barclays Bank in 1961 and starting his first post as a corporate banker and assistant to a senior General Manager in London. After a number of years gaining experience he transferred to Barclaycard operations in 1983 and in 1985 was appointed Chief Executive of Barclaycard, a position which he held until 1989. In that year he was head-hunted by the emerging TSB Bank plc and became Chief Executive of Retail Banking, charged with stimulating profit generation. In 1990 he was elected to the Group's main board as a director and added the Insurance arm of the bank to his responsibilities. At the time of the merger with Lloyds Bank

Peter Kenyon, Chief Executive of Chelsea FC and formerly Manchester United. Manchester United

in 1995, Ellwood was Group Chief Executive of TSB and following the merger was appointed Deputy Chief Executive of Lloyds TSB Group plc, a position which he held until 1997. Further changes brought him the ultimate accolade in the banking profession when he was appointed Group Chief Executive of Britain's biggest bank in 1997. Peter Ellwood was appointed CBE in 2001 and retired from Lloyds Bank in May 2003. Despite his intention to indulge his spare time with music and the theatre, he found time in his retirement year to return to King's School to give a lecture.

A Cestrian envied by many as having the job that most would perform for free is **Peter Kenyon**. Peter, born in Stalybridge in 1953, was once the Chief Executive of Manchester United, the largest and most powerful football club in the world. Peter was educated at West Hill Boys' School, Stalybridge, and set out in life as a trainee accountant with Gallahers in 1972. His first senior post came in 1979 as Divisional Director with Courtaulds. In the late 1980s he earned considerable respect by turning the loss-making Umbro sportswear to profit. As European head and then Chief Operating Officer his success was not lost on the American purchasers and he was persuaded to move his family to the US. However, the move was not a success and he resigned and returned to the UK with his family with no work alternatives in mind. By chance, via a former business associate, Peter Kenyon was offered the opportunity to join his favourite football club as deputy chief executive. Following the resignation of Martin Edwards in 2000 Kenyon stepped up into that most coveted of roles, Chief Executive of Manchester United. However pleasurable the job, the club commanded global attention and Peter Kenyon was charged with controlling the purse strings. Ever increasing costs had to be met with worldwide marketing of the brand name and related goods. Sponsorships had to be negotiated and transfer fees in and out are also an essential part of the role.

It is believed that Peter Kenyon had to forego a holiday with his family when he was involved with the transfer of Rio Ferdinand to Manchester United. It was after all a record for any British Football League club and with the buying price at £29.3 million any self-respecting accountant would want to be there. He was also involved in the much publicised and agonising transfer of David Beckham to Real Madrid for £25 million in June 2003. Although Peter is a life-long fan of the club he is also an accountant and a businessman and knew that the club must pay its way. But labour of love or not, the football world was rocked when seemingly out of the blue Peter Kenyon announced his resignation in September 2003 to take over as Chief Executive at Chelsea. The football world was staggered when Kenyon gave up the job at United, a club he had followed as a boy. However, the Chelsea owner, the Russian Roman Abramovich, having spent £111 million on players, was determined that Chelsea should be marketed as a brand name to match Manchester United. It is believed that he offered Kenyon more than £1 million per annum. Nevertheless Kenyon's departure was a shock.

Football also features prominently in the life of another successful Cheshire citizen. **Peter Johnson**, born in Birkenhead in 1940, spent several years after leaving school working in his father's butcher's shop. He was concerned by the struggle that many of his father's customers had to pay for their Christmas meats. With the true eye of an entrepreneur he thought up a scheme whereby people could pay in advance for their Christmas luxuries, a sort of weekly club with door-to-door collection of payments. Very soon his idea caught on and in 1967 he launched Park Food, his food hamper concept, and became the biggest employer of staff in Birkenhead. He moved to new premises near Tranmere Rovers's football ground and was able to combine his business interests with football when he joined the board. In 1983 the business, Park Group plc, took a full listing on the London Stock Exchange and became a national giant encompassing Park Hamper Co., with hampers for all occasions, Park Direct Credit Ltd, and a division offering marketing services. As his success continued he had the opportunity to join the board of Everton Football Club and jumped at the chance, but had to first resign from the Tranmere board. A real Merseyside lad, he still lived in Birkenhead and Everton was a dream come true. As a commitment to the region of his birth he launched and became Chairman of the Trustees of the Johnson Foundation, dedicated to supporting charitable causes primarily in the Merseyside area. Sadly dreams can often turn into nightmares and for Peter Johnson the Everton move was a failure and he sold his shares and resigned from the club in 2000. He still has a considerable holding in Park Group plc, which is still a major business in the UK, and now resides in the Channel Islands.

Another Cestrian to lead a nationally renowned company is **William John Anthony Timpson**, who was born in Altrincham on 24 March 1943. Educated at Oundle and Nottingham University, he joined the family business and was appointed Buying Director in 1970. However, after Timpson's was bought by UDS Group in 1973 he joined Swear & Wells as MD before returning to the family business in 1975, this time as MD. Shortly afterwards Timpson's became part of the Hanson Trust, which prompted John Timpson to lead a management buyout. In 1987 he sold the shoe shops and concentrated on the shoe repair and key cutting sector, while taking on watch repairs as a diversification. The metamorphosis was completed in 1995 with the purchase of Automagic and its 120 shops, making Timpson, with 330 outlets, the largest shoe repairer and key cutting business in the UK. What started out as a privately-owned family business has, after many turns of the wheel, returned to being a privately-owned family business. John Timpson still lives in Cheshire with his wife and family and has found time outside his love of sport and his years of fostering more than 70 children, to write a book, *Dear James,* which shares his experiences of his many years as Chief Executive and Chairman of Timpson Shoe Repairs Ltd.

Another small Cheshire family business which has turned into a national and international conglomerate is that of **Jones Homes**, the founding member of the Emerson Group, which is a privately-owned property development company. Jones Homes was started by **Peter Jones** and his wife Audrey in 1959. Peter, from Manchester, was a joiner by trade but had a vision of building quality houses. From their very first modest projects the company, based in Alderley Edge, set up regional offices in Yorkshire and Kent and now builds more than 600 houses a year in the UK. The company, which builds high and low rise apartments, mews style homes, town houses, detached luxury properties and also controls and manages more than 40 retirement home projects, has received a number of awards for both quality and environmental issues, including the National House Building Council Pride in the Job award, the What House Award that praised them for conservation and environmental care, and the prestigious Tree Council award that also recognised their care for the community by protecting mature trees. Certainly the Emerson Group is associated with quality and the family is still very much hands on, with sons Mark and Tony both on the Emerson board. Their reputation as quality builders of luxury properties in the UK is well established and their international projects now extend to Portugal and America. At the present time Peter Jones, now aged 67, is enjoying the challenge of building what appears to be a small town, Altamonte Springs, Florida. Not far from Orlando the project includes an hotel, a school and a golf course. A far cry from doing joinery work in Manchester, it is a testimony to what vision and hard work can bring to the determined.

Another small Cheshire acorn which has grown into a giant oak is the transport and haulage business of **Irlam & Sons Ltd**, which is based in Chelford. Started in the 1950s by **James Irlam** in Snelson, it was literally a one-man business with James transporting and selling his produce of tomatoes and cucumbers in the Manchester markets. From that tiny beginning, the family also started delivering milk, with James's four sons setting out every day at 5am on their various rounds. A little haulage was added with the collection and delivery of milk churns and then, following a number of changes, three of

A lorry of Irlam & Sons of Chelford, Haulier of the Year in 1996 and 2001.

the brothers consolidated the business into transport in 1980 and James Irlam & Sons was well and truly launched. Rapid expansion necessitated larger premises and the business relocated to Chelford, where its head office remains today. Irlams is now one of the largest and most successful haulage companies in the UK. Twice in recent years, 1996 and 2001, they have won the coveted title of 'Haulier of The Year' to add to their Lifetime Achievement Award for Road Transport awarded by Shell UK in 1999. The company has more than 350 trucks with uniformed drivers, who travel all over the UK. Their distinctive red lorries are very popular with the fans in the 'lorry spotting' culture. The business is still strictly a family business, very proud of its Chelford roots. **Ken Irlam**, the founder's son, is Chairman and his son **David** is the Managing Director, while **Stuart**, **Michael** and **Andrew** hold the respective positions of finance, operations and planning directors. The company gives its support to the community by giving much needed financial aid to Macclesfield Town football club, helping to secure their future in the Football League.

Another family business of a slightly different hue was established in 1762. **Greenalls**, the brewery, has undergone a complete metamorphosis since those days and particularly over the past 10 years under the influence of **Sir Peter Gilbert Greenall**, Lord Daresbury. Born on 18 July 1953, and educated at Eton, Cambridge and the London Business School, he entered the family business and became a director in 1982. In 1988 he was appointed MD of Greenalls Breweries plc until in 1991 the brewery was closed and Greenalls Inns was created with him as Managing Director. The conversion from brewing to the pub trade led to the eventual creation of the Greenalls Group plc with Peter Greenall as Chief Executive from 1997–2000. During this period he was able to negotiate the sale of the pubs and the company became part of the De Vere Group plc with Peter Greenall as Chairman in 2000. The restructuring of the Greenalls business was a difficult task in changing times. Today Peter Greenall, the seventh generation of the family, is non-executive Chairman of the De Vere Group, a much-respected name among the leading hotel groups in the UK. He remains chairman of Aintree race-course, was High Sheriff of Cheshire in 1992, and enjoys dairy farming on the family farm in Daresbury.

A business which wholly reflects the image of Cheshire to the outside world – lush, leafy country lanes, dairy farms, gardens and flowers – is Fryer's Nurseries Ltd of Knutsford. Founded by Knutsford man **Arthur Fryer** in 1912, in a small

field with a garden shed, his skill and passion for growing roses ensured that the business started to grow at such a rate that it moved to its present premises in 1928. Very much a family business, Arthur's two sons joined the business and after the war in 1946 they embarked on mail order sales and attended all the major shows. Soon they were producing over a million roses a year and were establishing an international reputation. Today the business is run by grandson **Gareth Fryer**, who was born in Bowden. The business was one of the first to be awarded the Queen Mother's International Rose Award in 1999, an accolade bestowed by the Royal National Rose Society for their outstanding contribution to developing new cultivars. In 2001 Fryer's won The Royal Horticultural Society Gold Medal for roses at each of the major shows that year: the

Fryer's of Knutsford's display at the Royal Horticultural Show at Tatton Park, 2003.

Chelsea Flower Show, Hampton Court and the Tatton Show in Cheshire. They followed that up with gold again at the 2002 shows at Chelsea and Hampton Court and achieved silver at Tatton. In a difficult 2003 growing season they achieved silver gilt awards at Tatton and Hampton Court and a silver at Chelsea. From that tiny field and garden shed in 1912, Arthur would be astonished at today's business with its Rose Garden, the Garden Centre and the café serving a range of quality meals with wine. No wonder then that this business, with over 200 varieties of roses, sells its products (through agents as they cannot export due to import regulations) to America, Canada, Australia and New Zealand and is one of the leading rose growers in the country.

A real rags-to-riches story is told by the rise to national and European recognition of a company which in 2004 will celebrate 150 years of business. **Arighi Bianchi of Macclesfield**, the high-class purveyor of furniture and furnishings, was founded by two Italians, **Antonio Arighi** who started it all when he arrived penniless from Italy in 1854, and **Antonio Bianchi**, a cabinetmaker from the same Italian village, who joined him in 1868. Furniture, upholstery and soft furnishings established their name far and wide and the firm eventually moved to its present site in 1883. The premises were extended in 1893 to keep pace with the growth in business. The extension gave the company its distinctive front, a façade which is a replica of the front of the Crystal Palace that housed the Great Exhibition of 1851. Horse-drawn vehicles bearing the Arighi Bianchi legend were followed by the first motorised vehicle to be used for commercial use in the Macclesfield area. Free delivery within a 30-mile radius and a pledge to respond on receipt to mail orders revolutionised the business.

If receipts are anything to go by, then Arighi

In 2004 the store celebrates 150 years in business in Macclesfield.

Bianchi's goods were sent to Marlborough House and to Sandringham at the time of Edward VII. By the 1930s they were importing materials from all over Europe, including tapestries, lace, velvet and damasks, and then had enormous success in designing and producing their own creations. At

One of Arighi Bianchi's early vehicles.

The Arighi Bianchi furniture store. The façade is a replica of the Crystal Palace built for the Great Exhibition of 1851. David Moore Photography, Congleton

one stage they were exporting to South America. World War Two put a stop to progress and for a time after the war business was very difficult. But a new generation of Bianchis soon had a greater threat – a compulsory purchase order to leave their site. The battle was long and hard, with even Sir John Betjeman involved at one stage, as government offices fought each other. Eventually the battle was won and the company embarked on a period of growth and development. The Coffee Shop was opened in 1988 and very quickly won acclaim for the quality of its food, and a Nursery Department was established, together with a new reception and several more departments, permitting a full and complete shopping experience. Leading brands of quality furniture, fabrics, and carpets are supported by a staff of more than 150, which includes carpetfitters and seamstresses, and Arighi's exclusive furniture. The business is still very much family-run with the third generation of Bianchis (all born locally), Anthony and Paul, operating as joint Managing Directors with Anthony's three sons and Paul's two sons and a daughter all working for the company. It doesn't come more family than that!

Another well-established family business is that of the brewery firm **Frederic Robinson** of Stockport. William Robinson bought the Unicorn Inn at Lower Hillgate in Stockport in 1838 and started to brew his own beer and in a very small way started to sell it to other local pubs. His youngest son Frederic joined him in 1865 but their partnership was cut short by the death of William shortly afterwards. Frederic bought the first pub and established the principle of 'tied houses'. When Frederic's own son, William, named after his grandfather, joined the business aged 14 in 1878, the company was modest, with two tied houses, a horse and a dray. However, by the time of Frederic's death in 1890 the brewery owned 12 houses and it was down to his widow Emma to take over the running of the business. In 1920 with steady growth continuing, the business was formed into a limited liability company with William's three sons, Frederic, John and Cecil, on the board of directors. Emma died in 1921. The business continues to thrive today as a family business, with Peter Robinson as Chairman and David Robinson as Head

Frederic Robinson Ltd.
The brewery in Lower
Hillgate, Stockport.

Brewer, and it has over 400 tied houses. It operates largely in South Manchester and Cheshire, North Wales, Cumbria and the north-west of England, but also enjoys free trade around the country. Internationally it exports to Italy and America and one of its beers, 'Old Tom', won an international award.

A lady who has succeeded internationally and nationally in the very difficult field of fashion is **Isabella Blow**. Although she was born in London in 1958, she was brought up in Cheshire until she was 21, before moving to New York. Isabella Delves-Broughton, as she was named, studied at Heathfield School where she became head of chapel and had a desire to become a nun. Her earliest recall of fashion influence was as an eight-year-old, when she tried on a huge pink hat and enjoyed being photographed in it. After school she enrolled in a secretarial college and then worked at a series of temporary jobs as a cleaner, waitress and shop assistant before going to New York in 1978 to study Chinese Art. After a year she left and started to work in the fashion world and received her big break in 1981, when through contacts she met and was appointed assistant to Anna Wintour, the fashion director of US Vogue. Soon she was organising fashion shoots and befriending the likes of Andy Warhol, but in 1986 she returned to London to work for *The Sunday Times* and the *Tatler*, where she eventually became editor.

She married Detmar Blow in 1989 and had a wonderfully productive spell of discovering talented people – Philip Treacy, Alexander McQueen, Stella Tennant and Sophie Dahl – all of whom have made their mark in the fashion industry. Isabella's reputation continued to grow and for four years she was the Fashion Director at *The Sunday Times Style* magazine. Today she acts as a consultant for Dupont Lycra, Lacoste and

Swarovski and in 2002 she was the subject of an exhibition at the London Design Museum, featuring many of the outrageous hats designed for her by Philip Treacy over the years. Isabella has already created a niche for herself as a leading guru for many of the young designers and her own outrageous tastes and willingness to try something different have provided a platform and the incentive for new ideas.

An inventor who came up with a simple but ingenious device, which not only earned him a fortune, but also the gratitude of many home-owners who were never ever able to paint, tile or paper around a radiator without having to call in a plumber to take it off the wall and shut off the water, is Cheshire-based **Paul Davidson**. Paul left school at the age of 15 and became an apprentice fitter with Shell in Manchester. After a spell working in the Middle East he returned to England and with great enterprise set up a thriving pipe fitting business which did well for several years before eventually failing. Not one to accept failure as inevitable, Paul set about utilising his experience in the pipe fitting industry and came up with an invention which allowed radiators to be swivelled from their position without being disconnected. A plastic inverted pipe, an oyster converter, was the solution which was a godsend to virtually every household. However, his early attempts to promote his invention fell on stony ground and indeed the company that first rejected his idea was later bought by Paul as his invention exploded on to the market. Davidson set up his own company in the Macclesfield area, Oystertec, to market and produce the product, which was floated on the stock market in 2001. He put in a management team to run the company while he pursued other interests and the promotion of other inventions. He bought the golf course operator Clubhaus in

2001 and in 2002 promoted the Galileo project, an inventors fund, and turned to the development of prestigious properties in Cheshire via PD Developments. It was, however, his involvement in a spread bet controversy which alleged that his bet helped underpin the flotation of a company, Cyprotex, in which he had a large stake, that hit the newspaper headlines in 2003. Paul Davidson sold all his shares in the company he had founded in 2002 because he was disenchanted with the way in which the company was being run. However this true entrepreneur and inventor is still, at the age of 48, loathe to sit on his laurels. Still very much involved with property, via Cheshire Estates, it is believed that he is now planning a considerable move into the area around the Costa del Sol, Spain, where he already has a number of assets, including a villa. His intention is to develop a chain of British-themed bars, starting with an opening in the elegant resort of Puerto Banus and expanding to maybe 50 in number. Paul and his family live in Prestbury, near Macclesfield, and despite the wonderful properties abroad which his success has deservedly brought him, I doubt that he will find anywhere more pleasing than the Cheshire countryside and a quaint country pub.

A Stockport man of foresight had the vision to recognise the huge potential of the revolution in technological communications, particularly with regard to mobile phones. **Martin Dawes**, born in Stockport in 1943, started his business career working in the television rental business owned by his father. It was during the 1980s that he started to investigate the mobile phone business and by 1985 he had set up his own telecoms business. The appeal was almost instant, with massive sales throughout the UK, and the business grew rapidly. In 1999 the company, Martin Dawes Telecommunications, moved from Warrington to splendid new premises at Preston Brook, Runcorn, with a workforce of more than 1,500. However, with the wisdom of an entrepreneur, Martin Dawes, later that year, sold his shareholdings in the company to British Cellnet at the top of the market. Good business from an astute businessman. His next venture, an investment in an Internet service provider, was regrettably not a success, but the Martin Dawes business interests cover a whole range of companies from Martin Dawes Systems based in Warrington to Martin Dawes Switched Service Ltd. Martin Dawes, despite his enormous success, has stayed true to his roots and still lives in Cheshire.

Although **Peter Neumark** was born in Blackburn in 1949 he created, with a business partner in 1982, Britain's largest independent express delivery company. From humble beginnings the company now has over 850 vehicles, employs almost 3,000 staff, and delivers more than 20 million parcels each year from 51 outlets all over the UK. Based in Warrington, it has regional depots in Manchester, Bristol, Dublin, Heathrow and conducts business in Europe, being a founder member of Netexpress Europe. When Peter Neumark started to build the business he lived for several years in Frodsham, but now, having sold his share of the business, he has moved to North Wales.

A Cheshire lady with a success story is **Barbara Catchpole**, who was born in Chester in 1946. Barbara is the Marketing Director of Elegant Resorts Ltd, an upmarket travel company specialising in quality holidays of an exotic nature around the world. The company was founded in 1988 in Chester by Barbara and partners and quickly found a niche in the travel market for holidays tailored to individual requirements. In 2002 Elegant Resorts was named 'Best Tour Operator' by the readers of Condé Nast Traveller, and Barbara Catchpole was listed as one of Britain's most successful women in a *Sunday Times* survey.

A Scotsman, **Brian Kennedy**, found his pot of gold in Cheshire. Born in Edinburgh in 1961 he set out in life as a bank clerk before venturing out into the retail world as a kitchen salesman. Tired of working for someone else, he took his first steps in business into the double glazing sector and like many before him failed. Undeterred, he continued to seek opportunities, and moved in to purchase the ailing Weatherseal Holdings which was based in Winsford. The business, double glazing, had been established since 1963 but at the time in 1992 was in the hands of the receiver. Weatherseal was to provide the cornerstone for a group of companies, all in the home improvements market and based in Cheshire, which Kennedy called the Latium Group. Conservatory roofs, glazed doors, PVC building materials and double glazing enjoyed a boom in consumer demand and created a very successful group. Like many other astute businessmen Brian Kennedy has begun to split up his original creation, the Latium Group, but still has a whole range of active companies within easy reach of his magnificent home near Congleton. He is also the owner of Sale rugby club, which no doubt provides him with a much needed avenue for relaxation.

It is pleasing to note that Cheshire's historic links with the soap industry from the past times of the Johnson Brothers and Lever Brothers, are maintained through a famous company, **Paterson Cussons**, whose headquarters are in Stockport. Now owned by Chairman **Anthony Green**, who was born in Altrincham, and family, the company was started in 1879 in Sierra Leone by two men, George Paterson and George Zochonis. They moved the company to London in 1884 and to Manchester in 1886, while setting up trading posts throughout Africa. The company, Paterson Zochonis, branched out into soap production in Nigeria and quickly added toiletries and pharmaceuticals to its product range. Today the company trades in 14 countries and employs more than 11,000 people. It manufactures throughout Africa, and also in China, Australia, Thailand, India and Indonesia. In 1975 Paterson Zochonis plc took over Cussons Group Ltd, the soap manufacturing, toiletries and household products company, which was also internationally respected in the industry. The group changed its name to Paterson Cussons and has invested heavily in its UK soap manufacturing factory in Nottingham. Once again familiar brand names frequent the national households, Imperial Leather, Pearl, 1001, Morning Fresh and Carex to name just a few. The company is highly regarded in financial circles and is truly a global giant with its headquarters in Stockport and its Chairman, a Cestrian, living nearby. It is pleasing to note that this 'local' firm was a heavy sponsor of the hugely successful Commonwealth Games held in Manchester in 2002.

The UK's largest and most respected name in that most modern of industries, cosmetic surgery, is the **Transform Medical Group** which is based in Cheshire with its headquarters in Halebarns. **John Ryan**, born in Doncaster, joined the company in 1975 when it was a small hair treatment concern based in Manchester. Over the years he helped instigate change and add to the product range and moved the company to Bowden. It now has 13 clinics throughout the country and is the acknowledged leader in its field. The company does not accept that you have to live with the body or face that nature gave you. It offers a seven days a week, 24 hours a day service to male or female and can alter, reduce, enlarge, enhance or remove virtually any part of the human body, surgically or non-surgically. Among the very many national figures who have utilised its services is Melinda Messenger, whose famous assets were enhanced by silicon implants made by John Ryan. The foresight and potential which John Ryan first detected in the industry helped him become the UK's largest specialist in cosmetic surgery and of course brought with it the rewards which come with the courage of pursuing a dream. He sold his shares in the company which he developed in December 2002 in order to pursue other activities

In the introduction to this section I mentioned that it was not just about wealth but about achievement and during the past few years a number of Cheshire businesses and their founders have been ranked by various surveys as being among the very best in Britain.

The boom in the property market, particularly in the north-west, enabled **Bruntwood Estates**, based in Cheadle and owned by **Michael Oglesby**

and family, to create a property and investments business through Abney Investments to rank with the very best in the UK.

Property and construction have placed the **Seddon Group**, now based in Macclesfield, as one of the country's leaders in house building. The company was started in 1897 and is still very much a family-run business under **John Seddon**. It is based in a delightfully preserved Elizabethan-style black and white house in the middle of a modern quality housing development in Tytherington, Macclesfield.

Another business to capitalise on modern requirements was **Mergebasic**, created by **Terence and Anita Coleman** from Alderley Edge. Their business, based in Manchester, made the Scorpion car alarm system and created national sales which placed it among the very best in Britain in terms of success.

John Newsome from Prestbury built a hugely successful business, **Mottram Group**, which he

The picnic area at Gawsworth Hall.

Gawsworth Hall.

started in 1982. Specialising in industrial plastics, the company employed more than 500 people at its peak and became one of the market leaders in the UK.

Having the courage of your convictions and pursuing ambition isn't always successful and failure can and often does lead to bad debt. Bad debts have to be collected, the piper must be paid. **Neil McRoberts** is one man who has been very successful in calling in and collecting bad debts. His family-owned Stockport-based **Moorcroft** company runs a business services debt recovery operation which should ensure that the 60-year-old McRoberts will never be the subject of recovery action himself!

A labour of love, but very much a business needing to survive by its own hard work and ingenuity, is the much-admired operation running one of Britain's finest historic manor houses, **Gawsworth Hall** near Macclesfield. Privately owned by **Timothy and Elizabeth Richards**, this most beautiful Manor House was the home of the Fittons and most famously Mary Fitton, maid to

Elizabeth I and thought by many to be the 'dark lady' of Shakespeare's sonnets. It was also the home of **Samuel Johnson**, featured in the Entertainers chapter as Britain's last professional jester, and it was also the subject of a tragic duel between Lord Mohun and the Duke of Hamilton, who both died during a dispute over the Gawsworth estates in 1712. The house is magnificent with its paintings, furniture, armour, artefacts and gardens, but requires expensive maintenance.

The Richards have an all-year programme of events embracing Craft Fairs, Antique Fairs, Plant Fairs, Classic Car Days and Christmas at Gawsworth, and the house and gardens are open from April to October. However, their annual Open Air Theatre, which commences in late June and finishes in mid-August, attracts crowds sometimes in excess of 1,200, mostly undercover but for particularly popular attractions on a warm summer night several hundred more sit out in the open. Crowds are encouraged to come early and to bring picnics as well as chairs, tables, some adorned with candelabra, gazebos with lights in, and champagne buckets while eating out by the lake. It is a combination of Ascot and Henley and much enjoyed. The entertainment programme is well balanced with popular music, like Bee Gees and Abba tribute bands; West End theatre music; brass bands; Viennese folk music; Andy Prior; Sinatra music; Humphrey Lyttelton and Acker Bilk, mixed with opera, Shakespeare plays and Gilbert and Sullivan. The Richards have shown what can be done to hold on to and to protect a most precious way of life. It is undoubtedly hard work but their efforts are well supported and long may they continue.

Although it has often been said and recognised that Cheshire was not a major beneficiary of the Industrial Revolution, nevertheless its industrialists made the most of what the county had. Salt, cotton, silk, railways, soap, ship building and chemicals provided the platform on which future generations continue to build. Chemicals and a link with soap still feature in Cheshire, but it is pleasing to note that the ingenuity, invention and entrepreneurial skills of later Cestrians have placed Cheshire at the forefront of this country's creative wealth: mobile phones, telecommunications, car alarms, cosmetic surgery, double glazing, travel, transport and the swivel radiator have seen Cheshire business respond to the demands of the modern world.

Business Titbits

- Britain's second largest DIY home improvement company, **Focus Do It All**, which has more than 250 stores throughout the UK, has its headquarters in Crewe.
- The **United Kingdom Atomic Energy Authority** sold its Cheshire sites at Culceth and Risley but retains at Risley, Warrington, a specialist team of planners, safety experts, technicians and engineers who are responsible for overseeing the UKAEA's nuclear sites in the UK, to ensure that safety and environmental issues are complied with.
- **Vauxhall** have been producing cars at Ellesmere Port since 1962 and in that time have turned out more than 3.5 million vehicles and have employed thousands of people. Models such as the Viva, which dominated the UK Saloon Car Championships in 1971, the Chevette, which was exported in the 1980s to Germany and the Astra, which was voted International Car of the Year in 1985, have kept the company, which is now part of General Motors, well to the fore. The latest model, the Vectra, is purported to be the most powerful road-going Vectra ever in the GSi. Today Vauxhall, with almost 4,000 staff, is still the largest private employer of staff in Cheshire and is proud of its involvement in the local community. It was the first vehicle manufacturer to use the Internet to sell its vehicles and created history when in 2002 the company's soccer team amazingly reached the first round of the FA Cup. They eventually went out to another Cheshire side, Macclesfield Town FC.
- **Sir Henry Royce** (1863–1933) lived in Knutsford for many years where he met Charles Stuart Rolls in 1904 and formed the famous partnership.

Index